Liturgy with a Difference

Liturgy with a Difference

Beyond Inclusion in the Christian Assembly

Edited by Stephen Burns
and Bryan Cones

scm press

© The Editors and Contributors 2019

Published in 2019 by SCM Press
Editorial office
3rd Floor, Invicta House,
108–114 Golden Lane,
London EC1Y 0TG, UK

www.scmpress.co.uk

SCM Press is an imprint of Hymns Ancient & Modern Ltd
(a registered charity)

Hymns Ancient & Modern® is a registered trademark of
Hymns Ancient & Modern Ltd
13A Hellesdon Park Road, Norwich,
Norfolk NR6 5DR, UK

British Library Cataloguing in Publication data

A catalogue record for this book is available
from the British Library

978 0 334 05740 6

Typeset by Regent Typesetting Ltd
Printed and bound by
CPI Group (UK) Ltd

Contents

Contributors

Teresa Berger teaches in the field of liturgical studies and in Catholic theology at Yale Divinity School and the Yale Institute of Sacred Music in New Haven, Connecticut. Her scholarly interests for many years lay at the intersection of these disciplines with gender theory. More recently, Professor Berger has turned her attention to liturgical practices in digital worlds. Her book @ *Worship* was published in the summer of 2017. Other publications include *Gender Differences and the Making of Liturgical History* (2011); *Fragments of Real Presence* (2005); and, as editor, *Dissident Daughters: Feminist Liturgies in Global Context* (2001). She co-edited, with Bryan Spinks, the recent volume *Liturgy's Imagined Pasts* (2016) as well as the collection of essays *The Spirit in Worship–Worship in the Spirit* (2009).

Stephen Burns is a presbyter in the Church of England and professor of liturgical and practical theology at Pilgrim Theological College, Melbourne, Australia, as well as being an international research consultant at the Queen's Foundation for Ecumenical Theological Education, Birmingham. His publications include *Christian Worship: Postcolonial Perspectives*, co-authored with Michael N. Jagessar (2011) and *Postcolonial Practice of Ministry*, co-edited with Kwok Pui-lan (2016) and *Liturgy* (SCM Studyguide) (second edition, 2018).

Bryan Cones is a presbyter in The Episcopal Church, a former book editor at Liturgy Training Publications, and was managing editor and columnist at *U.S. Catholic* magazine. He has served as adjunct faculty at the Episcopal Divinity School, Cambridge, Massachusetts, and is a doctoral candidate in liturgy and practical theology at Pilgrim Theological College, University of Divinity. His recent publications include 'On Not Playing Jesus: The Gendered Liturgical Theology of Presiding' in the June 2017 issue of *Pacifica: Australasian Theological Studies* and 'Diary of a Pilgrimage: An American Pilgrim under the Southern Cross' in the September 2018 issue of *Worship*. He is currently co-editing *Twentieth-century Anglican Theologians* with Stephen Burns.

Susannah Cornwall is Senior Lecturer in Constructive Theologies at the University of Exeter, UK, and Director of EXCEPT (Exeter Centre for Ethics and Practical Theology). She is the author of several books in the area of theology and sexuality, including *Un/familiar Theology: Reconceiving Sex, Reproduction, and Generativity* (2017), *Theology and Sexuality* (2013), *Controversies in Queer Theology* (2011) and *Sex and Uncertainty in the Body of Christ: Intersex Conditions and Christian Theology* (2010). She is the editor of *Intersex, Theology and the Bible: Troubling Bodies in Church, Text, and Society* (2015), and, with John Bradbury, *Thinking Again About Marriage: Key Theological Questions* (2016).

Miguel A. De La Torre is professor of social ethics and Latinx studies at the Iliff School of Theology in Denver, Colorado. He has served as the elected 2012 President of the Society of Christian Ethics and currently serves as the Executive Officer for the Society of Race, Ethnicity and Religion. De La Torre is a recognized international Fulbright scholar who has taught at the Cuernavaca Center for Intercultural Dialogue on Development (Mexico), Indonesian Consortium for Religious Studies (Yogyakarta), University of Johannesburg (South Africa) and Johannes Gutenberg University (Germany). He has also taken students on immersion classes to Cuba and the Mexico/US border to walk the migrant trails. De La Torre has received several national book awards and is a frequent speaker at national and international scholarly religious events and meetings. He also speaks at churches and non-profit organizations on topics concerning the intersection of race, class and gender with religion. His recent publications include *Embracing Hopelessness* (2017) and *The Politics of Jesús: A Hispanic Political Theology* (2015).

Edward Foley, OFM Cap., a Capuchin priest, is the Duns Scotus Professor of Spirituality, Professor of Liturgy and Music and founding director of the Ecumenical Doctor of Ministry Program at Catholic Theological Union. He has authored or edited 26 books, including *Integrating Work in Theological Education* (2017), *A Handbook for Catholic Preaching* (2016) and *Theological Reflection Across Faith Traditions* (2015). His *Catholic Marriage: A Pastoral-Liturgical Handbook* is currently at press. He has also produced 42 book chapters, 37 peer review articles and almost 200 encyclopedia, dictionary and pastoral articles translated into eight languages. A Lilly sabbatical Fellow and recipient of the Berakah lifetime achievement award from the North American Academy of Liturgy, he presides and preaches at Old St Patrick's Church in Chicago.

W. Scott Haldeman serves as Associate Professor of Worship at Chicago Theological Seminary. His first book, *Towards Liturgies that Reconcile* (2007), analyses the role of racism in the development of US Protestant worship. In queer religious studies, examples of his work include 'A Queer Fidelity' (2007), which was published in the journal *Theology and Sexuality*, and 'Receptivity and Revelation' (2008), which appears in the essay collection, *Body and Soul: Rethinking Sexuality as Justice-Love*.

Michael Jagessar currently serves as a minister of the United Reformed Church (UK) with responsibility for global and intercultural ministries and is an immediate past moderator of the General Assembly of the United Reformed Church (2012–14). He taught ecumenical theology, interfaith studies, and Black and contextual theologies and practice at The Queen's Foundation for Ecumenical Theological Education (Birmingham, UK) from 2002 to 2008, and liturgy and worship, and practical theology at the Cambridge Theological Federation from 2010 to 2014. From Guyana, Michael locates himself as a member of the Caribbean diaspora who embodies multiple identities and for whom 'home' is always elsewhere! Some of his publications include *Ethnicity: The Inclusive Church Resource* (2015), *At Home with God and in the World: A Philip Potter Reader* (2013) with Drea Fröchtling, Rudolf Hinz et al., *Christian Worship: Postcolonial Perspectives* (2011) with Stephen Burns, *The Edge of God: New Liturgical Texts and Contexts in Conversation* (2008) with Stephen Burns and Nicola Slee and *Black Theology in Britain: A Reader* (2007) with Anthony Reddie.

Rachel Mann is a parish priest, writer and poet. Formerly Poet-in-Residence at Manchester Cathedral, she is currently Visiting Fellow in English Literature and Creative Writing at The Manchester Writing School, Manchester Met University. Author of five books, her most recent volume is *Fierce Imaginings: The Great War, Ritual, Memory and God* (2017). She has contributed to several volumes of liturgical theology, including *The Edge of God: New Liturgical Texts and Contexts in Conversation* (2008), edited by Nicola Slee, Stephen Burns and Michael Jagessar. She is currently completing a new book on the poetry of Christina Rossetti, due to be published by Canterbury Press in 2019, and her debut full-poetry collection is due to be published by Carcanet in late 2019.

Bruce T. Morrill, SJ, a Roman Catholic priest and Jesuit, is the Edward A. Malloy Professor of Roman Catholic Studies at Vanderbilt University. Specializing in sacramental-liturgical theology, he has lectured widely and held visiting chairs and fellowships in North America, Europe and Australia. In addition to over 100 articles, book chapters and reviews, his eight books include *Anamnesis as Dangerous Memory: Political and Liturgical Theology in Dialogue* (2000), *Divine Worship and Human Healing: Liturgical Theology at the Margins of Life and Death* (2009), *Encountering Christ in the Eucharist: The Paschal Mystery in People, Word, and Sacrament* (2012) and *The Essential Writings of Bernard Cooke: A Narrative Theology of Church, Sacrament, and Ministry* (2016). In Nashville, Father Morrill provides pastoral-liturgical ministry at Christ the King Church, Riverbend Maximum Security Prison and to several house-based small communities committed to faith and justice, societal and church reform.

Frank C. Senn is a retired pastor of the Evangelical Lutheran Church in America, adjunct professor of liturgical studies at Garrett-Evangelical Seminary in Evanston, Illinois and a past president of the North American Academy of Liturgy and The Liturgical Conference. He has been a parish pastor and seminary professor and is a widely published scholar on the liturgy, including his magisterial *Christian Liturgy: Catholic and Evangelical* (1997), *The People's Work: A Social History of the Liturgy* (2010) and the recent *Embodied Liturgy: Lessons in Christian Ritual* (2016) and *Eucharistic Body* (2017), as well as numerous articles in liturgical and theological journals.

Kristine Suna-Koro is Associate Professor of Theology at Xavier University in Cincinnati, Ohio, USA. She is a Latvian-American diasporic theologian working at the intersection of postcolonialism, liturgical and sacramental studies, as well as migration and diaspora discourses. She teaches in field of modern historical theology at Xavier and is the author of *In Counterpoint: Diaspora, Postcoloniality, and Sacramental Theology* (2017) as well as numerous articles and book chapters. As a Lutheran pastor, she has served the diasporic Latvian Lutheran communities in Great Britain, Germany and the United States. Currently, Kristine serves as the convener of the Critical Theories and Liturgical Studies seminar at the North American Academy of Liturgy.

Foreword

ANN LOADES

This collection of stimulating and disturbing chapters should provoke vitally important exchanges and conversations between every person responsible for taking a lead in liturgy and those who think they know what 'ecclesiology' is all about. For it is clear from reading the chapters that there is a heartfelt need to find and express not just hospitality – essential and indispensable though that is – but grace and blessing to all who may be thought (quite mistakenly) to be 'marginal' when human beings gather in divine presence for the worship of God. To the contrary, for the 'marginal' themselves may well be the 'means of grace and blessing' sought. That is, attentively including them and listening to them alongside and among more familiar neighbours may provoke the re-invigoration and transformation both of worship as well as of community and politics beyond 'church' boundaries. So in a quite distinctive way, this collection is a summons to enjoying surprises and hence finding the courage for change, given all that we may learn from one another.

Ann Loades, CBE
Emerita Professor of Divinity, Durham University
Honorary Professor of Divinity, St Andrew's University

Introduction:
The Vivid Richness of God's Image

BRYAN CONES AND STEPHEN BURNS

In recent decades, Christian churches – as communions and denominations, and in local congregations – have taken some steps in their liturgical practice towards acknowledging the graced dignity of human variety. Some have started to value previously excluded forms of human difference, including correction of historical failures and acknowledgement of oppression. To a greater or lesser extent in different traditions, they have embraced some measure of inclusive or expansive language, at least with respect to male and female human persons, if much less commonly in naming towards God.[1] Many churches now ordain women and have begun to integrate the theological reflection of women and gender minorities into their liturgical resources.[2] 'Open and affirming' congregations and recent denominational authorizations of same-gender marriage in some contexts have expanded the participation of LGBTQIA+ Christians.[3] In North American contexts, new liturgical books and hymnals have gathered the treasures of African American and other musical traditions to places alongside the culturally dominant European musical heritage found in most historically white churches of European descent.[4] Around the West, the emerging hymnody of the so-called Third World has been incorporated in collections for assembly song.[5] Around the world, some churches have made efforts towards liturgies and resources that highlight the importance of generous use of diverse cultural forms and languages, consciously pursuing more authentic cultural and liturgical contextualizations and acknowledging the contextualized nature of historic resources themselves.[6] More recently, some liturgical scholars have engaged in efforts to acknowledge how racism, colonialism and cultural privilege are rehearsed and reinscribed in Christian liturgy.[7] These are steps worthy of acknowledgement, even celebration.

At the same time, the now-common language of 'diversity' and 'inclusion' can nevertheless occlude unacknowledged majoritarian norms that endure in many churches and assemblies. Women, trans and non-gender-binary clergy continue to operate in ecclesial systems long dominated by men, and find themselves serving in liturgies still shaped by the presumption of a clergy person who 'represents' the historical Jesus in his presumed gender. Resources drawn from the theological reflection of women of various backgrounds are relegated to 'supplementary' liturgical materials,[8] sometimes only regionally approved for denominational use and often published in flimsy paperback editions or as online ephemera. Liturgical resources in languages other than English suffer similar fates and are often mere translations of historic English texts rather than original compositions. Liturgical acknowledgement of human relationship remains limited to dominant heteronormative conceptions of marriage, while other relationships and family structures await recognition in the liturgical assembly. Unreformed gathering spaces assign anyone other than the 'temporarily able-bodied' to the backbenches as spectators. Differences of colour, gender, culture and history still await liturgical words and images worthy of them, as assemblies continue to rely on spent binaries of light and darkness, sight and blindness, male and female, which neither acknowledge the history of oppression wrought through the liturgical performance of such images nor propose pathways to reconciliation. In effect, even while the language of 'diversity' and 'inclusion' may sometimes be sprinkled around the churches, liturgical practices of exclusion still dominate, propelling much human difference to the shadows of the liturgical assembly rather than drawing those who bear such difference to the centre, where they arguably belong.

Liturgical theology has a crucial role to play in reflecting upon and reorienting liturgical practice towards liberation and reconciliation around human difference,[9] which liturgy rehearses at its best. *Liturgy with a Difference* gathers a broad range of international theologians and scholars to interrogate liturgical practice in order to unmask ways in which dehumanizing majoritarianisms and presumed norms of gender, culture, ethnicity and body, among others, remain at work in congregations in ways that continue to marginalize some persons. It asks such questions as: Who is excluded still, and how, and who is favoured? What pernicious norms still govern below the surface, and how might they be revealed? How do texts, gestures and space abet and enforce such norms? How might Christian assemblies gather multiple expressions of human difference to propose, through Christian liturgy, patterns of graced interaction both in the assembly itself and in the world around it? The overarching goal is to propose pathways for renewed liturgical practice that recognize and rehearse the vivid richness of God's image found in the human community and glimpsed, if only for a moment, in liturgical celebration. This collection points a way beyond talk of inclusion towards a generous embrace of the many differences that make up the Christian community.

Beginning with liturgical practice as a privileged location to explore the interactions of human difference in worshipping communities, each essay focuses on how particular differences disrupt, contest and decentre unexamined norms in the communities in which they appear, as well as contribute something new to the liturgical practice of assemblies that engage them. They may then go on to suggest how appreciation of the difference in question proposes new meaning with the potential to reconcile communities across difference as well as liberate those who bear such difference to full agency in the liturgical assembly. The overarching goal is, in the first place, to suggest practices of a renewed liturgical celebration, and secondly, to invite wider reflection for Christian mission in the world, at a time when that mission is in many places now deeply fraught by mistrust of churches for their public, real, imagined and enacted resistance, exclusion and rejection of many of those deemed to be different from its 'norms'.[10]

A particular contribution of this collection is that it foregrounds what is often judged 'exceptional' (minority sexual orientation, disability, migrant experience) as the norm. Building upon writing on Christian worship and human difference that tends to juxtapose 'traditional liturgy' with the practices of feminist and LBGTQIA+ communities, or propose the 'inculturation' of European liturgical forms in non-European contexts, this collection upholds the view that the bearers of marginalized differences are privileged sources of theological enquiry about the liturgy from which emerge new theological understandings accessible through Christian worship.

The essays are organized around four centres of enquiry about liturgy. The first makes the case for treating the assembly itself, and differences that appear among its members, as a 'primary symbol' of liturgical celebration. Beginning with a liturgy of foot washing, Bryan Cones explores how the differences that appear in an assembly, along with the relationships among them, add to and expand the 'public meaning' of the received 'biblical-liturgical heritage' captured in the Gospel narrative (John 13). Stephen Burns then explores the ecumenical *ordo* that shapes both much current liturgical theology and ecclesial resources, both to suggest 'an agenda for scrutiny' around liturgical practice and to point to openings where difference can be welcomed into liturgical celebration.

A second set of essays turns to questions of leadership and ministry broadly considered within the assembly, particularly in relation to gender. What changes, for example, when the role of presider at Eucharist, long reserved to apparently cisgender males, is open to others? How does an assembly's celebration of marriage change when its primary ministers – the couple – are no longer presumed to be opposite-gender? Rachel Mann opens this section with her own reflections on presiding as a trans priest and the ways that liturgical 'performance' gestures towards queer identities present in the assembly. Susannah Cornwall engages and questions Elizabeth Stuart's conception of gender erasure, critically suggesting that the specificity of gender in the person of the presider, and in the rest of the assembly, is an important dimension of the eucharistic mystery. Turning attention beyond eucharistic liturgies, Scott Haldeman questions the rapidly expanding practice of same-gender couples celebrating the same (or nearly the same) liturgies of marriage as those undertaken by opposite-gender couples. He proposes a more circumspect adaptation taking into account the critiques levelled by some queer thinkers regarding the heteronormativity of received marriage practice. Frank Senn concludes this section with a reflection on his own shift as a pastor and presider regarding the partners to a marriage, occasioned by the marriage of one of his sons to his same-gender partner.

A third group of essays settles around questions of culture, language and migration, along with attendant privilege or 'majoritarianism' in the liturgical assembly related to them. What are an assembly's languages of prayer, and why? What differences or cultural competences are privileged – English-language literacy, for example, or the ability to recall from memory a song from one's homeland – and which are not? How does a denominational resource or authorized liturgical text imagine the assembly that will pray it? What personal or cultural 'stories' and life experiences does an assembly's practice presume as shared? Is there any way around the inevitable privileging of some differences over others? Kristine Suna-Koro begins these reflections as a Latvian Lutheran 'magpie' in the US context, exploring the endurance of cultural heritage after migration – with its own dangers of exclusion. Bruce Morrill describes a different journey as a cultural outsider serving among Yu'pik Catholics in Alaska and the ways such intercultural engagement and exchange contributes new dimension to liturgy in pastoral contexts. Finally, Michael Jagessar troubles hopes of multicultural inclusion from a postcolonial perspective, roundly questioning whether any majoritarian centre can, or will, allow itself to be overturned by those it has cast to the margins.

A final group of essays addresses Christian mission and the relation of this assembly to the world around it. How does an assembly's practice account for those of other faith traditions, if at all? How does its practice imagine or address a religiously plural culture, including the 'nones' and the spiritual-but-not-religious in their contexts? How does its practice address the surrounding culture's patterns of injustice in relation to difference, whether based on conceptions of race or ethnicity, country of origin, gender or mental health, among others? How does this assembly's liturgy become 'public service' by rehearsing alternative visions of life together? Teresa Berger, reflecting on a popular hymn announcing that 'all are welcome', asks if there are limits to that 'all' in light of gospel visions of justice. Edward Foley proposes preaching as 'public theology', a way to speak into and provide 'public service' for the contemporary Areopagus in search of a new shared humanism that both authentically expresses Christian tradition and addresses those who do not share Christian faith. Finally, engaging the crisis of migration and the inhumane treatment of migrating persons, Miguel De la Torre highlights the practice of sanctuary as a critique of and an alternative to the traditional 'worship' of the churches, with attention to the divine rejection of prayer without justice in the prophets of the Hebrew Bible.

These exploration 'centres' surely overlap, and no contribution here or elsewhere can ever be the last word on its topic. Our hope is, however, that each voice here might lift up a new set of conversations about difference in the liturgical assembly, and that together they might constitute some new opportunities for compelling, focused and connected, and needed conversation.

Notes

1 Note Gail Ramshaw, 2012, 'A Look at New Anglican Eucharistic Prayers', *Worship* 86: 161–7, in which she notes that in the 'authorized rites of the Anglican Communion' for celebration of Holy Communion, naming God as mother appears just once. Note too that the binary of 'men and women', latterly incorporated into texts for prayer, is now confronted with new questions about gender fluidity. The literature on feminist liturgy is considerable, which makes its lack of impact on many official resources all the more inexplicable: on feminist collections of prayer, see for example, Janet Morley, 1992, *All Desires Known*, 2nd edn, London: SPCK; St Hilda Community, 1996, *The New Women Included: A Book of Services and Prayers*, 2nd edn, London: SPCK; Nicola Slee, 2004, *Praying Like a Woman*, London: SPCK; Nicola Slee, 2011, *Seeking the Risen Christa*, London: SPCK. On worship practices and communities, see for example, Rosemary Radford Ruether, 1985, *Women-Church: Theology and Practice*, San Francisco, CA: HarperCollins; Gail Ramshaw, 1998, *Liturgical Language: Keeping It Metaphoric, Making It Inclusive*, Collegeville, MN: Liturgical Press; Janet Walton, 2000, *Feminist Worship: A Matter of Justice*, Collegeville, MN: Liturgical Press; Jan Berry, 2009, *Ritual-Making Women*, Sheffield: Equinox; Nicola Slee and Stephen Burns (eds), 2010, *Presiding Like a Woman*, London: SPCK.

2 For ecumenical perspectives, see Janet Wooton, Kirsty Thorpe and Ian Jones (eds), 2008, *Women and Ordination in the Christian Churches: International Perspectives*, Edinburgh: T&T Clark. On women's ordination in the Anglican tradition, see Fredrica Harris Thompsett (ed.), 2014, *Looking Forward, Looking Backward: Forty Years of Women's Ordination*, New York: Morehouse Publishing, with its emphasis on the United States, marking the anniversary of the ordination of the 'Philadelphia Eleven' in 1974. For persistent campaigning in Roman Catholic contexts, see http://womensordinationcampaign.org/ [accessed 8 September 2018]. Women's texts for prayer included in ecclesial liturgical resources are likely to be anonymous, though sometimes acknowledged in back matter. For studies of women at worship, see among the work of a number of important scholars the insightful

trajectory by Teresa Berger, including 1989, *Women's Ways of Worship: Gender Analysis and Liturgical History*, Collegeville, MN: Liturgical Press; Berger (ed.), 2005, *Dissident Daughters: Feminist Liturgies in Global Context*, Louisville, KY: WJKP; Berger, 2005, *Fragments of Real Presence: Worship in Women's Hands*, New York: Crossroad; 2011, *Gender Differences and the Making of Liturgical History: Lifting a Veil on Liturgy's Past*, Aldershot: Ashgate.

3 The picture is quite patchy, with some churches welcoming LGBTQIA+ couples into marriage, and persons into ordination, while in other traditions sometimes harsh resistance to both prevails. In some denominations, while some congregations will welcome LGBTQIA+ persons to local roles in ministry, others will actively exclude. The US-based Episcopal Church, Scottish Episcopal Church and Uniting Church in Australia represent some of the more progressive possibilities in different Western contexts. In the United States, the LGBTQIA+-identified Metropolitan Community Church was the first Christian denominational body to affirm religious same-gender marriage. See Heather White, 2015, 'Gay Rites and Religious Rights: New York's First Same-Sex Marriage Controversy', in Kathleen T. Talvacchia, Michael F. Pettinger and Mark Larrimore (eds), *Queer Christianities: Lived Religion in Transgressive Forms*, New York: New York University Press, pp. 79–90. More recently, larger denominational bodies in the United States have extended their liturgies of marriage to same-gender couples. These include the United Churches of Christ (2005), the Evangelical Lutheran Church in America (2009), The Episcopal Church (2015) and the Presbyterian Church USA (2015), among others. See http://www.pew research.org/fact-tank/2015/12/21/where-christian-churches-stand-on-gay-marriage/ [accessed 22 November 2017]. For The Episcopal Church's initial rites of same-sex blessing, see https://extranet.generalconvention.org/staff/files/download/15668. For early collections of prayer by gay and lesbian persons, see Elizabeth Stuart, 1993, *Daring to Speak Love's Name: A Gay and Lesbian Prayer Book*, Harmondsworth: Penguin; Kittredge Cherry and Zalmon Sherwood (eds), 1995, *Equal Rites: Gay and Lesbian, Services, Ceremonies and Celebrations*, Louisville, KY: WJKP; Geoffrey Duncan (ed.), 2002, *Courage to Love: An Anthology of Inclusive Worship Material*, London: DLT; and from the Metropolitan Community Church, Robert E. Shore-Goss, Robert Bonache, Patrick Cheng and Mona West (eds), 2014, *Queering Christianity: Finding a Place at the Table for LGBTQI Christians*, Santa Barbara, CA: ABC-CLIO.

4 African American hymnody is included in piecemeal ways in a variety of US-produced hymnals, notably 2001, *The African American Heritage Hymnal: 575 Hymns, Spirituals and Gospel Songs*, Chicago, IL: GIA, the Introduction to which claims it to be 'probably the most important addition to Protestant hymnody in the past century'. See also 1999, *This Far By Faith: An African American Resource for Worship*, Minneapolis, MN: Fortress Press. A smaller representation of this genre may also be found in an international range of contemporary hymnals.

5 The publications of the Iona Community have perhaps pre-eminently represented this to churches in the West, for example in John Bell (ed.), 1991, *Many and Great: Songs of the World Church*, Glasgow: Wild Goose Publishing. The Christian Conference of Asia's 2000, *Sound the Bamboo*, Taiwan: CCA, is a fine example of a collection with a particular focus on one continent. C. Michael Hawn, 2003, *Gather into One: Praying and Singing Globally*, Grand Rapids, MI: Eerdmans, is an important study of such music.

6 Various publications of the World Council of Churches represent this approach, and 'multicultural worship' has been well-served by the US-based United Church of Christ press, Pilgrim Press and the likes of Maren C. Tirabassi and Cathy Wonson Eddy (eds), 1995, *Gifts of Many Cultures: Worship Resources for the Global Community*, Cleveland, OH: Pilgrim Press, and 2011, *Gifts in Open Hands: More Worship Resources for the Global Community*, Cleveland, OH: Pilgrim Press.

7 See Michael N. Jagessar and Stephen Burns, 2011, *Christian Worship: Postcolonial Perspectives*, Sheffield: Equinox; HyeRan Kim-Cragg, 2012, *Story and Song: An Interplay Between Christian Education and Worship*, Berlin: Peter Lang; Claudio Carvalhaes (ed.), 2015, *Liturgy in Postcolonial Perspectives*, New York: Palgrave; Kwok Pui-lan and Stephen Burns (eds), 2016, *Postcolonial Practice of Ministry: Leadership, Liturgy and Interfaith Engagement*, Lanham: MD: Lexington; Kristine Suna-Koro, 2017, *In Counterpoint: Diaspora, Postcoloniality, and Sacramental Theology*, Eugene: OR: Pickwick Press.

8 For example, the excellent resource of The Episcopal Church, 1998, *Enriching Our Worship*, New York: Church Publishing, is a relatively flimsy paperback, also available online in PDF format, in contrast to the BCP, which is mass-produced in boards and leather cover.

9 We adopt the pair 'reconciliation and liberation' from Robert W. Hovda, in whose 1976 'classic' of liturgical theology, *Strong, Loving and Wise: Presiding in Liturgy*, Collegeville, MN: Liturgical Press, the phrase recurs.

10 For example, *The Catechism of the Catholic Church* (1994) reasserts the view that homosexuality is 'objectively disordered'. Yet the Roman Catholic Church's as well as other churches' capacity to speak on such moral issues is seriously compromised by public mistrust following their failures relating to the abuse of the vulnerable young.

PART I

The Case for Difference

'How Beautiful the Feet': Discerning the Assembly's Path on Holy Thursday

BRYAN CONES

Among the many fruits of the twentieth-century North Atlantic liturgical movement has been the restoration of richer, deeper celebrations of the liturgies of the Triduum.[1] This three-day observance shared across many liturgical families carries assemblies who keep it from the end of Lent at sunset on Holy or 'Maundy' Thursday[2] through the Great Vigil of Easter. Each moment in the liturgical round recalls and makes present again significant events at the end of Jesus' life and ministry: his last meal with his closest followers, his suffering and death, and his passage from death to resurrection. On their face, these liturgies seem to 're-enact' or retell these events in a kind of ritual drama, yet how they are celebrated, and by whom,[3] can expand and develop the biblical-liturgical tradition[4] that provides their source material. Even more, attending specifically to the actual bodies that celebrate such liturgies, including the culturally encoded differences and relationships they bring with them, can bring new contour and significance to the tradition as it has been received. In effect, in their signifying through the liturgy, assemblies, in their members' 'full, conscious, and active participation',[5] *add to and further develop* the revelatory patterns borne in the liturgies they celebrate.

I experienced this most recently in my ministry as a presbyter and associate pastor in an Episcopal church in suburban Chicago, Illinois. The custom in the parish I served was to gather on Thursday before Easter for a festive meal in the parish hall to bring an end to Lenten observance and turn towards the Triduum liturgies. During the meal,[6] the gathered assembly listened to the biblical readings appointed for Maundy Thursday, which culminate in the unique Johannine account of Jesus washing his disciples feet 'on the night before he died'.[7] As the assembly finished the meal, a preacher expanded on the Gospel message, which then led to singing and a simple procession of those gathered to the other end of the parish hall, where a few chairs had been arranged with basins and pitchers for the assembly to embody in ritual the story just proclaimed. While in some assemblies, the foot washing is limited to the ordained presider and a number of pre-selected members of the assembly,[8] in this assembly, all so moved took turns washing feet and having their own feet washed.[9] As the presider in this assembly, I occupied a privileged position as a leader and 'participant-observer'[10] in the liturgy that unfolded.

In my own pastoral-liturgical experience, many assembly members experience the foot-washing liturgy as quite confronting[11] – leading some assemblies to prefer a more straightforward re-enactment or panto-mime of the Gospel passage, with the presider 'playing Jesus' and with a number of assembly members, at times restricted to men, standing in for the disciples, as is imagined in some liturgical books.[12] And on this night, as on others before it, there was some uncertainty as to who might take a seat to have their feet washed. This evening, however, it took no time at all. A two-year-old member of the assembly, Albie, who had been baptized just the summer before, leapt into a chair to have his feet washed to be quickly followed by other younger members of the assembly, who led the (reluctant) adults to their own 'full, conscious, and active' par-ticipation. That child then, with assistance from another clergy person, washed his mother's feet, with profound effect on her own participation.[13]

Over the next 20 minutes or so, the assembly continued to wash and be washed, emptying basins and refilling pitchers, replacing towels and smil-ing through some embarrassment. As the last members so moved washed others' feet, the assembly began to process into the church proper to celebrate the Eucharist. In those last moments one of our elders struggled to kneel and wash the feet of his spouse of many decades. Her physical health was rapidly declining, along with her awareness of the world around her. As he washed her feet, assisted – at times embraced – by another member of the assembly, I could not fail to notice his tears.

While all the ritual actors – mother and child, spouses long married, assisting disciples – reflected the story of Jesus the teacher washing his students' feet as an example, the liturgy they led refracted significance beyond the biblical story that provides its shape. Bookended by the unabashed leadership of children and the grief mixed with gratitude near the end of life's journey, this liturgy proposed a 'kingdom scene'[14] that gave flesh to the contention captured in a 1977 document of the US bishops' Committee on the Liturgy: 'Among the symbols with which the liturgy deals, none is more important than *this assembly of believers* ... The most powerful experience of the sacred is found in the celebration and the persons celebrating, that is, it is found in the action of the assembly: the living words, the living gestures, the living sacrifice, the living meal.'[15]

At the same time, however, the symbolic contour proposed by this particular liturgy of foot washing – its 'public meaning' – extended well beyond the 'official meanings' proposed by the received biblical-liturgical heritage as captured in liturgical books and other resources. Neither the liturgical books of, in this case, the US Episcopal Church nor the readings designated for this liturgy specifically include the participation of children or even elders as such, much less a married couple. As a rule, these resources tend to focus on Jesus' servant ministry among his followers with reference to his impending death,[16] the role reversal embedded in a rabbi washing his disciples' feet (rather than the other way around),[17] or the works of service to which all Christians are called by virtue of their baptism.[18] Yet it is precisely through relationships not imagined or included in the biblical-liturgical tradition as received and interpreted that this liturgy signified. Without these differences interacting as they did, this liturgy could not have borne such meanings. Indeed, I would argue that without attending to such difference in any assembly, the revelatory significance of this liturgy – its *theologia prima*[19] – is likely to be missed, or perhaps dismissed as a happy coincidence rather than an encounter with the living God.

Tracing the Assembly's Symbolic Footprint

The contention that the assembly itself – the church gathered to celebrate its liturgy – is the primary symbol of its celebration is, along with the renewal of the Triduum liturgies, another of the fruits of the North Atlantic liturgical movement. Hovda's contention that 'this assembly of believers' is the 'primary symbol' of the liturgy has become for me a foundational first principle of liturgical theology and practice, and I have experienced its significance many times in liturgical celebration – though equally often *not* experienced it. As I have explored the discipline of liturgical theology over the years, it is a claim that continually strikes me as, on the one hand, often completely taken for granted, present across the churches in various forms, yet often also simultaneously ignored, unconsidered or underexplored. It is the kind of claim that appears at the beginning of any book, essay or collection on liturgy or liturgical theology as a kind of calling card or shibboleth, which is then curiously left behind in favour of talking about some other dimension of the liturgy.

Nor is the claim that the liturgical assembly has a basic, even primary, symbolic and sacramental function to make Christ present in manifold ways[20] left to stand on its own. Especially in Roman Catholic theological reflection, the fullest symbolic expression of the assembly relies on it gathering as much 'difference' or diversity as possible. Louis-Marie Chauvet summarizes an oft-repeated claim that the 'diversified Sunday assembly' is the 'most typical [and] "sacramentally" exemplary of the church'.[21] Hovda, too, extensively comments on the importance of diversity in the assembly, asserting that 'the different gifts of different sexes, colors, classes, ethnic groups, lifestyles are reconciled in a unity of common daughters and sons, sisters and brothers, whose variety enriches all'.[22] Yet, other than highlighting the value of 'diversity', these acknowledgements of embodied human difference remain in list form and are rarely interrogated for what each term might suggest to the significance of the whole.

On the contrary, this fundamental affirmation is not without significant reservation, as if too much attention to a particular difference in the assembly might lead to problems. Hovda himself warns against groups that may 'indulge' liturgically 'in self-promotion and self-pity'.[23] Aidan Kavanagh, echoing many commentators, evokes the classic text from Galatians (3.28): 'For if here we have no abiding city, why should we be concerned with cities and the human groups – male and female, slave and master, Jew and Greek, black and white – which inhabit them?'[24] Thus, while a diverse assembly is the presumed goal and fullest liturgical symbol, it is an assembly in which all that difference is, to draw on Paul Bradshaw's categories of liturgical study, 'lumped' together into a harmonious unity, rather than 'split' in ways to make visible the diversity present – and to interrogate the relationships among those differences.

That 'lump', however, as Teresa Berger points out in her work on gender in liturgical history, inevitably occludes how differences in the assembly are being negotiated, especially how some are favoured over others, and her work makes clear that 'there is no moment in time when gender did not shape Christian faith (Gal 3:28 notwithstanding)'.[25] Hers is but one of many contemporary 'contextual' theological bodies of work that point out that Christian assemblies are full of liturgical 'indulgences' that privilege some and diminish others through often unacknowledged or occluded majoritarianisms, presumed norms and cultural privileges – Galatians 3.28 notwithstanding. All these are forms of what Gordon Lathrop tags *antiliturgica*: hierarchical and closed-circle distortions that either 'rank' some of members of the assembly over others or completely exclude some from participation.[26] The danger here is a 'whitewashed' assembly in which differences are unreflectively taken for granted rather than mined for the positive dimension they may add to the symbol of 'this assembly of believers'.

That positive dimension is of particular importance. While it is one thing to acknowledge *antiliturgica* in all its pernicious forms – manifest in clericalism, sexism and cultural privilege to name a few – it is another thing to seek the 'new thing' that might be revealed in and through the diversified Sunday assembly. Berger's work on gender in liturgical historiography leads her to suggest diverse *plena et actuosa participatio*[27] in the assembly based on such difference:

An elderly Pentecostal worshiper suffering from dementia participates in worship differently from a young Roman Catholic woman just completing her doctorate in liturgical studies. And the unborn child of a fervently evangelical mother is present differently from an adult Greek Orthodox worshiper who happens to be blind. A mentally disabled or neuro-diverse teenager in a Lutheran congregation participates differently from a neuro-typical, yet stressed, mother of twins.[28]

Bruce Morrill and others also enter this space, drawing out pastoral conclusions from Chauvet's work on the symbolic significance of the actual bodies gathered in the assembly. He writes:

[T]he actual local celebration of liturgy is always charged with bodily tensions encompassing gender, race, age, ethnicity, as well as the needs and gifts of the physically, intellectually, or emotionally challenged. The practical ways these questions and tensions are actually approached in real pastoral settings has everything to do with whether a given community is embracing the diverse complexity of our bodily living as opportunities for sacramentally encountering the gracious favor of God or suppressing the body as an obstacle to what is 'truly' holy and spiritual.[29]

My own work seeks to push these strands forward into a renewed liturgical and sacramental imagination that embraces 'the diverse complexity of our bodily living' by describing and interrogating the 'performed' liturgical theologies of assemblies. Key to that effort is taking seriously the difference gathered in 'this assembly of believers' *as a source for theological reflection* and, further, new appreciation of its 'signification' that unveils *a new dimension to the divine encounter* proposed in and through liturgical celebration.

Tracking the Assembly's Maundy Thursday Trail

Returning to 'this assembly of believers' on that one Holy Thursday night, then, suggests that the *plena et actuosa participatio* of these unique bodies and their relation to one another propose new contour and significance to the received biblical-liturgical heritage captured in the current liturgies for Holy Thursday. It may also unmask *antiliturgica* present in that biblical-liturgical heritage as it is currently articulated in some liturgical books. Taken together, the practice of this assembly proposes adjustments for that assembly's future practice, which may also benefit other assemblies in their own practice of this or other liturgies.

Discerning the *prima theologia* of this assembly requires attention in particular to the differences present and how they interact. The two-year-old 'leader' who began the assembly's foot washing highlights an absence not only in the biblical-liturgical tradition but in the Gospel story itself. In this 'memory' of Jesus' final meal with his disciples, there are no actual children – though Jesus does call his disciples 'little children' later in the proclaimed passage.[30] If they (or anyone else) were there, they were not deemed worthy of memory. The primary relationships imagined in the biblical-liturgical heritage are those of 'master/servant' and 'messenger/ one who sends'. And yet in the practice of the assembly, the *plena et actuosa participatio* of this assembly's newest initiated member both leads the assembly's practice and, in his body, recalls to 'this assembly of believers' other dimensions of Jesus' life and teaching, notably his admonition to become 'like children' to enter the reign of God.[31] In this the child is an embodied 'intertextual' reference; the juxtaposition[32] of his age and development with the absence of that difference in the story directs the assembly beyond this one 'moment' in the story of Jesus ('the Last Supper') to the life and teaching that informs the very act of foot washing. The child himself becomes a homily within this assembly of believers, one in particular that offers a foil to the (adult) Peter's refusal ('never!') to allow Jesus to wash his feet (John 13.8).

The fact that Albie was recently baptized, known to many in the assembly, offers further contour – foot washing is, after all, what baptized living 'looks like' in ritual. In this, Albie may also direct the assembly forward to its own shared baptismal commitment, which it renews at the Easter Vigil. His mother and co-participant in the liturgy discerned that 'baptismal' echo and the role reversal:

> Since my son's birth, I'd been living out the 'love one another' part of the 'new commandment' in a way that consumed all the minutes of my life. I'd cleaned his face after every meal, bathed him every night, and wiped his bottom countless times a day. But suddenly, here he was, at my feet, washing and drying me. Loving and serving me.[33]

The fact that Albie cannot 'know' any of this – or at least his manner of 'knowing' is not accessible to this 'participant-observer' – adds further dimension to 'this assembly of believers'. As Berger notes, he is participating 'differently' from the adults in the room, the more verbal children, the neuro-diverse members. His participation, and the contour he contributes to the signifying assembly, signals the kind of 'knowledge' liturgy produces. As Judith Kubicki points out, 'The type of knowing that occurs within worship can be described as neither rational nor scientific. Rather, because it is symbolic activity, it is primarily non-discursive and exhibitive.

That is, meaning is not asserted by means of propositional content in worship, but exhibited or manifested in the interplay of symbolic activity.'[34] Albie's participation makes clear that no member of the assembly really 'knows' what they are doing, perhaps least while they are doing it. The *theologia prima* of the assembly can only be caught in the act!

The 'kingdom scene' proposed as an elder washed the feet of his diminishing spouse, assisted by a younger adult member of the congregation, also provides contour not imagined by the biblical story it echoes. Jesus' relative indifference to marriage (at least as recounted in the synoptic Gospels[35]) aside, the image of one spouse washing another's feet after decades of presumed mutual love and service witnessed over time by 'this assembly of believers' provides dimension not possible in a story about a one-off event in the hours before Jesus' death. This elder couple instead extends the insight of that story over time: here is what 'foot washing' looks like after 50 years as it has unfolded in the lives of a single couple. This is no 're-enactment' or pantomime, not *mimesis* but *anamnesis*, not only making present once more but extending, interpreting and adding dimension to an as-yet unfinished story. The juxtaposition of the spousal relationship with those present in the biblical narrative opens reflection towards other kinds of relationships through which a life of 'foot washing' unfolds. Like the child, this couple also becomes an 'intertextual' reference, though in this case not so much to other stories of Jesus but to the church's own recognition (perhaps contrary to Jesus' own emphases) of marriage as a privileged pattern of Christian living. The relationship of marriage itself suggests others, such as relationships between parent and child, as ways of living the 'new commandment' the Gospel narrative itself suggests (13.34–35).

The care of a currently more able-bodied partner for a body in a weaker condition, along with the assistance provided by yet another person, suggests further contour to 'this assembly of believers' perhaps not imagined by the liturgy as proposed. While the emphasis in the biblical narrative and much pastoral practice is on direct imitation of Jesus, the shared care of a weaker member suggests a different kind of relationship, indeed of the dignity and value of one whose physical, mental or emotional function is either diminished from a previous condition or simply different from the majority. The willingness of the weaker partner to engage in that 'full, conscious, and active' participation proposes a juxtaposition with the seemingly able-bodied Peter's initial refusal to have his feet washed. Here, the 'weaker' member signifies the willing response that Peter initially withheld. Even more, the advanced age and diminished condition of both washer and washed suggest the particular 'share' of Jesus' path Peter was resisting, a share in his death. Though not in proximate danger of death themselves, this elder couple and their diminishment could not but call to the assembly's attention the following day's recollection of Jesus' passion on Good Friday.

Stumbling Blocks on the Assembly's Path

Admittedly, the rich signification in 'this assembly of believers' apparent to this participant-observer is not necessarily common, as Thomas O'Loughlin documents in his study of foot washing in Roman Catholic contexts.[36] It is heavily dependent upon their *plena et actuosa participatio*, which, after all, is the 'aim above all else' identified by the Second Vatican Council's Constitution on the Liturgy in liturgical reform.[37] However, as expressed in some liturgical books and resources, that participation may well be limited to sitting and watching, perhaps singing, while the presider (perhaps along with other clergy and assistants) washes the feet of a selected few members of the assembly. Some liturgical books direct such a limited performance of the foot-washing liturgy; at best, such ritual performance will produce a contemporary re-enactment with the unfortunate effect of identifying the presider with the person of Jesus in the story, occluding any contemporary significance in 'this assembly of believers'. As Martin Connell notes,

> Efforts to re-enact the world of Jesus and his followers as an end in itself are more of an impediment to rather than an inspiration for paschal prayer and piety ... Liturgies are futile if the celebrations stop at mere imitation, for the communal actions are the ritual media for discerning and receiving the church's vocation today, as the community of faith orients itself once again to the word of God and to the practice of the sacraments.[38]

That is not to say that the 'difference' that appears in the presider, assistants and those whose feet are washed cannot propose some of the meanings suggested thus far. Media accounts have made much of the Bishop of Rome, Pope Francis, washing the feet of a young woman of Muslim faith, prisoners and those experiencing homelessness – a 'public service' that indeed troubles a straightforward mimesis of Jesus washing the feet of his inner circle, which has, in turn, provoked further reflection on the practice.[39] Yet such performance does not trouble the direct identification of the presider with Jesus, nor does it suggest a liturgy in which all participants are full and conscious actors, both as those washing and those being washed. In the end, even the best such examples maintain actors and 'audience'.

It is likely, then, that the biblical-liturgical tradition and its various receptions continue to inscribe a hierarchical *antiliturgica*, one that in this case emphasizes the identification of clergy with the person of Jesus, ironically turning a ritual act proposed as embodying humility and service into one that sets the presider apart from the rest of the assembly. Such practice limits rather than extends the full Christic significance of the assembly in and through its difference, collapsing an open-ended and multivalent liturgical symbol (embodied in the assembly as a whole) into a more or less straightforward sign (embodied in the single presider who 'represents' Jesus, with some 'representatives'). At best, such performance produces accessible ritual drama; at worst, it undermines the full christological and symbolic significance of the assembly as a whole. Such practice is unlikely to foster the 'adjustment to deep change caused in the assembly by its being brought regularly to the brink of chaos in the presence of the living God',[40] which Aidan Kavanagh describes as the 'ontological condition' of theology itself.

The clear and present danger of limiting any assembly's practice of foot washing, and the revelatory power of doing the opposite, is clear. As O'Loughlin notes (and who could argue?), contemporary societies 'are riven by distinctions based on wealth, ecclesiastical status, color, ethnicity, gender, and sexual orientation. Mutual foot-washing challenges these divisions, calling on us to recognize our human commonality and equality as creatures, and the bonds that unite us, in the Christ, as sisters and brothers in the Father's family.'[41] Indeed, reflection on the practice of foot washing, in this case from Reformation-era churches that have recovered the practice as part of their celebration of the Lord's Supper, testifies to its power to propose new relationships. Writing as one who has 'drunk the sin of racism with our mother's milk', Mennonite Marc Thiessen Nation eloquently describes the effect of a foot washing that crossed boundaries of colour in his own church. Writing of his encounter as a white man with an African American parishioner, Ralph Ferguson, through the practice of foot washing, Nation writes: 'It never occurred to him [Ferguson] – a profoundly Christian man – not to pick up a towel, place my feet, the feet of a white man, in the basin and wash my feet and allow me to wash his',[42] which Nation experienced, along with the embrace that followed the washing, as 'revolutionary signifiers of new life' – even if that sign is not a reality in the world around. It would not be hard to imagine other relationships to which this Mennonite 'basin ministry', as they call it, might propose new and liberating alternatives.

Clearing the Assembly's Path

Assembly practices that take seriously the differences gathered in an assembly and the *plena et actuosa participatio* of those who bear them propose new opportunities for the continued development of Christian *theologia prima*. In the case of the liturgy of foot washing, the juxtaposition of differences of age, development, ability and relationship visible in this small assembly on one Holy Thursday suggests liturgical practice that diminishes any direct mimesis of a particular biblical passage, complete with identification of contemporary individuals with the characters in the scene. Rather, both the story and the ritual pattern it suggests might better be received as templates to engage and inhabit rather than a kind of 'ritual pedagogy' that retells the story by acting it out. On the contrary, the participation of children, elders and persons with bodies impaired or diminished by age or illness adds something to the heritage that has been received, making up for what is lacking in the foundational narrative and, more, extending it into new and revelatory territory.

In the case of the liturgy of foot washing, a continued development of fuller participation in the ritual itself – the opportunity to wash and be washed – appears as an obvious necessity, along with a surrender of unnecessarily narrow interpretations of the liturgy's 'meaning'. Taking 'this assembly of believers' seriously as the liturgy's 'primary symbol' suggests that its most fulsome signification can be found in its fullest expression: each member participating according to their own gifts and ability, with provision made for them to do so,[43] and the presumption that they are so invited. This goal will require pastoral liturgists to be both proactive in ensuring access to participation for all members and vigilant for insidious *antiliturgica* that value some over others, particularly clergy and those most closely associated with them. As Thomas O'Loughlin beautifully puts it: 'I become Christ-like when I adopt the role of the servant and wash another's feet; I discover my dignity within Christ when an *alter Christus*, another disciple, washes my feet.'[44]

These adjustments may or may not require abandoning some of the received interpretations of the biblical-liturgical heritage, though some may drop away or reveal new contour. More positively, some of what has been received – for example, the connection between Holy Thursday and ordained ministry or (in some traditions) 'priesthood' – may only need to be reframed with reference to the whole. Thus if the presider by virtue of leadership in the assembly may refer to Christ, she does so by exemplifying that presence in the assembly as a whole and in her leadership inviting the assembly's members to engage and experience their own share in Christ's priestly ministry. Celebrating foot-washing liturgies beyond Holy Thursday, as is the custom among some Mennonite congregations and is encouraged by O'Loughlin in his own proposals for this liturgy, would also help reduce both the clerical cast and the mimetic tendencies of some foot-washing liturgies.[45]

Beyond this, two further things are likely desirable, at least to ensure that the pastoral-liturgical and theological reflection presented here is not limited to privileged participant-observers such as this presbyter and pre-sider. The first is formation: while the goal of *plena et actuosa participatio* may indeed be the 'aim above all else' in the renewal of the liturgy, it is a difficult goal if pastors, preparers and people do not have the tools to take their 'full, conscious and active' part. Peter Jeffrey in his own critique of current Roman Catholic practice notes the right of assemblies 'to be taught and nourished by the complete and authentic liturgical tradition' – to which he adds participation in the reform of the rites themselves.[46] Not least among the elements of this formation is recognition of the theo-logical value and significance of the difference gathered in the assembly.

The second task is *mystagogia*: if *theologia prima* is indeed 'primarily non-discursive and exhibitive', it requires the thoughtful reflection of those who engage it to detect its movement and follow the 'adjustments' proposed by their encounter with the living God. Such shared reflection might draw out the connections between washing feet and initiation, as in the case of Albie, or washing feet and Christian marriage, as in the case of the assembly's elders. Both have the possibility of bringing to an assem-bly's awareness meanings that may well be part of the biblical-liturgical heritage but are rarely explored, such as the practice of foot washing as part of the rites of initiation among some ancient Christians,[47] or the con-nection between Jesus' washing his disciples' feet and Mary of Bethany's anointing of Jesus' feet in the passage preceding this one.[48] It also may invite the assembly to make connections across its own practice, from the baptism of a child to the marriage of its members. As O'Loughlin points out,

> Reflection on the experience, both as a washer and as one whose feet have been washed, is an essential part of the event. In this the community needs to give itself space to let individuals articulate their discomfort with the action and in the process reframe it. It is the totality of the experience – discomfort, practical messiness, surprise, and thoughtful hindsight – that make this a mystagogical occasion and a moment on the path of discipleship.[49]

Such reflection might well begin by looking back to discern the prints and trail of all those unique and beautiful feet for the embodied records of its encounter with the living God.

Notes

1 This restoration began in 1951 with a revision of the liturgies of the Triduum in the Roman Catholic Church, renewed in 1956 and integrated into the 1970 liturgies after the Second Vatican Council's liturgical reform. See, for example, Martin Connell, 2006, *Eternity Today: On the Liturgical Year, Vol. 2: Sunday, Lent, the Three Days, The Easter Season, Ordinary Time*, New York/London: Continuum, pp. 121–4. Connell notes that the rites of the Three Days are shared in the liturgical books of 'Lutheran, Episcopal, Presbyterian, and Methodist' churches (p. 129, n. 50). What follows below references liturgies from those traditions, as well as some Mennonite and Anabaptist reflection on foot washing, which does not necessarily coincide with Holy/Maundy Thursday. See, for example, Bob Brenneman, 2009, 'Embodied Forgiveness: Yoder and the (Body) Politics of Footwashing', *The Mennonite Quarterly Review* 83: 7–28.

2 'Maundy' refers to the 'new commandment', *mandatum*, of John 13, recalled during this liturgy.

3 I take for granted the widely held position that, while often rooted in denominational and other resources, liturgy is an action best described as 'performance', with its many meanings. See, for example, Richard McCall's 2007, *Do This: Liturgy as Performance*, Notre Dame, IN: University of Notre Dame Press, especially the summary on pp. 76–7.

4 Robert Hovda uses this expression to capture the broad range of texts and practices inherited and engaged by assemblies. He writes, 'The liturgical book offers only the ritual skeleton and structure, gifting the faith community with the biblical and ecclesial tradition.' See his 1983, 'Sunday No Better – After All This Betterment', *Worship* 57: 527. In the case of foot washing, both the Gospel story proclaimed from John 13 and the enacted practice of that story comprise the foundation of the assembly's reception of the tradition.

5 Constitution on the Sacred Liturgy *Sacrosanctum concilium*, 1963, para. 14, in Austin Flannery (gen. ed.), 1975, *Vatican Council II: The Conciliar and Postconciliar Documents*, New York: Costello Publishing, p. 8.

6 The Episcopal Church's *Book of Occasional Services* [BOS] offers a template for a Maundy Thursday celebration including a meal, which is not to be confused in any way with a Jewish Passover Seder. See 'Agapé Meal for Maundy Thursday', in BOS, 2003, New York: Church Publishing, pp. 95–6.

7 The Episcopal Church's lectionary follows the Revised Common Lectionary and proclaims John 13.1–17, 31b–35. This passage, or some portion of it, is routinely included in liturgies of foot washing on Holy Thursday and other times. The exclusion of some verses (13.18–31a), which reference Jesus' betrayal by Judas, is worth noting, as their absence shapes the possible interpretation of the liturgy. While exegetical analysis of the text may highlight the purpose of these verses, their significance will not likely appear in the liturgy, rendering some exegesis on the passage less apropos to the liturgy's interpretation.

8 The current edition of the *Roman Missal* until 2016 specified that '*viri selecti*' (chosen men) had their feet washed by the presider (always a presbyter). At the direction of Pope Francis, the Congregation for Divine Worship and the Discipline of the Sacraments issued a revised rubric indicating '[t]hose who are chosen from amongst the people of God' may participate, indicating the group can include 'men and women … young and old, healthy and sick, clerics, consecrated men and women and laity'. This change did not affect the rubric indicating that 'the Priest' be the one to wash those chosen. See Congregation for Divine Worship and the

Discipline of the Sacraments, Decree *In missa in cena Domini*, 6 January 2016, http://www.vatican.va/roman_curia/congregations/ccdds/documents/rc_con_ ccdds_doc_20160106_decreto-lavanda-piedi_en.html [accessed 3 August 2018]; and 'The Sacred Paschal Triduum: The Washing of the Feet', nos. 10–11 in *The Roman Missal: English Translation According to the Third Typical Edition*, 2011, London: Catholic Truth Society, pp. 331–2. The Church of England's *Common Worship* simply indicates, 'The president may wash the feet of some members of the congregation'. See *Common Worship: Times and Seasons*, 2000, 'The Liturgy of Maundy Thursday', https://www.churchofengland.org/prayer-and-worship/ worship-texts-and-resources/common-worship/churchs-year/times-and-seasons/ passiontide-and-holy-week#mmm173 [accessed 31 July 2018].

9 The Episcopal Church's *Book of Common Prayer* [BCP] simply states, 'When observed, the ceremony of the washing of feet appropriately follows the gospel and homily'. See BCP, 1979, New York: Church Publishing, p. 274. Other liturgies provided in BOS make some provision for other members of the assembly to wash feet, such as 'Maundy Thursday Rite of Preparation for the Paschal Holy Days', which proposes foot washing as an opportunity for renewal of baptism and/ or reconciliation. See BOS, pp. 144–5. The more standard 'On Maundy Thursday, at the Footwashing', however, presumes the ordained presider is the one washing feet, with its pastoral introduction (spoken by the presider) noting, 'I invite you … who share in the royal priesthood of Christ, to come forward, that I may recall whose servant I am by following the example of my Master.' See BOS, p. 93. Other resources, and much pastoral practice, however, extends this gesture to the whole assembly. *The United Methodist Book of Worship*, for example, insists, 'Mutual footwashing among pastor(s) and laypersons should be clearly visible.' See United Methodist Church, 1992, *The United Methodist Book of Worship*, Nashville, TN: The United Methodist Publishing House, p. 351.

10 I draw the language of 'participant-observer' from Margaret Mary Kelleher, who proposes this method to ascertain the 'public meanings' of liturgy as it is celebrated, which she relates to the 'official meanings' proposed by official resources and the 'private meanings' proposed by individuals. See her 1998, 'Liturgical Theology: A Task and a Method', *Worship* 62: 2–25, along with her 1985, 'Liturgy: An Ecclesial Act of Meaning', *Worship* 59: 482–97. For more on Kelleher's approach to the different 'meanings' present in liturgy, see Jan Michael Joncas, 2003, 'Ritual Transformation: Principles, Patterns, People', in *Toward Ritual Transformation: Remembering Robert W. Hovda*, Gabe Huck and others (eds), Collegeville, MN: Liturgical Press, pp. 49–69.

11 Liturgical books themselves betray some anxiety about this ritual. *United Methodist Book of Worship* encourages 'Careful advance planning and advance notice' for foot washing (p. 351). The Uniting Church in Australia's *Uniting in Worship* 2 twice repeats that foot washing be 'voluntary' with 'no element of coercion'. See Uniting Church, 2005, *Uniting in Worship* 2, Sydney: Uniting Church Publishing, pp. 610, 603, respectively.

12 Thomas O'Loughlin is particularly critical of both Roman Catholic resources and liturgical celebration in this regard, judging them as 'mime', echoing a critique by Peter Jeffery, who focuses on the exclusion of women in such 'scenes'. See O'Loughlin, 2014, 'From a Damp Floor to a New Vision of Church: Footwashing as a Challenge to Liturgy and Discipleship', *Worship* 88: 137–50, at 141; and Jeffery, 1990, '*Mandatum novum do vobis*: Toward a Renewal of the Holy Thursday Footwashing Rite', *Worship* 64: 107–41.

13 Albie's mother, Meghan Murphy-Gill, a friend and colleague, wrote of her own 'participant-observation' and the meanings she derived from it in her 2017 essay, 'As I Have Loved You', *U.S. Catholic* 82 (2017, no. 4): 45–6. Her son's name is used with her permission.

14 Hovda proposes that liturgy makes possible a 'powerful corporate consciousness of God' marked by a 'sense of mystery and reverence', which upends distinctions among persons. While affirming the 'scene', however, the 'distinctions' present in this assembly are, to my eye, key to interpreting the gospel relationships there proposed. See Robert Hovda, 1976, *Strong, Loving, and Wise: Presiding in the Liturgy*, Washington, DC: Liturgical Conference, pp. 75–6.

15 United States Bishops' Committee on the Liturgy, 1977, *Environment and Art in Catholic Worship*, Washington, DC: United States Catholic Conference, para. 28, emphasis added. Robert Hovda was among this document's primary authors.

16 See, for example, Gordon W. Lathrop's 2012, *The Four Gospels on Sunday: The New Testament and the Reform of Christian Worship*, Minneapolis, MN: Fortress Press: 'In this meal ... Jesus serves the participants with his serving love, with his very death' (p. 137).

17 Exegetical studies of John 13 frequently point out the unusual situation of a teacher washing disciples' feet, noting that even Jewish slaves were not required to provide such service, and that hosts generally provided water for guests to wash their own feet. See, for example, Raymond Brown, 1970, *The Gospel According to John: XIII–XXI (The Anchor Bible)*, Garden City, NY: Doubleday & Company, Inc., pp. 564–5. John Christopher Thomas provides an exhaustive study of foot washing in ancient and biblical contexts in his 1991, *Footwashing in John 13 and the Johannine Community*, Journal for the Study of the New Testament Supplement Series 61, Worcester, UK: JSOT Press.

18 *Evangelical Lutheran Worship* provides a representative example of a common interpretation in the presiding minister's words introducing foot washing: 'Our commitment to this loving service is signified in the washing of feet, following the example our Lord gave us on the night before his death.' See *Evangelical Lutheran Worship: Leader's Desk Edition*, 2006, Minneapolis, MN: Augsburg Fortress, p. 632. Reformed traditions without official liturgical resources that practise foot washing also tend to focus on 'mutual service' as the ritual's primary meaning. As Keith Graber Miller writes of the practice among some Mennonites, 'The Mennonite bodily practice [of foot washing] itself has carried with it not only the sense of humbling oneself, but humbling oneself for mutual service to another person.' See his 1992, 'Mennonite Footwashing: Identity Reflections and Altered Meanings', *Worship* 66: 148–70, at 167.

19 Aidan Kavanagh defines an assembly's *theologia prima* as 'adjustments' that 'will affect [an assembly's] next liturgical act, however slightly'; in this case, the *theologia prima* can be discerned through the interaction of difference in the assembly. See Kavanagh's 1984, *On Liturgical Theology*, Collegeville, MN: Liturgical Press, p. 74. Gordon Lathrop defines *theologia prima* as 'the communal meaning of the liturgy exercised in the gathering itself'. See his 1993, *Holy Things: A Liturgical Theology*, Minneapolis, MN: Fortress Press, p. 5.

20 *Sacrosanctum concilium*, para. 7.

21 Louis-Marie Chauvet, 2001, *The Sacraments: The Word of God at the Mercy of the Body*, Collegeville, MN: Liturgical Press, p. 34.

22 Robert Hovda, 1984, 'Cultural Adaptation and the Ministry of Reconciliation', *Worship* 58: 252–3.

23 Robert Hovda, 1990, 'The Relevance of the Liturgy', *Worship* 64: 62–3.

24 Kavanagh, *On Liturgical Theology*, p. 52.

25 Teresa Berger, 2008, '"Wisdom Has Built Her House" (Proverbs 9:1): Gendering Sacred Space', *Studia Liturgica* 38: 176.

26 Gordon Lathrop, 2003, *Holy Ground: A Liturgical Cosmology*, Minneapolis, MN: Fortress Press, pp. 181–2.

27 *Sancrosanctum concilium*, para. 14.

28 Teresa Berger, 2015, 'Gender Matters in Worship: An Ecumenical Theme Across a Divided Church', *Liturgy* 30, no. 4: 42.

29 Bruce Morrill, 1999, 'Initial Consideration: Theory and Practice of the Body in Liturgy Today', in Bruce Morrill (ed.), *Bodies of Worship: Explorations in Theory and Practice*, Collegeville, MN: Liturgical Press, p. 4.

30 John 13.33, NRSV.

31 For example, Matthew 18.3.

32 Gordon Lathrop proposes juxtaposition for the purpose of 'breaking' a received symbol, yielding something new – 'one thing set against another across silence', which Lathrop identifies as 'the poetic tradition of Christian liturgy – the way liturgical celebration makes meaning'. See his *Holy Ground*, p. 194.

33 Murphy-Gill, 'As I Have Loved', p. 46. It is worth noting that Sandra Schneiders excludes such relationships of dependent service (including mother to child) in her own oft-cited hermeneutic exegesis of John 13, arguing instead that in washing his disciples' feet, 'Jesus has transcended and transformed the only onto-logically based inequality among human beings' (p. 87). Thus, Murphy-Gill's own imputed meaning to the ritual may actually critique and expand the narrative as pro-claimed and interpreted, with its focus on hierarchical relationships (even upended ones). Schneiders's exegetical method, however, makes room for Murphy-Gill's own 'reading' when Schneiders writes: '[T]he text mediates a meaning which is not behind it, hidden in the shroud of the past when the text was composed, but ahead of it in the possibilities of human and Christian existence which it projects for the reader' (p. 77). See Schneiders, 1981, 'The Foot Washing (John 13:1-20): An Experiment in Hermeneutics', *The Catholic Biblical Quarterly* 43: 76–92.

34 Judith Kubicki, 2006, *The Presence of Christ in the Liturgical Assembly*, New York: Continuum, 15.

35 For example, Matthew 19.10–12.

36 O'Loughlin, 'A Damp Floor', pp. 137–8.

37 *Sacrosanctum concilium*, para. 14, in *Vatican Council II*, p. 8.

38 Connell, *Eternity Today*, p. 107.

39 Thomas O'Loughlin begins his reflection with Pope Francis's practice of foot washing. See 'A Damp Floor', p. 137. O'Loughlin has also explored a further renewal of foot-washing practice in Roman Catholic contexts in his 2015, *Washing Feet: Imitating the Example of Jesus in the Liturgy Today*, Collegeville, MN: Liturgical Press.

40 Kavanagh, *On Liturgical Theology*, p. 74.

41 O'Loughlin, 'A Damp Floor', p. 147.

42 Mark Thiessen Nation, 2011, 'Footwashing: Preparation for Christian Life', in Stanley Hauerwas and Samuel Wells (eds), *The Blackwell Companion to Christian Ethics*, 2nd edn, Chichester: Wiley-Blackwell, pp. 479–90, at 487. Fellow Mennon-ite Bob Brenneman writes similarly of the power of foot washing to signify racial reconciliation in the US context. See his 'Embodied Forgiveness', p. 21.

43 The United Church of Christ's *Book of Worship* signals the need to provide

provision for assembly members to participate according to their ability: 'Adjustments will need to be made for those whose abilities do not include some of these physical movements.' See 'Order for Footwashing', in United Church of Christ, 1986/2012, *Book of Worship*, Cleveland, OH: United Church of Christ, p. 205.

44 O'Loughlin, 'A Damp Floor', p. 143.

45 The United Church of Christ's *Book of Worship* (p. 197) notes 'service of footwashing may be held at any time'. In *Washing Feet*, O'Loughlin proposes a number of 'liturgical scenarios' that might offer appropriate opportunities, including small-group gatherings, the beginning of Lent, liturgies commissioning ministers and ecumenical services. See *Washing Feet*, pp. 87–111.

46 Jeffery, '*Mandatum novum*', p. 136.

47 Connell, for example, is at pains to highlight the initiatory character of the liturgies of the Triduum as a whole, beginning with foot washing on Holy Thursday and culminating in the rites of initiation at the Great Vigil: '[T]he Three Days is the climactic time of renewing the baptismal vocation of the local church as a whole.' See *Eternity Today*, p. 108.

48 Almost all exegetical studies of John 13 note the connection between Mary's anointing of Jesus 'for his burial' and Jesus' own action and its connection, in the dialogue with Peter, to a share in Jesus' death, a connection largely absent from denominational resources and much preaching, with their focus on service in some form. Harold Weiss, for example, draws particular attention to 'love and devotion' in the action of Mary, a contour suggested by the elder married couple. See Weiss, 1979, 'Foot washing in the Johannine community', *Novum Testamentum* 21: 298–325.

49 O'Loughlin, 'A Damp Floor', p. 149.

2

Acts of Uniformity

STEPHEN BURNS

Acts of Uniformity refer in the first place to a series of measures by the British Parliament in the sixteenth and seventeenth centuries.[1] The first such Act, concerned as it was with 'uniformity of service and administration of the sacraments', established the Book of Common Prayer (BCP) of 1549 – a new compilation and composition largely by Archbishop Thomas Cranmer – as the only legal form of worship in England. The Act, dated 21 January 1549, held that violators were to be punished with incrementally harsh penalties: for clerics refusing to use the book, in the initial breach six months' imprisonment and loss of income, then longer imprisonment and loss of livelihood, and on the third violation, life imprisonment. Further Acts of Uniformity followed with subsequent editions of the BCP, next in 1552 with the second, more Protestant, version of the book, which added to an expanded list of punishable violations absence from worship. Another Act followed in 1559, and another on 16 May 1662, following the publication of the book that has served as something like the 'definitive' edition of the BCP, becoming, through migration via mission and colonization, the main source of prayer across what would become the 'Anglican Communion' around the world.

One immediate effect of the 1662 Act was the ejection of perhaps 2,500 ministers who refused to abide by the book, and hence the tradition of 'non-conformity'. That 1662 Act was allied to other acts which temporally framed it, such as the Corporation Act of 1661, which required persons in civil office to partake in Communion in Anglican churches – so effectively excluding non-conformists from leadership in public life – and the Conventicle Act of 1664, which forbade unauthorized gatherings for worship by more than five persons from more than one household – and hence meant to restrict non-conformists from free religious practice.

The first Act of Uniformity to enforce a particular text for use in worship was also known as the 'Act of Equality'. Equal it may have made persons in their access to newly defined legal acts of worship, thwarting the different 'uses' of rites in Latin, the best known and most widely used of which had been Sarum. But unfolding restrictions from subsequent Acts of Uniformity, Corporation and Conventicle Acts seriously curtailed freedoms – and this despite a subsequent so-called Act of Toleration in 1689 that allowed for some meetings of non-conformists, without lifting civil restrictions upon them, nor being applied to Roman Catholics. While uniformity and equality may have been used together in the first Act, equality and uniformity were not then, nor are now, corresponding in meaning, as reference in the first Act itself to 'the king's dominions' gives the clue, quite apart from the realities of sanctioned retribution for deviation from enforced norms seen in the Acts and their allied parliamentary manoeuvres.

This essay is concerned about acts of uniformity, not only of the kind just mentioned, but dimensions of liturgical celebration that presume or pressure for uniform participation in our own times. While sixteenth- and seventeenth-century parliamentary measures were one means of imposing a certain kind of sameness, a range of dynamics are even now at work in Christian liturgy that resist or contest the presence of difference. In the following pages, I chart some such dynamics, also noting several openings where more space could be made for better recognition of difference.

More positively framed, it might be said that at least some of the dynamics pressing for sameness serve to promote unity. By no means do I intend my reflections to counter ways in which liturgy might enable recognition of a certain commonality, and even create it. My concern is rather that common prayer should not erase difference, nor deny the presence of those who are or wish to be there, currently excluded or as it were incognito because of majoritarian pressure and 'the tyranny of normality'[2] manifest in the assembly's order, practices and talk. Indeed, I think that liturgy can and might yet invite, celebrate and foster differences that have not always been recognized, or are not now widely recognized, in many gatherings for worship. Therefore, questions about the limited kinds of unity that are all that liturgy often shows forth remain close to the surface in what follows, seeing that some liturgical domains are becoming increasingly – in some respects, disturbingly – uniform. For example, the point that Christian assemblies can sometimes be marked by quite limited inclusion can be felt with some force when one recognizes the prevalence in some contexts of what Gary Bouma, an Australian sociologist of religion, dubs 'geriatric assemblies'.[3] In the Anglican tradition in its Australian setting, the kind of brittle Anglo-Catholicism that prevails in some parts of the country – largely in ineffective opposition to the encroaching conservative evangelicalism of Sydney Diocese – is vulnerable to Bouma's descriptive tag. At the time of writing, a once cardinal 'catholic' parish in Melbourne Diocese has just published its parish profile, in search of a new vicar. With 80 per cent of its congregation over 60 years of age, and 50 per cent over 70, the parish is a fine example of what Bouma means by a geriatric assembly – and its determination not to change its ways of worship, stated quite openly in the profile, is unlikely to make for future flourishing. It might well be said that, to allude to the title of a book on Anglo-Catholicism by Geoffrey Rowell (*The Vision Glorious*[4]), if the glory has not yet departed, it is heading for the door, perhaps to fritter out in a series of grand funeral processions. While the sense of the communion of saints may currently be alive in this parish, whatever might be said about its self-understanding of the like of 'stand[ing] with Christians throughout history and around the world today',[5] no one young is marching in such that there can be confidence that the 'tradition' will continue. It is not being handed on.[6]

Resistance to change is wider than any one church style, of course – a point well made by Steven Croft and others[7] in their insistence that 'fresh expressions of church' are not simply an evangelical affair. At the current time in contexts across both international and ecumenical lines, fresh expressions are attempts to engage with – in hope of eventual reverse of – the reality of decline in churches of liturgical predilections of all kinds. The literature on evaluating fresh expressions raises many apt – as well as sometimes bitter – critiques[8] and important questions about the capacity, indeed intent, of fresh expressions to sediment communities of like-kind persons. Just one ambiguous example of the risk might be glimpsed in the movie *Fight Church*,[9] centred on mixed martial arts as a medium around which a church can be organized. While in a way the whole Christian tradition – like its parent religion in Israel – emerges out of Jacob's wrestling,[10] Fight Church is a distinctive phenomenon, and its embrace of violence is troubling. But not all like-kind churches need be as stark as Fight Church. They may indeed be as innocuous as 'family': a somewhat ironic billboard for a Uniting Church in Melbourne advertises a weekly event of 'Family Church' – with every person pictured a senior/seasoned citizen. That church may be a family of sorts, with the word capturing the close, loyal or intimate sense of kinship felt by those inside the experience, but if so it is a family that does not appear to have intergenerational dimensions – and evidently includes no children, nor perhaps the next two generations up from the young – and is another example of a geriatric assembly. These snapshots make the point that the potential risk in fresh expressions to narrow to a certain demographic is not something to which fresh expressions alone are prone. 'Traditional' contexts can be deeply entrenched in the same problems, making for situations in which various kinds of difference have all but disappeared. But how might difference be embraced?

An Agenda for Scrutiny

The rest of this essay makes some notes 'Concerning the Celebration'[11] organized around the notion of the ecumenical *ordo* – itself a construct, and not least one that can be interrogated about its capacity for 'ideology'.[12] The shape of the ecumenical *ordo* by no means influences all Christian assemblies, in either traditional or 'fresh' modes. But its pattern at the very least suggests an agenda for scrutiny around which in what follows I assemble what are in large part reminders, reiterations and amplifications of fragments of reflection, brought together to enquire how to open space in which many kinds of difference might be invited, named, acknowledged, enacted, blessed.

Gathering

It is a commonplace of contemporary liturgical theology that the assembly is the primary symbol of the liturgy. An uncompromising statement of such is made in the US Roman Catholic bishops' statement *Environment and Art in Catholic Worship*: 'Among the symbols with which liturgy deals, none is more important than this assembly of believers.'[13] The author of that statement was Robert Hovda, who in his own voice sometimes suggested a slightly modified, possibly gentler, variant: 'the gathering of the sisters and brothers is a primary sign of the Sunday assembly, a primary part of the symbol'.[14] The conviction manifests in the affirmation that 'the assembly is the celebrant', as the International Anglican Liturgical Consultation, among many others, put it.[15] One would barely know this in many assemblies, however, given that the leadership effectively expropriates from the rest of the people all liturgical ministries, while the rest of the people effectively become spectators.[16] Prayer books and liturgical resources may in part be to blame for such scenarios, as these can sometimes rather suggest that if the people have read designated lines of dialogue text, one or two persons have stepped up to read a Scripture portion (unlikely the Gospel portion, which is perplexing, whatever the weight of history) and again one or two have further 'assisted' in serving Communion – likely carrying a chalice rather than a plate – then they have participated.[17] Furthermore, the prayers of the people, often the freest place in the *ordo* for local text and extemporary voice, are forced into being a very freighted symbol of an actively engaged assembly. Over the past 50 or so years of liturgical scholarship, nuancing notions of Vatican II's sparkling idea of 'full, conscious and active participation'[18] may have led to deeper appreciations of quietude and contemplation as means of such participation, but these attractive preoccupations are by no means always what are going on when laity have minimal involvements in vocal and focal shared leadership of celebration. It may just as well be that the assembly has been rendered lumpen and sidelined. While introductory passages of some prayer books may suggest that 'the congregation is not an audience',[19] convincingly enacting this idea is not widely in evidence, and sometimes rubrics seem to have no idea about how or intent to enact it. Such it is that ceremonial scenes, whether crafted by rubrical directives in a liturgical resource, uncritically inherited in the absence of rubrics from some official source or locally composed, can all too easily compound the problems of expropriation from the people of their role and status in the celebration.[20] Ceremonial proposals to animate the conviction that the assembly is celebrant are rare, and much needed: as a countersign of what they have to confront, I recall a deplorable liturgy in a Melbourne theological college chapel in which an archbishop was censed multiple times, his presbyteral sidekick two or three times and the entire assembly (admittedly small) just once for the lot. Appreciation of either the people's 'worth[iness] to stand in [God's] presence and serve [God]',[21] let alone the assembly as the celebrant seemed quite unlikely to be absorbed from the malformed and mal-forming ceremonial.

A basic requirement for attention with respect to gathering remains care for the seating of the people[22] – a spatial environment that from the get-go suggests that the assembly is not an audience of spectators sitting in on the leaders' show. Pioneering feminist contributions to liturgy in both woman-church (a fresh expression, ahead of its time?[23]) and other modes, have tended to prize the conversation circle, the round table and what Rosemary Radford Ruether calls the 'communalization' of roles in such formation,[24] and these are lamentably neglected, to great loss, yet full of ideas as to making amends to some of the problems. The more commonly addressed question among feminists of fully humanly inclusive presidency is certainly important, but relates to a wider range of dynamics in liturgy that need to conspire together to change the scene for the better,[25] with the question of the assembly as celebrant prior to special consideration of the presiding celebrant among the rest of the people.

If the differences of various kinds constituting an assembly – sex and gender identity among them – are to be celebrated, the assembly in its diversity needs to be better seen, more able to move, and its status as celebrant better understood than is oftentimes the case.

Word

Without doubt, the Bible richly funds some of the liturgical problems that resist diversity. Notions such as 'all [being] one in Christ Jesus' can all too easily be employed to 'level' differences both by authors of biblical texts and by others in their subsequent interpretation. Most notable is the form of this phrase in Galatians 3.28: 'There is neither Jew nor Gentile, neither slave nor free, nor is there male and female, for you are all one in Christ Jesus' (NIV). As Teresa Berger notes, however, 'there is no moment in time when gender has not shaped Christian faith (Gal 3:28 notwithstanding)'.[26] Sometimes claimed even by conservative Christians as a statement of 'gospel inclusivity',[27] this text from Galatians is evidently oftentimes not read as presuming equality – and perhaps it should not be, in order to remain clear that the Bible's prevalent view that 'women are always "at fault" unless they are subordinate to males' means that it needs to be 'criticised not just for being ambiguous, but for being most profoundly mistaken'.[28]

Paula Gooder's study of the World Council of Churches' *Baptism, Eucharist and Ministry* (BEM) – as Gooder cites, 'the most widely distributed, translated, and discussed ecumenical text of modern times'[29] – surveys the use of the Bible in that document and notes not only that Galatians 3.28 is cited more than any other biblical portion, but that its frequent use in BEM 'requires the text to bear a lot of theological weight',[30] not all aspects of which are obvious. She identifies six ways in which BEM draws on the verse (and its immediately prior one, Gal. 3.27), notably the verse's use in the section of BEM on ministry, under the heading 'the ministry of men and women in the church'. At that point ('Ministry', para. 18), BEM claims that 'where Christ is present, human barriers are being broken down' and speaks of the church's calling to 'convey to the world the image of a new humanity'. Then the document *almost* echoes Galatians 3.28, suggesting that 'in Christ no male or female' means that both women and men 'must discover together their contributions to the service of Christ in the Church'. It further asserts that the church must discover the ministry which can be provided by women, recognizing that while different churches would agree on this need, they 'draw different conclusions as to the admission of women to the ordained ministry'. The commentary following the paragraph elaborates on the supposed sources for such different conclusions and calls for 'joint study and reflection within the ecumenical fellowship of all churches'.[31] As Gooder notes, however, Galatians 3.28 is widely held to be an early – and possibly pre-Pauline – baptismal formula, which raises questions about whether the unity it purports refers to baptism in particular or to Christian community in some more general sense. If it is deemed to be a text about baptism, then it is not so much about status within the community but access to the community – through the waters of baptism: 'in other words it does not matter if you were a Jew or a Gentile, slave or free, male or female before, what matters is being baptized into Christ'.[32] Moreover, the text may have originally referred not to gender but to marital status, given the subtle distinction made in the text between 'Jew nor Gentile', 'slave nor free', and 'male *and* female'. While not stating her own view – though it is quite public knowledge that Gooder is a supporter of the ordination of women in her own tradition, the Church of England[33] – she suggests that if the passage is in fact about marital status, as some scholars have claimed, 'then Galatians 3:28 cannot really be used to support statements about a new humanity, the need for appropriate relationships nor to argue that there is no male or female in Christ'. Indeed, she goes on to suggest that 'the use of Galatians 3:27–28 in BEM cautions against the natural tendency to have a favourite passage which is used regularly' and that its 'overuse' 'dilutes its value as a revolutionary early text within Christianity because it has been made to mean too much'.[34] At the very least, it is curious how this much-used text is employed both to argue for something it was not intended to support and then to scramble notions of unity and equality.

Whatever portions of Scripture can be 'made to mean', liturgical practices that foster diversity in the ministry of the word are not commonplace – and this despite the fact that 'Bible' is itself plural, meaning 'books', and is a collection of writings in multiple genres, from diverse periods and addressed to different kinds of hearers.[35] Moreover, it is – contra theologies of the Bible that over-egg its singularity – best conceived as conversation.[36] At their best, lectionary sequences can suggest some of the diversity of voice in the Bible – albeit at other times too tidy, missing parts of the argument and occluding differences there to be found in the canon. Juxtaposition of scriptural texts with visual images,[37] contrapuntal reading[38] with historical and contemporary texts of different kinds and intelligent use of sacred texts from 'other' faiths in inter-religious readings[39] all present fecund possibilities for conversing with the Hebrew and Christian Bible in Christian worship. And while Bible reading in lectionary sequences and preaching may indeed always involve an element of 'dialogue' – not least the reception of a message or messages by hearers such that what is heard is enacted in their lives,[40] the practice of dialogical preaching – 'where two preachers converse together about the scriptural texts ... or the whole congregation can be actively engaged in discussing the texts'[41] – remains quite uncommon, despite more expansive understandings of the sermon in contemporary liturgical resources. Take *New Patterns for Worship* as one clue to opening some possibilities:

The term 'sermon' includes less formal exposition, the use of drama, interviews, discussion, audio-visuals and the insertion of hymns or other sections of the service between parts of the sermon. The sermon may come after one of the readings, or before or after the prayers ...[42]

But despite suggestions such as these, the notion of questions, interruptions and counterpoints to a preacher, or more than one preacher, or no preacher, or of some other mode of exploring portions of the Bible in relation to one another and the contexts of its readers is often unheard of. And even where ideas like *New Patterns for Worship* are taken up, it still needs to be remembered that

> since scripture itself is so pervasively patriarchal (with some scholars estimating that women appear in only about one tenth of the text), preachers need to be intentional about making women's lives fully present in the sermon ... Since Christian tradition has been, until very recently, so pervasively Eurocentric and racist, then again, preachers need consciously to think about how to stand against that tradition and proclaim the word in ways that embrace all.[43]

Feminist communities often have led the way on enacting dialogue sermons, and with sensitivity to those whom the text elides.[44] Emergent church communities have often pioneered the former if not always the latter dynamic, finding creative ways to 'say, "Here is what the Christian faith is. What do you think?"'[45] If various kinds of difference are to be voiced, models like these will be needed.

Table

Biblical texts also conspire with liturgical actions that propose the oneness of participants. An interesting action in this respect is the fraction, or breaking of bread, in the rite of Communion, which in various traditions is accompanied by a text that draws on New Testament ideas in 1 Corinthians 10.17. The Church of England's default text, an alternative to silence, is:

> We break this bread to share in the body of Christ.
> **Though we are many, we are one body**
> **for we all share in one bread.**[46]

These words function 'not only as a practical action before the distribution, but also as a symbol of the unity of the church'.[47] Part of this text is, notably, a unison text, of the kind that appear not only in the table-section of the *ordo*, but throughout, and a form that Marjorie Procter-Smith has firmly in her sights for critique.[48] Unison texts may be presented differently, in bold, capitals or with some prompting rubric, characteristically 'All:'. And as Procter-Smith points out, they 'present the participants with texts which do not need to ask ("Do you believe?" "Have you sinned?")

because they begin from the presumption of consent: "Say what you believe". "Confess your sins".[49] But these presumptions are by no means always shared around the assembly. One striking example I recall transpired when a child, then excluded from Communion in the polity of the church in which he was baptized, responded to the statement 'though we are many, we are one body for we all share in one bread' with a loud retort: 'No! We don't,' pointing to himself, brothers and peers.

Procter-Smith links unison prayer to Nancy Jay's description of 'A–Not A' thinking, which thrives not only on dichotomy but exclusion, and Procter-Smith deftly adds the point that early attempts at unification of the church's public prayer coincided with repression of women's leadership as well as identification of women with heresy. A unitary voice, she continues, can serve as 'a defense against critics and attackers', confirming group identity and operating as a means of setting boundaries. But as Procter-Smith also points out in her own contribution to counter-hegemony, univocality is never actually achievable, 'because of the diversity of participants'.[50] What is not always the case, however, is that such diversity is *apparent*, and its voice is certainly often smothered or silenced, with adjacent practices like psalm-singing, which flattens the vast emotional range of the psalter into an undemonstrative range of chant, Gregorian, Anglican or whatever,[51] emphatically *not* helping to enable expression of difference. As Procter-Smith attests, supposed pray-ers may be 'defecting in place' as well they might need to. And feminists and others may be 'praying between the lines', refusing to join in, uttering alternatives and countering the dominance towards which unison text can tend. At the very least, unison prayer needs to revise the prefix 'All:' for something – albeit more cumbersome – more open-ended, seeking consent and not assuming agreement, perhaps 'Some/one/many/none/those so moved ...'.

If difference is to be embraced, words and the actions they accompany may need to be more congruent, and more voices – in what Procter-Smith calls 'heteroglossia' – invited, so that polyphonic alternatives to unison text – and, again, especially alternatives to unison text that is prescribed to be spoken by all – can emerge.

Sending

One possible danger of emphasizing the assembly as primary symbol, the assembly as celebrant, is that this, without complementing emphases, could suggest a kind of clericalization of the laity, giving the impression that 'gifts' from God are for exercise in the gathered assembly rather than by the assembly dispersed. A complementing emphasis is therefore needed on the wider world of which the assembly is a part, as well as on the representative vocation of the celebrants – both ordained and lay – in their lives beyond the liturgy,[52] and the like of what The Episcopal Church (TEC) calls 'The Baptismal Covenant', and other traditions, following TEC's lead, 'Commitment to Mission', 'Affirmation of Commitment' or something akin:[53] among other commitments, proclaiming the good news by word and example, seeking and serving Christ in all persons, striving for justice and peace. The 'worldly calling' of members of the assembly might be invoked and emboldened in various kinds of possibilities in liturgy itself, such as testimony about participants' lived struggle for peace and justice; the enervating work of seeking and/or bestowing dignity among neighbours and opponents; sending in blessing to places of work, study and recreation; representations of the realities of diverse compositions of households, families, marriages and how they may embody 'the many kinds of awesome love'[54] in sexual and other kinds of intimacy; and focus on particular locations within the local community and wider scene that stretch passing reference in prayers of the people – assuming that any concrete reference appears there.

The final part of the form of the Baptismal Covenant used by TEC, enquiring about commitment to 'respect the dignity of every human being', is notably and most curiously elided in the Church of England's appropriation of it, shifting the focus to 'acknowledging Christ's authority over human society, by prayer for the world and its leaders'[55] – so the Act of Uniformity's concern with 'the king's dominions' bounces back. The shift is perhaps a significant insight into how differences are likely to be welcomed. Such variant wordings may well be suggestive of the hospitality of a gathering, of presumptions about who may 'preach' – especially as a representative of the church, a clue to who may preside and bear sacraments to others – their bodies holding 'the body of Christ' in eucharistized bread, or touching the bodies of other persons in the vulnerability of baptism, frailty of sickness, face of death and so on. To propose anything like a fully robust and liberative version of the assembly, with that assembly manifesting 'liturgy with a difference', convictions like those of the Baptismal Covenant will need to be in place. If they are not, 'the different' from majoritarian and assumed norms must needs search elsewhere for a different liturgy.

The *ordo*, because widely followed, is an important locus for reflection about difference, and yet it invites a series of scrutinies through the optics of difference. Essays in this volume will press further into various such optics. I hope that the *ordo* is one place, among others, where readers will return with their questions.

Notes

1 On the BCP, see Charles Hefling and Cynthia Shattuck (eds), 2006, *The Oxford Guide to the Book of Common Prayer: A Worldwide Survey*, New York: Oxford University Press; Stephen Platten and Christopher Woods (eds), 2012, *Comfortable Words: Polity, Piety and The Book of Common Prayer*, London: SCM Press; and Stephen Burns and Robert Gribben (eds), forthcoming, *When We Pray: The Future of Common Prayer*, Melbourne: Coventry Press.

2 Find this phrase developed in Stanley Hauerwas, 1986, *Suffering Presence: Theological Reflection on Medicine, the Mentally Handicapped, and the Church*, Notre Dame, IN: University of Notre Dame Press.

3 Gary Bouma, 2011, *Being Faithful in Diversity*, Adelaide: ATF Press, p. 11.

4 Geoffrey Rowell, 1991, *The Vision Glorious: Themes and Personalities in the Catholic Revival in Anglicanism*, Oxford: Clarendon Press.

5 A trigger line to introduce recitation of the creed in the Anglican Church of Kenya, 2002, *Our Modern Services*, Nairobi: Uzima Press.

6 See Stephen Burns, 'Faithfulness or Betrayal? Tradition in "Geriatric Assemblies"', in Jione Havea (ed.), forthcoming, *Horizons of Contextuality*, Lanham, MD: Lexington Books.

7 See Steven Croft, 2010, 'Persuading Gamaliel: Helping the Anglo-Catholic Tradition Engage with Fresh Expressions of Church', and others' essays in Ian Mobsby and Steven Croft (eds), *Fresh Expressions in the Sacramental Tradition*, Norwich: Canterbury Press, pp. 36–51, etc.

8 Julie Gittoes, Brutus Green and James Heard (eds), 2015, *Generous Ecclesiology: Church, World and the Kingdom of God*, London: SCM Press, represents some pathways beyond the impasse of Andrew Davison and Alison Milbank, 2010, *For the Parish: A Critique of Fresh Expressions*, London: SCM Press.

9 https://www.imdb.com/title/tt2118623/ [accessed 8 September 2018]. Thanks to my colleague John Flett for informing me about this film.

10 Genesis 32. For an insightful comment on this text, see Diarmaid MacCulloch, 2010, *A History of Christianity: The First 3,000 Years*, Harmondsworth: Penguin, p. 50.

11 The phrase adopted in The Episcopal Church, 1979, Book of Common Prayer, New York: Church Publishing, for example, p. 322 on Eucharist.

12 See Stephen Burns, 2014, 'A Fragile Future for the *Ordo?*' in Glaucia Vasconcelos-Wilkey (ed.), *Worship and Culture: Foreign Country or Homeland?*, Grand Rapids, MI: Eerdmans, pp. 146–60.

13 US Bishops' Committee on the Liturgy, 1978, *Environment and Art in Catholic Worship*, Chicago, IL: LTP, para. 28.

14 Robert Hovda, 2003, 'The Sacred: Silence and Song', in Gabe Huck et al., *Toward Ritual Transformation: Remembering Robert W. Hovda*, Collegeville, MN: Liturgical Press, pp. 15–28, at p. 22.

15 David Holeton (ed.), 1998, *Our Thanks and Praise: The Eucharist in Anglicanism Today*, Toronto: ABC, p. 261 (Principle 2). In Hovda's words, 'the entire assembly is the primary minister in liturgy, and the variety of specialized ministries ... are all in the service of the assembly, dependent in many ways on that assembly' (Hovda, 'The Sacred', p. 21).

16 The notion of expropriation is found in Rosemary Radford Ruether, 1985, *Women-Church: Theology and Practice*, San Francisco, CA: HarperCollins, p. 87.

17 Stephen Burns and Bryan Cones, 2014, 'A Prayer Book for the Twenty-first Century?' *Anglican Theological Review* 96: 336–60.

18 *Sacrosanctum Concilium*, para. 14, http://www.vatican.va/archive/hist_councils/ii_vatican_council/documents/vat-ii_const_19631204_sacrosanctum-concilium_en.html [accessed 8 September 2018]. See discussion in Stephen Burns, 2006, *Worship in Context: Liturgical Theology, Children and the City*, Peterborough: Epworth Press, Chapter 2.

19 Methodist Church of Great Britain, 1999, *Methodist Worship Book*, Peterborough: Epworth Press, p. vii; Uniting Church in Australia, 2005, *Uniting in Worship 2*, Sydney: Uniting Church Press, p. 131.

20 The term 'celebrant' applied to the presider is part of the problem, and is discussed in Burns and Cones, 'A Prayer Book for the Twenty-first century?', p. 652.

21 Church of England, 2000, *Common Worship, Services and Prayers for the Church of England*, London: Church House Publishing, p. 190, echoing *The Apostolic Tradition*, an early extant text of eucharistic prayer.

22 Note Richard Giles's comments at http://www.praytellblog.com/index.php/2011/03/04/teaching-liturgy-where-do-i-begin/ [accessed 8 September 2018]; see also his creative book of 2004, *Creating Uncommon Worship: Transforming the Liturgy of the Eucharist*, Norwich: Canterbury Press.

23 See Stephen Burns, 2012, *Worship and Ministry: Shaped Towards God*, Melbourne: Mosaic Press, Chapter 10.

24 The term 'communalization' is found in Ruether, *Women-Church*, p. 91. See discussion in Stephen Burns, 2010, '"Four in a Vestment": Feminist Gesture for Christian Assembly', in Nicola Slee and Stephen Burns (eds), *Presiding Like a Woman*, London: SPCK, pp. 9–19.

25 See Stephen Burns, 2014, 'From Women Priests to Feminist Ecclesiology?' in Fredrica Harris Thompsett (ed.), *Looking Forward, Looking Backward: Forty Years of Women's Ordination*, New York: Seabury Press, pp. 99–110.

26 Teresa Berger, 2008, '"Wisdom Has Built Her House" (Proverbs 9:1): Gendering Sacred Space', *Studia Liturgica* 38: 171–82, at p. 176; see also Teresa Berger, 2011, *Gender Differences and the Making of Liturgical History: Unveiling Liturgy's Past*, Aldershot: Ashgate.

27 https://keswickministries.org/about/who-we-are [accessed 8 September 2018].

28 Ann Loades, 2004, 'Women in the Episcopate', *Anvil* 21: 113–19, at p. 114.

29 Paula Gooder, 2004, '"According to the Scriptures …" The Use of the Bible in *Baptism, Eucharist and Ministry*', in Paul Avis (ed.), *Paths to Unity: Explorations in Ecumenical Method*, London: Church House Publishing, pp. 75–90, at p. 75.

30 Gooder, 'Scriptures', p. 82.

31 World Council of Churches, 1982, *Baptism, Eucharist and Ministry*, Geneva: WCC, pp. 23–4, with commentary at p. 25.

32 Gooder, 'Scriptures', p. 85.

33 https://www.theguardian.com/world/2012/nov/20/campaigners-women-bishops-foiled-laity [accessed 8 September 2018].

34 Gooder, 'Scriptures', p. 86.

35 Michael Vasey, 1998, 'Scripture and Eucharist', in Holeton, *Our Thanks and Praise*, pp. 147–61.

36 Arnold Browne, 1997, 'Yesterday, Today and Forever: The Dynamic of Scripture', in Stephen Platten, Graham James and Andrew Chandler (eds), *New Soundings: Essays on Developing Tradition*, London: DLT, pp. 13–37, at p. 13.

37 For a good example, see proposals in rubrics relating to expression of lament in *Uniting in Worship 2*, pp. 199–202.

38 For discussion, see Michael N. Jagessar and Stephen Burns, 2011, *Christian Worship: Postcolonial Perspectives*, Sheffield: Equinox, Chapter 4.

39 See Monica J. Melanchthon, forthcoming, 'Scripture and Scriptures in Worship Space', *Liturgy* 34.

40 See anecdotes related by Marva Dawn, cited in Stephen Burns, 2006, *SCM Studyguide to Liturgy*, London: SCM Press, p. 91.

41 Nicola Slee, 2008, 'Word', in Stephen Burns (ed.), *Journey*, Norwich: Canterbury Press, pp. 36–61, at p. 54.

42 Church of England, 2002, *New Patterns for Worship*, London: Church House Publishing, p. 14.

43 Slee, 'Word', p. 55.

44 Slee, 'Word', p. 54 for the example of the St Hilda Community.

45 Mary Grey-Reeves and Michael Perham, 2010, *The Hospitality of God: Emerging Worship for a Missional Church*, London: SPCK, p. 65. See further their chapter, 'Appropriating the Church's Faith', pp. 58–66.

46 *Common Worship: Services and Prayers ...*, p. 179.

47 Paul Bradshaw, Gordon Giles and Simon Kershaw, 2002, 'Holy Communion', in Paul Bradshaw (ed.), *Companion to Common Worship: Volume 1*, London: SPCK, pp. 98–147, at p. 130.

48 Marjorie Procter-Smith, 1995, *Praying with Our Eyes Open: Engendering Feminist Liturgical Prayer*, Nashville, TN: Abingdon Press.

49 Procter-Smith, *Praying with Our Eyes Open*, p. 42.

50 Procter-Smith, *Praying with Our Eyes Open*, p. 26.

51 Don E. Saliers, 1997, 'David's Song in Our Land', in Blair Gilmore-Meeks (ed.), *The Landscape of Praise: Readings in Liturgical Renewal*, Valley Forge, PA: TPI, pp. 235–41.

52 The Uniting Church in Australia, 2008, 'Ministry and Ordination in the Uniting Church in Australia', in Geoff Thompson and Rob Bos (eds), *Theology for Pilgrims*, Sydney: Uniting Church Press, pp. 328–99.

53 The Episcopal Church, 1979, BCP, p. 306; Church of England, 2000, *Common Worship: Services and Prayers...*, p. 152; Uniting Church in Australia, 2005, *Uniting in Worship 2*, p. 82.

54 Nicola Slee, 2002, 'So Many Kinds of Awesome Love', in Geoffrey Duncan (ed.), *Courage to Love: An Anthology of Inclusive Worship Material*, London: DLT, pp. 62–3.

55 See discussion of this shift in Jagessar and Burns, *Postcolonial Perspectives*, Chapter 6.

PART 2

Leadership and Ministry
Through Liturgy

3

'The Performance of Queerness': Trans Priesthood as Gesture Towards a Queered Liturgical Assembly

RACHEL MANN

Around the turn of the millennium, I went through selection for training and formation in ordained ministry in the Church of England. As I progressed through the various stages of selection, I paid careful attention to theologies of priesthood. I felt called to priesthood. Thus, I reasoned, it was important I came to some mind on what that meant. Conceptions of priesthood I discovered at the time – most especially those which understood priesthood as more of an ontological rather than functional matter – remain significant for me. Yet, there remained and remains a niggle about these theologies. I am a trans woman and I am alert to how my body is non-normative and my identity is variant. For nearly 20 years I've wrestled with the extent to which conceptions of priesthood have been derived from white masculine performance and asked to what extent priesthood under such conditions requires the erasure of difference, not least of women's and trans people's and black people's bodies. This essay attempts to interrogate the impact of trans-priestly performance on gathered liturgical assembly and vice versa. It argues that patriarchal-masculine constructions of priestly performance create traces and effects that make the erasure of 'difference' normative for liturgical gesture and assembly. This erasure constructs representations of liturgical assembly as the gathered 'holy' Body of Christ that prioritize 'vanilla', heteronormative readings of community, subjectivity and the body.

'What's the Problem? A Priest Is a Priest Is a Priest'

It might be argued that my anxiety that classic understandings of priesthood and liturgical assembly erase difference and variety is just that: anxiety. While some academic attention has been given to the extent to which embodied particularity generates interesting effects on priestly ministry and identity,[1] it might be argued that what makes a priest 'a priest' in the liturgical assembly transcends distinctions of gender, sexuality, class, colour and so on. Indeed, the very fact that my own church has male and female priests, LGBT* priests and priests from every cultural and ethnic background underlines this claim.

One famous statement of priesthood that, implicitly at least, indicates the indifference of priestly identity to particular context is that stated by Archbishop Michael Ramsey in the 1970s' classic, *The Christian Priest Today*.[2] It was, perhaps, the defining text in my initial priestly formation. In it, Ramsey suggests, in effect, that priesthood is an office that gathers up all those things that make the church 'the Church'. He suggests that the priesthood is 'a gathering up of roles which belong to the whole Church'.[3] The priest, Ramsey adds, is 'a man of theology', a 'minister of reconciliation', 'a man of prayer' and 'the man of the Eucharist'. Leaving aside, for the moment, the gendered language in Ramsey's claim, what is striking in Ramsey's understanding of priesthood is the lack of interest in 'personal' aspects of ministry. This is a picture of priesthood that is more interested in the office of priesthood rather than the personal make-up or particularity of the individual minister, something which perhaps reflects his un-foregrounded assumption that all priests will be, for example, male and of a relatively similar background (white, middle-class, university-educated, etc.).

Writing from a more evangelical Anglican perspective, Steven Croft suggests that to be a presbyter or priest is to be a minister of word and sacrament. First, he suggests that, 'at the heart of the presbyteral dimension of ministry in Scripture and the tradition is the call to preach and to pray'.[4] He locates eucharistic ministry within the latter category: 'For the most part this ministry of the sacraments finds its roots and origins in prayer with or on behalf of individuals and the whole community on different occasions to which the apostles promise to give themselves in Acts 6.'[5] He adds, 'The Eucharist is seen as a focusing of the prayer and worship offered on behalf of the Church, appealing to Christ's sacrifice of himself. There the person presiding at the Eucharist, offering thanksgiving and intercession, is described in priestly and cultic language.'

Given the brief pictures of priestly ministry – as a theological category – one can see how it might be argued that concerns over the erasure of embodied distinctiveness are ill-founded. For, according to the pictures I've sketched, particularity is of less concern than the general nature of priestly ministry. What matters is not so much that this or that person presides or celebrates in the liturgical assembly, it is the office or the orders to which they have been ordained. At one level, I do not want to question this. It is a theologically potent point, but it risks ignoring the lived, embodied realities of ministry. Liturgical assembly does not happen in imagined and imaginary space (or merely so); it is the business of bodies. Liturgical assembly is something done by the people and priest/minister together in a lived, gathered way.

Furthermore, it remains the case that, in different traditions, not all bodies are treated equally in the liturgical assembly. In Roman Catholicism and in some parts of the Anglo-Catholic tradition, bodies coded as female are disallowed from presiding over the liturgical assembly. In the Church of England, the bodies of LGBT* people remain under question: LGBT* people can be ordained, but should they contract equal/same-sex marriages they can be prevented from presiding. If one accepts that eucharistic presidency can be characterized as having generic and typical components (the use of the *orans* position, perhaps having generic gestures during the epiclesis, words of institution and so on), specific bodies matter. Not every body is permitted to preside, and those that are permitted are regulated, sometimes ruthlessly. In short, at the performative and phenomenological level, presiding resists genericized or 'vanilla' ideas of liturgical assembly. Particular bodies preside, not generalized ones.

This performative particularity has been brought out by the likes of Andrea Bieler and David Plüss. In a chapter on performativity in priesthood, they reflect on the differing experiences of two Caucasian clergy women in their 40s when pronouncing blessing at the close of the Eucharist.[6] One, Heather, talks about the experience of opening her arms to pray and how 'the exposure of my torso – my breasts and my belly – leaves me with the fear of losing my protection'.[7] Bieler and Plüss note, 'The exposure of vulnerability that this ritual gesture releases for Heather does not belong to her common repertoire of body language in the public square.'[8] Indeed, 'she experiences it as a threatened terrain. Her upper body especially is vulnerable and needs protection. She also describes a momentary sense of shame at what seems like the inappropriate unveiling of her breasts in a worship service.'[9] This contrasts with the experience of Julie who experiences the ritual of blessing, 'in a deep felt sense of motherhood … [where] her breasts are the symbolic terrain of nurturing'.[10] They conclude, 'There is definitely not a single "natural" meaning to this part of the body … this terrain carries very ambiguous connotations.'[11]

What Bieler and Plüss bring out in these miniatures is the embodied divergence in the performance of presidency even among persons who might be coded as relatively similar (middle-aged, white, female and so on). It gives an insight into the embodied possibilities and complexities of presiding at the liturgical assembly; the 'vanilla' representations of priesthood I outlined earlier in this chapter are exposed as exactly that: lacking in lived colour and embodied reality. Bieler and Plüss claim that:

Presiding at a worship service and performing a particular gender have both to do with the subconscious and conscious showing of some-thing[:] ... an interactive, communicative practice in which we engage certain ways of embodied knowing what it means to be a woman as well as a presider who offers leadership in liturgical celebration.[12]

In the following section, I want to reflect on these claims in relation to certain aspects of my experience of being trans and a presider, indicating the places where my embodied knowledge brings living colour into the eucharistic liturgical assembly. By being attentive to my own embodied ministerial performance as an out trans priest negotiating eucharistic liturgies which erase difference, I want to indicate some subtle gestures of queering embedded not only in my own bodily performance but in the structure of Eucharist itself.

Being Trans and a Priest in the Church Today: Unexpected Intersections?

One of the intersections between being a priest and being trans is that both, in many ways, are concerned with the notion of 'being one's true self'. Indeed 'becoming one's true self' is a conservative classic of the faith journey: a process of growing into the likeness of Christ. In the previous section, I drew attention to Ramsey's classic statement of priesthood. Arguably, running behind its understanding of priesthood is the claim that becoming a priest is a matter of ontology. Ramsey suggests that priesthood is the gathering up of those aspects of the church that make the church 'church' – forgiveness, reconciliation, sacramental gesture and so on. Through ordination, a priest becomes someone who embodies the church's self-understanding. As Croft notes, 'the Catholic tradition has emphasised the concept of what ministers are or become'.[13] Even in less ontologically pressured contexts, the crucial matter is character: being or becoming the kind of person who has the character of priesthood. Doing or function is secondary. Of course, some emphasize the functional aspects of ministerial identity – 'can you do "x" and "y"?' 'are you competent?' 'can you lead this?' – though even here the inner dimension of holiness or moral purity tends to override the functional. Perhaps most broadly, the priest exists in a place of meeting, grounded in Christ: of ordination to a public, visible office which finds its meaning through time and space in being – character, or virtue or, if one is bold, in ontology.

Trans subjectivities are as diverse as trans people. Yet, there is one obvious intersection with standard pictures of priesthood. Many trans people speak of becoming their true selves, of working out, typically in publicly effective ways, an inner conviction to conform the body in some significant way to a pre-critical, inner representation of self. Jay Prosser's study of trans subjectivities has indicated that trans people may face specific issues when negotiating issues of authenticity and 'truth'.[14] Judith/ Jack Halberstam suggests, '[Prosser's] formulation of the role of narrative in transsexual transition has established itself in opposition to what he understands to be a queer preference for performativity over narrativity.'[15] While, for the likes of Judith Butler, the trans person acts as an icon of gender performativity, exposing (by the 'disconnect' between 'gender' and 'sex') the constructed 'non-naturalness' of sex and gender for all subjects, Prosser indicates an issue raised by some trans people: 'there are … transsexual trajectories that aspire to what this scheme devalues. Namely, there are transsexuals who seek very pointedly to be non-performative, to be constative, quite simply to be.'[16] Halberstam glosses this as, 'many transsexuals do not want to represent gender artifice; they actually aspire to the real, the natural, indeed the very condition that has been rejected by the queer theory of gender performance.'[17] Prosser indicates a powerful subjective 'force' in some trans identities: the desire to be 'conformed' to 'the natural'. I've felt the pre-critical force of this in my imaginary: I should like to be able to 'have' a womb, ovaries, give birth to children and be a mother. At the level of theory, it's relatively straightforward to bring critical pressure on that 'desire' from various angles. However, at the level of pre-critical, expressive and 'confessional' living, my hunger to embody the 'natural' fecund and my acknowledgement that this cannot be the case has been emotionally and psychologically resonant.[18]

However, while the axis between 'inner' and 'outer' offers fruitful lines of enquiry into Christian and trans subjectivities, insofar as trans or priestly 'formation' is based always on naturalistic and reified ideas of authentic selfhood, it runs the risk of eliding and parodying the complexity, particularity and contingency of both trans lives and lived realities of priestly performance more broadly understood. Insofar as the praxis of priesthood is predicated on inviting persons to perform normative concepts of subjectivity (either grounded in a normative white masculine subjectivity or divided along normative gender or sexual lines), it will place trans and other identities coded as subaltern at peril.

Trans-inclusive approaches to priestly performance entail a queering of the notion of 'growing into the likeness of Christ' or representing Christ or representing the church; in short, this entails reading priesthood subversively by being alert to performative and constructed dimensions of gendered and sexual subjectivities. That is, by being alert to provisional and flexible meanings as opposed to timeless, reified ones. I say this not to be offensive to sincere, naturalistic discourses around both priesthood and trans subjectivities; however, given the power-dynamics that can accrue to discourses that privilege the natural, the normative and so on, it's surely wise to interrogate Christian and/or trans narratives predicated on humanistic notions of subjectivity which state there is a 'self' that one truly is or could be, and that this self is fundamentally whole and integrated, or hoping to achieve wholeness. I fear that naturalistic discourses do a disservice to the queerness of a God liberated from patriarchal, reductive representations; the latter are inclined to prioritize denotative ideas of meaning, while the queer is fascinated with connotative notions of language. Rather than saying, 'This is what x is or means for all time', the queer is more concerned with metaphor, play and possibility, with going astray from that which is received.

On a pre-critical level, then, the authentic 'priestly subject' finds one kind of analogue in a humanistic reading of trans identity – as a return to true self. Of course, beguiling as this picture might be in outline, it may not resist the concerted pressure which terms like 'self', 'natural' and 'authenticity' have been placed under by queer, poststructuralist and feminist discourse of the past 40-plus years.[19] The dream of the humanistic unitary self has been problematized as one kind of beguiling mirage, a dream of a Symbolic Father who guarantees meaning; and, insofar as these strategies of exposure have been effective, in the place of the self emerges an interest in temporary, fractured and provisional subjectivities. As Hélène Cixous – someone more alert than most to the theatrical, performative and positional nature of subjectivity – suggests, the question one should ask is not 'Who am I?', but 'Who are I?'[20] For if there are ways we are expected to perform a unitary social self, the truth is that we are multiples and doubles of our selves with no guarantees of stable selves.

What Are the Implications of Embodied Complexity in the Liturgical Assembly? What Are the Implications of Liturgical Assembly for Embodied Complexity?

A range of performative, playful yet profoundly serious ways of dwelling in the trans-priestly body present themselves. Writing specifically about women's relationship with poetry, Yopie Prins and Maeera Shreiber make a helpful general observation about the etymology of the verb, 'to dwell'. They remind us that the notion of 'dwelling' gestures towards 'a process of perpetual displacement, [reclaiming] the wayward etymology of "dwelling" not as a hypothetical house to inhabit but as a verb that also means to go astray, leading us away and unpredictably elsewhere'.[21] If priestly identity is ultimately located in God in Christ – as Word who dwells in the world and dwells in eternity – then so is one's habitation of priestly being. It is a place we inhabit yet creatively go 'astray from'.

The 'going astray' is no cause for 'moral concern' – rather it is the social, cultural and aesthetic condition that leads us into 'the new'. It is in our departures from established meanings, practices and ideas as much as in our traditions that we are faithful to the Word's poetic indwelling.[22] Theologically, Jesus Christ as the incarnated Word of God – fully human, fully divine – represents the definitive reconciliation point between the material and the divine; yet this reconciliation is not static, but dynamic. God's making or *poiesis* is not to be reduced to the initial creation and ongoing sustaining of the world; Christ acts as an icon of remaking and re-creating the world. The Word is before the world, but also participates in the world's redeeming. As St John has it, the Word became flesh and dwelt among us. God's fundamental *poiesis* indwells the world and remakes it. In our participation in Christ – in church, in Eucharist, as part of the Body – we participate in that creative work and our material reality is transformed. In another context, I suggest that the eucharistic liturgical assembly is fundamental to this disruptive encounter between bodies, those of the priest, the people and Christ:

> In the assembly of faith, priest and people gather to re-enact the breaking of bread and wine outpoured, participating in an act of remembrance that is also communion and a renewal of commitment to service. The Christian re-membering of Christ is a constant practice of making 'present' and yet is a disappearing act. The embodiment of Christ in organic matter – in bread and wine – is a constant reinscription of fragility. Christ is not made to be cast in bronze or gold or stone like an idol. Christ is precisely not the golden calf.[23]

The power of the eucharistic assembly is such that it disrupts or queers all presumptions of settled and preordained identities and meanings. 'Dwelling' with and in God is both a recapitulation of the world and a going 'astray' from ready-made meanings. But if that is our vocation in community, it is specifically central to that ministry which gathers those things that make the church 'the church' – the priesthood. And even if we abstract the dimensions of priesthood ('forgiveness and reconciliation' and so on), it is first an incarnated matter. That is, it is 'enfleshed' and located and dwelt within. Incarnated priesthood comprises the set of practices and ways of being that might be said to make up 'the habitus' or the 'warp and weft' of ministry. Participating in 'the poetic' – God's making, our making and the making of others – is part of the proper habitus of ministry. It draws us deeper into relationship with God, the ecclesial community and the world.

Well, that's all very fancy and neat, but being trans, being other, being non-normative, is a place of exile from many of the conventional

performances unthinkingly available to many priests. In my own liturgical praxis, especially pre-coming out definitively in 2012, I felt the strain
of feeling 'caught between'.[24] To use terms I shall shortly explain, I felt
caught between 'passing' as a conventional priest by using 'stealth' and
my own sense of joy in my 'trans-ness'. When – to use a specific example
of liturgical gesture – I raised my hands in the *orans* position to lead the
people's worship in the eucharistic prayer, I would often feel a mix of
delight that I, as an ordained trans person, was exercising my calling, as
well as a sense of anxiety. At the heart of this anxiety, I think, was a fear
of exposure. To open one's arms to pray as one does in the eucharistic
assembly is very exposing; I had a sense that I didn't want to expose too
much. I felt I was exposing not just my breasts and tummy and other parts
of my body, but my whole inner life, that few in the assembly knew about.
At an almost pre-conscious level, I had a sense that in leading the prayers
over the Table, I was both 'outing' myself as who I really was (a priest, an
authentic human being), and yet expecting someone to either laugh at me
or tell me I should be barred from serving the community in this way. I
was caught between 'stealthy passing' and being congruent with who God
called me to be.

'Stealth' and 'passing' may be unfamiliar to many outside the trans community. They're terms that are part of the habitus of trans communities
and, yet, remain indicators of the complex, often heterogeneous nature
of trans identities. The notions of 'stealth' and 'passing' are problematic
and problematized terms in trans self-understanding, yet they remain a
significant part of many trans narratives.

For anyone unfamiliar with the notions of trans 'stealth' and 'passing',
perhaps the easiest explanations can be provided by using my own experience as an example. When I transitioned in the early 1990s, one of the key
requirements from NHS psychiatrists who 'treated' me – a condition of
becoming a recipient of hormone replacement therapy and being recom-
mended for surgery – was undertaking the so-called Real-Life Test. I
needed to 'live as a woman' for two years and work for one year as such,
too. When I met with my psychiatrists, the litany of questions always
included some about how I was seen: did I 'pass', did I think I 'passed',
what kind of gaze did I think was directed at me? The imperative, both
spoken and unspoken, was to 'pass' as a woman, to achieve invisibility
and blend in, that is, to not be seen as trans but as what is now known as
'cis'.[25] 'Success' – from a psychiatric, medical point of view – was measured
by being seen socially and publicly as 'just like' any other 'cis' woman.

Of course, running alongside this was the conservatism of the psychiatrists who were treating me. Their ideas about what, for example,
constituted a woman were of an essentially conservative kind: a woman
wears make-up, wears a skirt or dress, is attracted to men and so on. I

learnt to 'act up' to their stereotypes on initial visits to Charing Cross Gender Identity Clinic – it simply made my life easier and I was more likely to get what I wanted (my hormone prescription, the prospect of surgery) if I 'performed' their script. Those who disobeyed – because they saw themselves as gender-neutral or genderqueer, for example – were likely to run into trouble. It's possible to see why the notion of 'passing' as a narrative of disappearance might be controversial and significant for the trans community. For, on the one hand, I – like many trans people – was rather desperate to 'pass' (not least because I so completely wanted to be seen/read/accepted as a woman); however, on the other, the notion of 'passing' can be read as an introject generated by medical, social and cultural expectations. The fundamental demand of the psychiatric script is to be 'conformed' to social and medical normative ideas of 'woman', 'man', 'femininity' and so on.

The notion of 'passing' can easily be connected to an allied concept, 'stealth'. Again, my own experience can readily illuminate this concept. As I transitioned, I was keen to pass, and perhaps had certain social advantages in a visually prejudiced culture. Like many trans people who – on these terms – 'successfully' transition, I saw the social and personal advantages of 'going stealth', that is, effectively excising all performed reference to my trans identity. I enacted my disappearance into cis-normative society by living as if I were a cisgender woman. Letting people know I was trans became the exception rather than the norm. This practice is sufficiently controversial among trans people that – while it is understood as a practice with a history, and therefore, one might say, part of the trans tradition – it has been seen by some in trans communities as an example of internalized transphobia.[26] In other words, to 'go stealth' is to act as if one is so fearful and anxious about one's status as trans that one seeks to pretend or act as if one is not trans. Yet, there is no escape from cost and loss. Those who perform or foreground their trans identities face regular abuse and the threat of violence, but those who go stealth will live in the terror of discovery and outing. One of the indicators that we live in a cis-normative culture is the prevalence of the narrative that trans people are duplicitous and tricksterish.

On a Sunday morning, at weekday Mass, as I take funerals and baptize, as I dwell in those things which make the church the church, I think I often pass quite well as a priest among priests. I spent years going stealth. And perhaps that shows that the being of the priest encompasses all other particular subjectivities, including trans and cis, black and white, male and female and so on. And there's something to this. Perhaps there's something to priestly performance that gestures towards the universal.

Yet, as I've sought to suggest in this chapter, even if one wishes to emphasize the performative at all cost, there is an inner horizon. Judith

Butler suggests that gender – perhaps like many categories – acts as a copy without an original and that it is constituted through repetitive inscription.[27] Trans subjects like me who happen to be priests expose the performative structure of priestly identity; we suggest that the priest (and the church and God whom she/he/they represent) works in queered time and space rather than univocal, authoritarian time and space; in short, our presence at the altar (even when we perform conventional subjectivities) exposes the constructed nature of priestly performance. The authority of the priest and the gathered community she represents may (because of the effects of certain readings of history, power and voice) cluster around performances of univocity, power-over, monarchical authority, but the trans priest exposes the performative, non-essential nature of that. Even if she chooses to go stealth or pass as the normative priest, even if she chooses to perform disappearance for the sake of survival, that performance is already a work of creative subversion. When she doesn't, the trans priest acts – within the gathered community – as an icon of Christ's queerness. She works in the midst of the community as critique of the church's pernicious love of kyriarchal power.[28]

Conclusion

A huge amount of work remains to be done to explore the dynamics between the liturgical assembly, presiding and queer identities. At best, this essay has sought to indicate a number of creative intersections which show that 'vanilla' conceptions of the priest in the assembly of God are inadequate to capture the embodied variety of priestly and liturgical performance. Despite the power of normative/patriarchal constructions of 'liturgy' and 'priest', I conclude that such constructions cannot fully erase vibrant, disruptive resources already contained within liturgy and gathered assembly; 'the Body of Christ' (so often fetishized as a conservative picture of community and formation to which 'we' must all be conformed) is an already queered set of representations that not only 'uncovers' erasure and injustice, but re-forms community, liturgical gesture and priestly subjectivities in liberative, queered directions. It should also be clearer that my own embodied ministerial performance, as a trans priest negotiating eucharistic liturgies that seek to erase difference, contains gestures of queering embedded within it. I take these gestures as a sign of encouragement and hope rather than grounds for anxiety; they indicate God's utter commitment to embedded ministry and the discovery of grace in actual, human bodies.

Notes

1 For example, Nicola Slee and Stephen Burns (eds), 2010, *Presiding like a Woman*, London: SPCK.

2 Michael Ramsey, 1972, *The Christian Priest Today*, London: SPCK.

3 Ramsey, *The Christian Priest Today*, p. 6.

4 Steven Croft, 1999/2005, *Ministry in Three Dimensions: Ordination and Leadership in the Local Church*, London: DLT, p. 98.

5 Croft, *Ministry in Three Dimensions*, p. 121.

6 Andrea Bieler and David Plüss, 2010, 'In This Moment of Utter Vulnerability: Tracing Gender in Presiding', in Slee and Burns, *Presiding*, pp. 112–22.

7 Bieler and Plüss, 'In This Moment', p. 112.

8 Bieler and Plüss, 'In This Moment', p. 112.

9 Bieler and Plüss, 'In This Moment', p. 113.

10 Bieler and Plüss, 'In This Moment', p. 113.

11 Bieler and Plüss, 'In This Moment', p. 113.

12 Bieler and Plüss, 'In This Moment', p. 113.

13 Croft, *Ministry in Three Dimensions*, p. 106.

14 See Jay Prosser, 1998, *Second Skins: The Body Narratives of Transsexuality*, New York: Columbia University Press.

15 Judith Halberstam, 2005, *In a Queer Time and Place: Transgender Bodies, Subcultural Lives*, New York/London: New York University Press, p. 50.

16 Prosser, *Second Skins*, p. 32.

17 Halberstam, *In a Queer Time and Place*, p. 50.

18 It's certainly the case that one of the most difficult aspects of negotiating being trans is accepting that I cannot 'bear' children. In my late 20s and early 30s, despite 'knowing' – at an intellectual level – that I can't and will never bear children, I struggled to accept it at an emotional level.

19 For example, Jacques Derrida, 1978, *Writing and Difference*, translated by Alan Bass, London: Routledge & Kegan Paul; Jacques Lacan, various years, *The Seminar of Jacques Lacan*, translated by Jacques-Alain Miller, New York: W. W. Norton and Co.

20 Hélène Cixous, 1994, *The Hélène Cixous Reader*, translated by Susan Sellers, New York: Routledge, p. xvii.

21 See: Yopie Prins and Maeera Shreiber, 1997, *Dwelling in Possibility: Women Poets and Critics on Poetry*, Ithaca, NY/London: Cornell University Press, p. 1. In Old English, 'dwellen' means 'to lead astray', developing into 'tarry, stay in place' in Middle English.

22 For an extended analysis of the Word, Dwelling and Priesthood, see Rachel Mann, 2016, 'The Priest Attends to the Word', in Jessica Martin and Sarah Coakley (eds), *For God's Sake: Re-Imagining Priesthood and Prayer in a Changing Church*, Norwich: Canterbury Press, pp. 78–90.

23 Rachel Mann, 2017, *Fierce Imaginings: The Great War, Ritual, Memory and God*, London: DLT, p. 25.

24 For more on my experience of coming out as trans, see Rachel Mann, 2012, *Dazzling Darkness: Gender, Sexuality, Illness & God*, Glasgow: Wild Goose.

25 'Cisgender', as a gender theory term, has its origins in the Latin-derived prefix 'cis', meaning 'to the near side'. In this context, 'cis' refers to the alignment of gender identity with assigned gender.

26 Monica Roberts, 2013, 'Stealth Doesn't Help the Trans Community', *The TransAdvocate*, https://www.transadvocate.com/stealth-doesnt-help-the-trans-community_n_9817.htm.

27 Butler says, 'Gender is a kind of imitation for which there is no original; in fact, it is a kind of imitation that produces the very notion of the original as an effect and consequence of the imitation itself.' See Judith Butler, 1991, 'Imitation and Gender Insubordination', in Diana Fuss (ed.), *Inside/Out: Lesbian Theories, Gay Theories*, New York: Routledge, pp. 13–31 at p. 21.

28 See Elisabeth Schüssler Fiorenza, 1992, *But She Said: Feminist Practices of Interpretation*, Boston: Beacon Press, for a classic definition of 'kyriarchy'.

4

All Things to All? Requeering Stuart's Eucharistic Erasure of Priestly Sex

SUSANNAH CORNWALL

What should a priest be?
All things to all
Male, female and genderless.[1]

Introduction

Elizabeth Stuart, the Catholic queer theologian, has done extensive work showing how Christian liturgy at the sacramental moments of Eucharist and baptism disrupts and disturbs assumptions about identity and demarcation. She points to an embodiment (in the priest at Eucharist, or the new Christian at baptism) of the end of sex, race, class and divisive identities obsolete in Christ.

Two essays in particular focus on how these moments might lead to 'sexlessness', subverting culturally imposed narratives about legitimate gender and sex. Stuart's assertion that the priest's sex is 'under erasure' in the Eucharist goes far to queer the gender symbolism inherent in the liturgy. However, ultimately, her argument risks denying non-normative bodies and sexualities. I suggest that the priest's *continuing* sexed specificity is queer, *not* its erasure, and that Stuart's claim that identity is predicated upon exclusion does not acknowledge the nature of redeemed, overlapping identities in Christ.

The Priest at the Altar

In a 2009 essay,[2] Stuart analyses François-Marius Granet's[3] painting *Priest at the Altar*. The priest faces the altar, back to the viewer, hands raised. Granet would not have meant to depict anything but a male priest, says Stuart; nonetheless, in a world where some priests are women, we may view it otherwise:

The vestments and gesture serve to wipe out sex and gender leaving just the human, ... in whom sex is rendered unreadable if it is not simply assumed ... There is something about the Catholic priesthood in its defining act of celebrating the Eucharist that renders it trans-sexual ... [It] demands that sex is taken up into the mystery of redemption where it is erased under a matrix of sacramental signs, symbols and displacements. Sex is placed under eucharistic erasure and the priest is the central player in that drama.[4]

This 'desexing' begins when Jesus' body 'becomes bread and wine, non-sexed corporeality, able to be ingested in other bodies, becoming one flesh with them. Sex is erased from embodiment.'[5] This affects not just Christ's body, but his Body, 'Multi-sexed, multi-social, national and cultural and multi-dimensional ... Dualisms and divisions are dissolved and in the process the thickness of these categories is dissipated to the point of nothingness so that the Bride, like the Lamb, emerges from the tomb of sex as something different.'[6]

But must this transformation necessarily involve distinction and particu-larity ebbing away? Passionate debates in recent years have surrounded similarity, difference and tensions in mixed-constituency groups. Can LGBT groups adequately champion lesbians, gay men, bisexuals *and* transgender people, critics ask, or will the interests of the majority – likely 'L' or 'G', not 'B' or 'T' – inevitably dominate? Is 'queer' a good 'catch-all' for resist-ing normativity, or is it assimilationist and amorphous, failing to represent any constituent group's special needs? The risk of melting away diversity is that strong, strident identities remain the longest, becoming ostensibly 'neutral' identities which really continue to privilege the dominant.

But it is not that human sexed difference as only male and female with clear, concomitant gender identities is divinely ordained: far from it. Nor do I believe that the persistence of priestly sex at Eucharist means that only males may preside. Rather, I suggest that the significance of sex is trans-formed *even as* humans remain sexed in particular ways. Accordingly, the president's existence in the liturgy signifies humanity transformed not into indistinctness, but into creatures whose creatureliness *in particularity* is preserved, even as hierarchies based upon it crumble.

For Stuart, the 'erasure' of priestly sex is amplified by *how* the Eucharist is celebrated:

In the celebration of the Eucharist (particularly if celebrated *ad orien-tem*)[7] the priest leads the Church away from a world of male and female towards the divine world in which subjectivity is defined purely in terms of union with God ... As the person at the front line of the eucharistic action, it is imperative that the priest embodies the end of sex. This is much harder to do in a celebration of the Eucharist *contra populum* where the priest is positioned physically as a mediator between people and divinity and the sex of the priest is evident for all to see.[8]

In this account, priests who face the people can less effectively point beyond themselves, for priestly sex is 'evident for all to see'. But this is not quite right: *gender* might be clear (though it might not, depending on the signals sent by hairstyle, build, face and shoes, and local conventions about their significance, as well as whether the priest is already known to members of the congregation), but *sex* is not. Sex has variously been held to reside in chromosomes, gonads, gametes, hormones and genital appearance, but none of these is evident from looking at a clothed person (and some would still not be even if the priest were completely naked).

Human sex is not always clear and self-evident. People with physical intersex characteristics, sometimes called DSDs,[9] have bodies not easily classified as male or female. They may have unusual genital anatomy, or some 'female' and some 'male' physical characteristics. Scholars of the representation of intersex people in culture and history note that intersex disrupts sex in general, since the boundaries between maleness, intersex and femaleness are not always clear-cut.[10] Many people assume sex is obvious because they have no reason to think otherwise, but a surprising number of us might, if we were to undergo chromosomal analysis, find that, for example, we have both XX and XY chromosomes.

Stuart's queer advocating of the 'end of sex' is attractive, but some queer, intersex and transgender people may suspect it is too soon to stop celebrating difference and particularity, especially for sexes which are all too easily erased. Stuart says,

> The sacrifice of the Eucharist which is enacted by the priest acting *in persona Christi* is to some extent a sacrifice of sex. When the priest performs the consecration and utters the words, 'This is my body … This is my blood' s/he gazes at a piece of bread and a cup of wine, at an embodiment made strange and sexless.[11]

But while sacrificing sex might make sense if male privilege, hegemony, incontrovertibility and power are ceded, this sacrifice is less evidently good if we acknowledge that *all* sex is, already, ultimately unstable and shifting. In that case, *remaining* sexed might be as queer as, or more queer than, becoming unsexed.

So priests *may* embody the end of sex in some symbolic way, but priests *also* remain sexed human beings, even as they mediate Christ. Of course, this is partly why some people, like the Anglo-Catholic E. L. Mascall, writing in the 1970s, have opposed women's presidency altogether:

Priesthood belongs to Christ as the *Son* of the eternal Father ... The fact that he has only one sex, and that the male, does not make his humanity incomplete. Humanity belongs to him fully in the mode of masculinity; he does not need to be a hermaphrodite[12] in order to be fully human, any more than he needs to be a eunuch to avoid favouring one sex over the other. And because the ordained priest is not exercising a priest-hood of his own but is the agent and instrument through which Christ is exercising *his* priesthood, he too must be male.[13]

Why must Jesus' *maleness* be reflected by all priests when other charac-teristics are not?[14] Mascall would likely retort that sex is an *ontological* difference in a way that race, class and so on are not; indeed, the Church of England House of Bishops said so explicitly in 1988 when they wrote, 'Sexual differentiation ... belongs to a fundamental differentiation in the created order and has necessarily a significance over and above any sig-nificance that can be claimed for any other particularity.'[15] However, this argument is dubious on at least three counts. First, sex might also be understood as socially constructed and read into bodies;[16] second, asser-tions about sexed ontology are rarely grounded in sex at all but in gender;[17] and third, the unambiguity of even Jesus' male sex is not self-evident.[18]

When debates about women's ordination took place in the Church of England in the 1980s and 1990s, some men – like Bishop Graham Leonard, the retired Bishop of London – said they would be unable to keep their minds on higher things if women presided, because they would be overcome by desire.[19] This is obviously problematic – painting women as peculiarly sexual in a way men are not, and men as inherently lustful, undisciplined creatures – but does touch on something Stuart under-plays, namely that priests continue as sexed and sexual creatures even when embodying broader truths about God's indwelling of humanity. Eucharistic sex may not mean exactly what it meant before, but it is still present.

Some female priests have written of a special awareness (in themselves and others) of the potency of celebrating Eucharist while pregnant, with feeding and fecundity swelling visibly in their bodies. Kate Moorehead describes undergoing her first pregnancy when newly ordained. She says, 'We need the gospel to be enfleshed not just in the sacrament but also in the life of the one who officiates the sacrament ... Pregnancy forced me to integrate my human frailties into my ministry. There was no avoiding my physical needs, my sexuality or health.'[20] Lucy Winkett concurs: 'When pregnant women preside ..., the congregation has to acknowledge the visible unavoidable presence of sexuality within the liturgy.'[21] Of course, women are not *uniquely* sexual or embodied, and pregnancy does not somehow make pregnant women more sexed than other women, but advanced pregnancy is nonetheless a peculiarly *observable* reminder of sexuality and fertility.

For Stuart, priests enact the erasure of sex on behalf of others, embodying the birthing of non-sex into a sexed world. But while she is right that 'no other identity except that of Christ has ultimate concern',[22] I think she is mistaken to imply that the identities of human priests *this side of the eschaton* do not carry continuing significance. For humans, identities may be exclusive – though they may not: many theologians have written of what it means to carry apparently contradictory identities, like being a queer Asian-American Christian. But in Christ, identities can and do overlap. Christians' identities have in some sense ended, but also in some sense persist. Essence, *Gestalt*, is carried forward. Otherwise, it would be too easy to define some identities as legitimate and good reflections of God, and others as problems to be healed or perfected away.

I doubt this is what Stuart means to imply. Elsewhere she says: 'The beliefs that the resurrection involves some kind of bodily change and that bodies continue to bear the scars of human contingency are not necessarily incompatible. Indeed, they are mysteriously connected.'[23] In that work, she insists on an eschatology for people with physical impairments which is inaugurated but not fully realized, because this affirms that while they are certainly oppressed by social construction and interpretation, they are also, often, oppressed by physical experiences of pain.[24] So in 'The Priest at the Altar', she means simply that sex and gender cannot be considered *ultimate* identities, among the aspects of our natures that *must* continue as they were.

This almost works, but not quite. The insignificance of sex is right, but not because sex disappears: sex is insignificant *precisely because* it continues to exist, even in the moment that discloses its penultimacy. Stuart says a 'eucharistic theology of sexuality' resists the idea that sex is 'stable, thick and truthful'.[25] But it need not appeal to erased sex in the priest's body in order to do this. Queerness in liturgy involves highlighting *contingency* – of isolated biblical texts, human agendas and understandings of the divine.[26]

I suggest that what is queer about priestly sex in Eucharist is precisely its continuation, specificity and rootedness in particular embodiment. The priest's sex is queer not because only males can image Christ, but because *all* human sex is, simultaneously, specific and uncertain. The priest could be male, female, intersex, transgender or another sexed-gendered identity; they might be multiply inscribed as sexed and/or gendered, by themselves and others. Nonetheless, their sex remains specific. It does not matter *what* it is, but it matters *that* it is. This specificity is queer: Christ's incarnation happens in rooted, specific (yet provisional) embodiment.

The Sex of the Body of Christ

In terms of baptism, Stuart asserts,

> Into the font are plunged sex and age and what emerges is a new creation, the product of the resurrection. It is this new creation which the priest represents before God, a sexless humanity, a humanity looking into the tomb living on transformed bread and wine. This is humanity whose identity is erased by the very excess of it. No one is excluded and the act of inclusion obliterates identity which is always predicated upon exclusion.[27]

But is identity really always predicated on exclusion? Must identity claims always necessitate exclusion? Saying, for instance, that I am female as far as I know is an affiliation and a trajectory: it represents my female history and my probable female future, but without claiming femaleness as a best or sole possibility. 'Obvious' physical sex is, in fact, often merely *assumed* physical sex. Stuart is right that baptism initiates believers into a new creation (which they also co-create), but this new creation is lived and brought into existence in and through people who are still fully human, and thereby fully sexed in their various ways.

Importantly, this does not mean that we need fall back into essentialism, or insist that maleness, femaleness and sex in general are *a priori* 'real' in a way that gender identities are, at least by followers of Judith Butler, no longer believed to be. Scholars including Butler herself, Georgia Warnke and Thomas Laqueur have argued that sex is no more 'real' than gender or 'race' are, and that what we see in sexed bodies is deeply affected by what we expect to see – that is, what our cultural upbringing communicates about what sex can and should be like.[28] A body might be defined as male according to one definition and female according to another. In this sense, its sex shifts; but it can never disappear entirely.

However, I agree with Graham Ward that biologically essentialist theologies 'fail to understand the nature of bodies and sexes in Christ'[29] (while also agreeing with Virginia Burrus that Ward himself may do too little to disrupt the sexism historically reinscribed through assertions about Christ's maleness).[30] Like Stuart, Ward points out that sex for Christians is also constituted by their multiple existence: 'Bodies have no stable or autonomous identity. Bodies are not self-grounded and self-defining. A person's physical body, the "one flesh" of the nuptial body, the church's ecclesial body, the eucharistic body and Christ's eschatological body map upon one another.'[31] For Ward, maleness and femaleness have a reality, but a theological rather than (or as well as) a biological one. He argues, via Karl Barth, that male and female are 'tropes' or types, carriers of difference which generate desire for the other and (therefore) dynamism. But while theology and liturgy must 'sanctify' sexual difference, difference exists between same-sex couples as well as heterosexual couples.[32] It is difference that matters, not that that difference is fixed as desire for an 'opposite' sex.

Ward himself does not explore the implications of his argument for intersex and transgender people, nor the implications of transgender and intersex for his argument (though he does, in passing, express doubt about whether there are only two sexes).[33] Ward's logic is precisely what needs to be outworked in the eucharistic president's body – but cannot be outworked if, as Stuart says, priestly sex is under complete erasure. Ward, like Stuart, is correct that Christians' sexed bodies, like the other bodies in which they participate, should be understood as malleable, ambiguous, porous, hybrid, even queer;[34] but Ward acknowledges an ongoing concrete reality in differentiated sexed human bodies. For Ward, sex and gender are *queered* in Christ but not *erased*:

It is not that gender disappears. Gender is not transcended. It is rather rendered part of a more profound mystery; the mystery of relation itself between God and human beings. I am found in God most myself, my sexual, gendered and gendering self – but I have to be taught what it means to be such a self by the Christ who draws me into a relationship with him. It is then the very male specificity of the body of Jesus Christ that comes to determine how I understand my own embodiment.[35]

I would suggest to Ward that the *maleness* of Jesus' body is less significant than the *specificity* of Jesus' sex whatever that may be – since Jesus' assumed maleness is not incontrovertible.[36] Nonetheless, Ward is right that only in a specifically sexed body which remains specifically sexed can other specifically sexed bodies – no matter what their sex – be transformed and redeemed.

In a 2010 essay, Stuart revisits the notion of the queer-eucharistic self, not *sacrificed* but *constituted* by the liturgy. Here, the 'non-gendered, non-sexed, non-raced, non-classed self, the baptized self' has been colonized and 'written over by hetero-patriarchy and cultural constructs',[37] but can be re-membered – put back together – liturgically. Stuart appeals to Christians to reclaim their 'given' selves rather than holding on to their 'scripted' selves, the ones influenced by culture and history. Her focus shifts from priestly sex to the sexed nature of the *whole* Christian community constituted in Eucharist:

The chief characteristic of this body is its extraordinary diversity – all sexes, sexualities, races, classes are part of it ... The body of Christ in which our individual bodies find their meaning is the perfect queer community, a body in which all forms of identity are rendered slippery and unstable.[38]

Echoing Butler, Stuart argues that gender is not stable or certain, but performed. We do not necessarily perform it freely, because we are influenced by culture, and our carts roll most easily in the grooves made by those who drove their genders across the landscape of identity before us. But it is interesting that Stuart refers to the non-gendered, non-sexed self as the *given* self. The language of givenness is more often used, theologically, by those insistent that sex and gender are *themselves* 'God-given', that God has a divine plan involving males identifying as men attracted to women, and females identifying as women attracted to men.[39] Stuart seems to say, rather, that what is God-given *preceded* all this: perfect selves from which the shiny accoutrements of culture have lured us away.

I go far with Stuart here. Her claim that 'the Eucharist ... reminds us that the unity between Christ and his church, and the creation of one-fleshness, is not only, or indeed primarily, established through sexual relating'[40] is persuasive. The Christian community is built on children adopted as well as born into it, and relationships of love and loyalty which transcend kinship groups and biological reproduction. But for Stuart, this happens in and through Christians' refusal to recognize boundaries of embodiment, and this is more problematic. Boundaries are sometimes healthy and necessary: refusing to respect them can lead to psychological destruction. Furthermore, boundaries do not always entail hierarchies of identity. Ancient diagrams representing the mystery of the Trinity insisted that the Father is not the Son, the Son is not the Spirit and the Spirit is not the Father, though all three are God. Christians whose agency and bodily integrity are already at risk – especially intersex and transgender people – may, reasonably, be especially wary of erasing sexed boundaries.

This is the crux. All sexes, sexualities, races and classes *cannot* be part of this Body if they have *already* ceased to exist. If they have already ceased to exist, they cannot be taken forward into their own redemption. The priest's role is to take up multiplicities of embodiment, but not by eliding them; for priests are understood as 'embodying and remembering at the altar the new creation that the Eucharist makes possible'[41] in and through their *distinctively* sexed bodies.

The changes in sacred gendered space will surpass those identified by Andrea Bieler and David Plüss[42] and others as occurring when women priests inhabit the sanctuary, for they will acknowledge human sex *already* existing multiply and uncertainly. Indeed, they will also exceed the gender transcendence identified by Stuart in Eucharist and baptism; crossing and uncertainty will be shown as *already* existing at the heart of

the story of human sex. Slipperiness and instability are important quali-
ties. But they already exist in all sexed bodies, because all sex is already
slippery and unstable even (and especially) where it is not named as such.
These identities' instability does not, therefore, equal their cessation. It is
for the same reason that Ward does not go quite far enough when he says,
'In being transposable, while also being singular and specific, the body of
Christ can cross boundaries – gender boundaries for example. Jesus' body
as bread is no longer Christ as simply and biologically male.'[43] Actually,
Christ's maleness is not simple and biological, for *even in simple bio-
logical terms* – prior to the queer disruptions and disturbances Ward and
Stuart identify in the Eucharist – it is uncertain.

Conclusions

Divisions of function based on gender are dangerous, both because they
solidify into chains of command and because they inevitably exclude or
write out of existence those whose gender stories do not fit the neatly
gendered picture. Stuart is right that Eucharist disrupts even the gender
of the priest, pointing to Jesus' existence, in and through the people, as
transcending human norms and categories of gender and sex. How bodies
behave in eucharistic presidency sends messages about power, authority,
potency and hierarchy: Letty Russell, Janet Walton, Rosemary Radford
Ruether and others therefore suggest that changes in the postures, rubrics
and even furniture and vestments used might disrupt unacknowledged
patterns of gendered and other inequality.[44] The presidency of women
priests, suggests Anita Monro, may be understood as particularly ambivalent, since 'feminine' priests re-play a 'masculine' act which is itself already
'feminine' (echoing Christ's motherly feeding with his body), so that
women must either repeat this suppression of the feminine or be excluded
from presidency altogether.[45] James Walters adds that bodies priestly and
lay are 'reconceived, even symbolically regenerated, within the symbolic
interactions of liturgy'.[46]

Nonetheless, I suggest, this cannot mean erasing sex at the moment of
celebration. The real, continuing specificities of sexed-gendered embodiment in those who preside must not lead to stereotypical or homogenizing
assumptions about what particular kinds of bodies 'mean' when leading liturgical worship. For Sarah Coakley, the eucharistic president's
existence at the boundary between humanity and divinity (repeatedly
crossing between them) renders the priest's presence in Eucharist deeply
subversive of gender normativities. However, *erasing* gender is not the
answer. Rather, Coakley describes the shifting, liminal status of the priest
as participation in divine fluidity.[47]

Coakley's account is still problematic. She still portrays the priest's disruptive role as a crossing *between* genders, ostensibly fluid and dynamic but nonetheless understood as 'both' (that is, in only binary terms). Furthermore, she views androgyny as necessarily negative, since it would (she suspects) entail uncritically splicing stereotypical femininity and masculinity.[48] She also does too little to acknowledge the non-gendered hierarchies and subordinations which the eucharistic president's 'crossing' movements might evoke.[49] However, Coakley's conviction that erasing gender in the priest's body ends up reinforcing a 'male neuter' is well made, and chimes with the point I have attempted to set out: that eschatological transformations of sex can be instituted, but not fully realized, for as long as sexual inequality persists.

But I part from Coakley, as from Stuart, by suggesting that even claims about a priestly mixing or erasure of sex in the Eucharist unwittingly reinforce the notion that human sex was stable, evident or clear to begin with. Rather, I suggest, the continued reality and persistence of the priest's particular sexed physicality (regardless of what that sexed physicality is) itself signifies a divine resistance to the elision of types of bodily sex.

Ward says, 'The displacement of the body at the Eucharist effects a sharing, a participation. We belong to Jesus and Jesus to others through partaking of his given body.'[50] 'Givenness' rears its head again: but here, it references not only the incontrovertibility or otherwise of a particular body, but also its existence as *gift*. At Eucharist, Jesus' body is displaced and queried, like the priest's body. Both bodies are given over for the community. Stuart might hold that this 'giving over' entails the erasure of priestly sex because only in its erasure is the significance of maleness in the priesthood disrupted. But I suggest that giving over continues to happen in bodies that retain their sexed specificities, while simultaneously refusing to say any more about the significance of that sex than that it exists. This profoundly alters the terms of the game, rendering 'ambiguously' sexed and gendered bodies (which are actually entirely *un*ambiguous, being perfect examples of their own specific sexed nature) no more problematic than male and female ones, and male and female bodies just as shifting and uncertain as intersex and trans ones. In this way, all bodily sexes are shown to be penultimate (as Stuart insists) *even before* they have been taken up into the cosmic queering of normativity which takes place again and anew in each act of liturgical celebration.

Stuart focuses on priests and their specific role in liturgy. But there is a noble Christian tradition of seeking and endorsing the 'priesthood' of all Christians, acknowledging that each of us mediates Christ in and for the world. In this way, each and every one of us, priest or not, is also called to queer and question gender in our own lives, even as we remain specifically sexed persons.

Notes

1 Stewart Henderson, 1997, 'Priestly Duties: A Poem', *Limited Edition*, Winona, MN: Plover Books, no page number.

2 Elizabeth Stuart, 2009, 'The Priest at the Altar: The Eucharistic Erasure of Sex', in Marcella Althaus-Reid and Lisa Isherwood (eds), *Trans/Formations*, London: SCM Press, pp. 127–38.

3 Granet, a French painter, lived between 1775 and 1849.

4 Stuart, 'Priest', p. 127.

5 Stuart, 'Priest', p. 129.

6 Stuart, 'Priest', p. 130.

7 'Ad orientem', meaning 'to the east', refers to a celebration of Eucharist in which a priest stands in front of the altar facing the east wall of the church with his or her back to the congregation, and may be understood as symbolic of the priest's partnership with the people in their worship. When this occurs, however, it is not possible for the congregation to see the priest's face and it may be more difficult to see his or her actions and to hear his or her words. Current Roman Catholic guidance specifies that, where possible, the Eucharist should be celebrated with the priest facing the people.

8 Stuart, 'Priest', p. 131.

9 DSD (disorder of sex development) began to be used as an alternative term for intersex in the mid 2000s, having been endorsed by Intersex Society of North America and, subsequently, Accord Alliance, a US-based organization seeking to promote improved medical treatment. 'DSD' has rapidly overtaken 'intersex' as the commonly used term in medical contexts. Proponents of the term consider that it escapes some of the associations of 'intersex' with queer theory, LGBT identity politics and gender identity problems, which may have dissuaded parents of children with these conditions from seeking help from intersex groups. However, some intersex support and activism groups reject 'DSD' since they consider the term 'disorder' stigmatizing and view 'DSD' as having been imposed on them by medics (and reinforcing a medical, rather than social, model of intersex). A few critics suggest retaining the 'DSD' shorthand, but changing the long version to 'difference of sex development' or 'divergence of sex development'. See Milton Diamond and Hazel Glenn Beh, 2008, 'Changes in Management of Children with Differences of Sex Development', *Nature Clinical Practice: Endocrinology & Metabolism* 4, no. 1: 4–5. See also Elizabeth Reis, 2009, *Bodies in Doubt: An American History of Intersex*, Baltimore, MD: The Johns Hopkins University Press, p. 159. For more on the ongoing debates surrounding terminology, see e.g. Emi Koyama, 'From "Intersex" to "DSD": Toward a Queer Disability Politics of Gender', keynote speech presented at Translating Identity conference, University of Vermont, February 2006, http://www.ipdx.org/articles/intersextodsd.html [accessed 26 July 2018]. See also Ellen K. Feder and Katrina Karkazis, 2009, 'What's in a Name? The Controversy over "Disorders of Sex Development"', *Hastings Center Report* 38, no. 5: 33–6. See also Georgiann Davis, 2011, '"DSD Is a Perfectly Fine Term": Reasserting Medical Authority Through a Shift in Intersex Terminology', *Advances in Medical Sociology* 12: 155–82.

10 Alice Domurat Dreger, 1998, *Hermaphrodites and the Medical Invention of Sex*, Cambridge, MA: Harvard University Press; see also Reis, *Bodies in Doubt*.

11 Stuart, 'Priest', p. 131.

12 Note that 'hermaphrodite' was also used in the past with reference to intersex people but is now considered inaccurate and stigmatizing and is no longer used in medical parlance.

13 E. L. Mascall, 1978, 'Some Basic Considerations', in Peter Moore (ed.), *Man, Woman, and Priesthood*, London: SPCK, pp. 9–26 at p. 23.

14 Rosemary Radford Ruether, 1985, *Women-Church: Theology and Practice of Feminist Liturgical Communities*, San Francisco, CA: Harper & Row, p. 70; Susan Dowell and Jane Williams, 1994, *Bread, Wine and Women: The Ordination Debate in the Church of England*, London: Virago, p. 23.

15 Central Board of Finance of the Church of England, 1988, *The Ordination of Women to the Priesthood: A Second Report by the House of Bishops*, London, Church House Publishing, p. 26.

16 Thomas Laqueur, 1990, *Making Sex: Body and Gender from the Greeks to Freud*, Cambridge, MA, Harvard University Press.

17 Susannah Cornwall, 'Intersex and Ontology: A Response to *The Church, Women Bishops and Provision*', Manchester: Lincoln Theological Institute, http://lincolntheologicalinstitute.com/iid-resources/ [accessed 26 July 2018], pp. 9–10, 16. Consider, for example, one of the House of Bishops' justifications for the maleness of the priesthood in 1988: 'In terms of our relationship to God we are essentially "female-like" and feminine and he is "male-like" and masculine. God always has the initiative and our duty is to respond. Because, psychologically and symbolically and, to an important extent, biologically, taking the initiative is male, it was therefore appropriate that the Word was incarnate as a male human being and not as a female human being. The particularity of maleness assumed in the incarnation and taken into the Godhead signifies divine initiative' (Central Board of Finance, 'The Ordination of Women', p. 27). This deeply stereotypical picture of masculine initiative and feminine response and receptivity seems to rest in older understandings of the female role in reproduction.

18 Cornwall, 'Intersex and Ontology', p. 15. As I have argued elsewhere, the existence of 'invisible' intersex conditions that cause no genital ambiguity means that even people whose maleness or femaleness is never called into question might unknowingly have some intersex characteristics. Since we cannot analyse Jesus' chromosomes or gonads, we cannot know whether or not they 'matched' his presumably male-looking genitalia.

19 Dowell and Williams, *Bread*, p. 33.

20 Kate Moorehead, 2000, 'Preparing for Luke: Reflections by a Pregnant Priest', in Nathan Humphrey (ed.), *Gathering the Next Generation: Essays on the Formation and Ministry of GenX Priests*, Harrisburg, PA: Morehouse Publishing, pp. 121–30 at p. 129.

21 Lucy Winkett, 2010, 'Why is That Priest Singing in a Woman's Voice?' in Nicola Slee and Stephen Burns (eds), *Presiding Like a Woman*, London: SPCK, pp. 94–101 at p. 95.

22 Stuart, 'Priest', p. 134.

23 Elizabeth Stuart, 2010, 'Disruptive Bodies: Disability, Embodiment and Sexuality', in Marvin M. Ellison and Kelly Brown Douglas (eds), *Sexuality and the Sacred: Sources for Theological Reflection*, 2nd edn, Louisville, KY: Westminster John Knox Press, pp. 322–37 at p. 328.

24 Stuart, 'Disruptive Bodies', p. 322.

25 Stuart, 'Priest', p. 137.

26 Michael N. Jagessar and Stephen Burns, 2011, *Christian Worship: Postcolonial Perspectives*, London, Equinox, p. 74.

27 Stuart, 'Priest', p. 132.

28 Judith Butler, 1993, *Bodies That Matter*, New York: Routledge; Georgia

Warnke, 2001, 'Intersexuality and the Categories of Sex', *Hypatia*, 16, no. 3: 126–37; Laqueur, 'Making Sex'.

29 Graham Ward, 1999, 'Bodies: The Displaced Body of Jesus Christ', in John Milbank, Catherine Pickstock and Graham Ward (eds), *Radical Orthodoxy: A New Theology*, London: Routledge, pp. 163–81 at p. 177.

30 Virginia Burrus, 2006, 'Radical Orthodoxy and the Heresiological Habit: Engaging Graham Ward's Christology', in Rosemary Radford Ruether and Marion Grau (eds), *Interpreting the Postmodern: Responses to 'Radical Orthodoxy'*, New York: T&T Clark International, pp. 36–53.

31 Graham Ward, 1998, 'The Erotics of Redemption – After Karl Barth', *Theology and Sexuality* 8: 52–72 at 63.

32 Ward, 'Erotics', pp. 71–2.

33 Ward, 'Bodies', p. 178.

34 Graham Ward, 2004, 'On the Politics of Embodiment and the Mystery of All Flesh', in Marcella Althaus-Reid and Lisa Isherwood (eds), *The Sexual Theologian: Essays on Sex, God and Politics*, London and New York: T&T Clark, pp. 71–85 at p. 85.

35 Ward, 'On the Politics', p. 72.

36 Ward's argument (here and in 'Bodies') focuses on the theological and political implications bound up in Jesus' circumcision. But even circumcision is not necessarily a marker of unambiguous or indisputable maleness, since some intersex conditions present with male-related genitalia including a penis-sized phallus with foreskin, but in combination with some unseen 'female' characteristics such as XX chromosomes and/or ovarian tissue.

37 Elizabeth Stuart, 2010, 'Making No Sense: Liturgy as Queer Space', in Lisa Isherwood and Mark D. Jordan (eds), *Dancing Theology in Fetish Boots: Essays in Honour of Marcella Althaus-Reid*, London: SCM Press, pp. 113–23 at p. 119.

38 Stuart, 'Making No Sense', p. 122.

39 Oliver O'Donovan, 1982, *Transsexualism and Christian Marriage*, Nottingham: Grove Books, p. 15; Evangelical Alliance Policy Commission, 2000, *Transsexuality*, London: Evangelical Alliance, p. 67; Archbishops' Council, 2003, *Some Issues in Human Sexuality, A Guide to the Debate: A Discussion Document from the House of Bishops' Group on Issues in Human Sexuality*, London: Church House Publishing, p. 233.

40 Stuart, 'Making No Sense', p. 122.

41 Winkett, 'Why', p. 97.

42 Andrea Bieler and David Plüss, 2010, 'In This Moment of Utter Vulnerability: Tracing Gender in Presiding', in Slee and Burns, *Presiding*, pp. 112–22.

43 Ward, 'Bodies', p. 168.

44 Letty Russell, 1993, *Church in the Round: Feminist Interpretation of the Church*, Louisville, KY: Westminster John Knox Press; Janet Walton, 2000, *Feminist Liturgy: A Matter of Justice*, Collegeville, MN: Liturgical Press; Ruether, *Women-Church*; Slee and Burns, *Presiding*.

45 Anita Monro, '"And Ain't I a Woman": The Phronetic Dramaturgy of Feeding the Family', in Slee and Burns, *Presiding*, pp. 123–32 at p. 124.

46 James Walters, 2012, *Baudrillard and Theology*, London: T&T Clark, p. 116.

47 Sarah Coakley, 2004, 'The Woman at the Altar: Cosmological Disturbance or Gender Subversion?', *Anglican Theological Review* 86, no. 1: 75–93 at 92. Coakley explicitly rejects the idea that this should be understood as 'a queer protest against gender stability' (p. 92), but this seems to be largely because she assumes queerness

as necessarily secular rather than a refusal of human hegemony already existing within the divine. See also Rupert Shortt, 2005, *God's Advocates: Christian Thinkers in Conversation*, Grand Rapids, MI: Eerdmans, p. 77; Susannah Cornwall, 2011, *Controversies in Queer Theology*, London: SCM Press, pp. 235–7.

48 Coakley, 'The Woman', p. 92.

49 Cornwall, *Controversies*, p. 237.

50 Ward, 'Bodies', p. 169.

5

The Queer Body in the Wedding

W. SCOTT HALDEMAN

The wedding, as a classic 'rite of passage', marks (and effects) the movement of persons from the social status of 'the single' to the social status of
'the married'. Being married is, for some, to enter a new ontological status
– joining one's spouse in a permanent sacramental union. For others, it is
more mundane – one gains certain new social and financial benefits (such
as inheritance without taxation or access to one's partner's health insur-
ance) and accepts certain responsibilities (such as to provide resources and
support to one's spouse and any dependents) that are legally enforceable
in family court through laws governing divorce. For most, the wedding is
somewhere in the middle, involving:

- a reaching for the ideals of unifying love;
- a joining not only of the couple but their families and a community of
  friends as some sort of new relational unit;
- a making of a solemn, public vow of commitment;
- a receiving of blessings and gifts and good wishes from their newly configured network of support; and, of course,
- a legitimating, even honouring, of their sex practices.

To be permitted to 'wed' requires that the participants, the 'couple',
match some criteria. In most US states, these involve a minimum age and
some proof of lack of blood relationship.[1] Until recently, these have also
included a certain gender configuration: one man, one woman. Meeting
the criteria, one is able to plan the wedding and to stand before witnesses
and make vows – and then have an authorized agent sign a piece of paper
that moves one from single to married in the eyes of the state, one's
family/community and, if the ceremony involves a community of faith,
the church and, even, God. These are wedding fundamentals.

Religious communities also have an interest in who can marry (and,
apparently, who should not) and how they are wed. Denominations and
local congregations tend to have more complex criteria for who can plan
a wedding and make vows and be declared married and have a document
signed than civil jurisdictions. These may include:

- membership in the particular congregation that owns the building in which the ceremony will take place;
- the ability to pay for the space and for the time and talent of professionals, such as an organist and a pastor/presider;
- submission to certain preparatory activities such as premarital counselling, and/or;
- a certain gender configuration that may or may not match the configuration the state requires.

Because of the legislative and judicial successes of the marriage equality movement in the United States, as well as globally, churches tend to be stricter than the state; many refuse to wed same-gender couples still.

Certainly, the wedding has 'performed' certain relations and dynamics between the two dominant genders for millennia. These have changed but remain operative. Gladly we are beyond (in most places) a baldly property-based dynamic – when the wedding is arranged as an economic transaction in which the 'bride' is transferred from the ownership of her father to that of her husband – this is, after all, what 'husband' means: 'the owner/head of a household'.[2] Gone, too, are coverture laws through which the wife's legal and financial identity was subsumed by the husband. Women keep their own names or couples create new family names together. Marital rape and domestic violence, while still too prevalent, at least have legal redress. No fault divorce allows for the dissolution of destructive relationships. This is real progress.

History – theological, ecclesial and civil – contains other ambiguities, mutabilities and contradictions, as well. Jesus called his closest followers away from their homes and families (e.g. Matt. 4.18–22) and promises that in heaven there will be no marriage – and that this will make us more rather than less like angels (Matt. 22.30). Paul counsels that it is better to marry than to burn with lust, but that it is better still to remain single and (presumably) celibate (1 Cor. 7.9). The early church blessed couples but not at the altar.[3] The wedding joined the lofty realm of 'sacrament' only in the twelfth century – as a theology of marriage as a perpetual, exclusive and indissoluble union also developed.[4] This was tempered in the Reformation as the couple's companionship in the midst of a fourfold covenant between couple, clergy, state and God came to the fore as the paramount purpose and gift of blessed coupledom.[5] And, then, of course, 'love conquered marriage' in Coontz's apt phrase, placing romantic bliss before all else starting in the Victorian era.[6] In the United States, the wedding not only helped to govern gender dynamics but also racial ones – as we now remember again as we note the recent fiftieth anniversary of *Loving v. Virginia*,[7] which allowed bi-racial couples to be legally wed – in 1967. And, in 2015, *Obergefell v. Hodges* expanded the circle of eligibility to include same-sex couples across the United States.[8]

Beyond all this, there remains something more about weddings – about their centrality in our lives, both individually and culturally. Weddings are the stuff of dreams. They shimmer along the horizon – on that day, we will be fulfilled, find and claim ourselves, establish our maturity, begin life truly … or so the myths have it. Weddings also figure in larger trajectories of human thought. When J. L. Austin proclaimed what is both obvious and elusive – that we can 'do things with words', he used the wedding vow as his first and most central example.[9] Since Austin, and so within all subsequent conversations about language – and its efficacy and performativity and citationality – phrases such as 'I thee wed' and 'I now pronounce you' hover, even as they also structure and enforce heterosexual desire. There does, in fact, seem to be 'something about "marry"!'[10]

When first-graders, even those who have never been to a wedding, can describe the 'perfect' ceremony that they plan to have someday,[11] when many remain convinced that a vast and diverse society is dependent for its fundamental stability on the valorization of the heterosexual couple and its offspring,[12] when most churches prioritize in budgets and programming the support of couples and parents – even in an era with growing visibility and acceptance of alternative structures of intimacy and support – can we ever hope to escape the fundamental gender structure of the wedding? This is the question to which this essay attempts an initial answer. More specifically, I, below and all too briefly, look at the three most common types of union services for same-sex couples through a lens of Butlerian performativity:[13]

- When a traditional ceremony is used and yet two women stand up and asked to be blessed, are the norms escaped, challenged or reinscribed?
- When a new ceremony is proposed that begins with the assumption that it should 'work' for both different-sex and same-sex couples, is this a laudable goal or a misapprehension? and,
- When a new ceremony is proposed that begins with the assumption that it should 'work' specifically for same-sex couples and their distinct needs, again, is the underlying dynamic escaped or not?

But, before focusing on our three specific examples, it may help to think again about the wedding through the lens of theology, ritual theory and queer theory. What is a wedding for, in a theological sense? What is 'Christian' about it? How does it function in relation to larger cultural systems? And, for our purposes here, what might also be 'queer' about it? These reflections lead to a consideration of bodies – those of the couple and that of the church as Body of Christ.

The Wedding: Christian? Queer?

Every religion – and every so-called secular society as well, I would contend – develops a series of practices that shape adherents/citizens in relationship to both stated and implicit values or beliefs. This may be called a ritual system – tools, techniques, pathways and processes that define the way things are and who we are becoming over time. The system may be more closed or more open, more coercive or more voluntary, but it is always there. In certain times and places, those who define, maintain and enforce a community's doctrines or worldview are also those who shape rites to inculcate preordained teachings. In other circumstances, practices bubble up and bodies-in-motion improvise, such that new teachings, new knowledges emerge – perhaps themselves to be codified and institutionalized over time.[14]

Christian ritual systems are, of course, multiple and vary in all these ways – from rigid to flexible, from doctrine-heavy to exploratory, from secretive to socially dominant. Within such a system, the wedding serves as one way to commence a new phase of one's faith journey, 'from this day forward' with a more or less permanent companion.[15] The human is not meant to live alone, we read (Gen. 2.18). But, of course, many live alone – even when married. Marriage does not define the best or only way to live out one's vocation of discipleship – but it is one way, and so should be ritually marked. Another way to live out one's vocation is as a member of the clergy – so ordination ceremonies parallel the wedding in many branches of the church. Beyond these two rites, ways to honour and celebrate varied specific vocations of discipleship grow thin. Sanctuaries filled with tools on Labor Day. The naming and blessing of church school teachers – and perhaps all teachers. The commissioning of lay leaders, of missionaries and seminarians. Veterans' Day sermons. Mothers' Day flowers. These are a start. And they are paltry, and often problematic. The point is that a Christian wedding is Christian, first, when it humbly marks one way of living that the church honours and blesses – but not to the exclusion of other paths.

Given the complex societies in which we live, it is also true that our rites are one part of a larger matrix of social structures, which can nurture life and keep peace and distribute goods (with equity or, more often, without), but which also create such stabilities through mechanisms of normalization and naturalization. For instance, what it means to be a 'man' or to be a 'woman' clearly changes over time and across cultures, but in any discrete time and place is said to reflect simply 'the way things are'. Further, such identities or roles or characters – because, in fact, they are actually fictions – are always vulnerable to the messiness of reality. Threats of instability produce still further anxious strivings to secure boundaries and clarify categories. Mary Douglas observes that the more a group values structure, the more it fears disruption: 'Pollution is a type of danger which is not likely to occur except where the lines of structure, cosmic or social, are clearly defined.' She continues: 'A polluting person is always in the wrong.'[16] In terms of gender, Judith Butler argues: 'Discrete genders are part of what "humanizes" individuals within contemporary culture; indeed, we regularly punish those who fail to do their gender right.'[17] Conformity is enforced and yet is never totalizing. Butler, again:

> The abiding gendered self [is then] shown to be structured by repeated acts that seek to approximate the ideal of a substantial ground of identity, but which, in their occasional *dis*continuity, reveal the temporal and contingent groundlessness of this 'ground'. The possibilities of gender transformation are to be found precisely in this arbitrary relation between such acts, in the possibility of a failure to repeat, a de-formity, or a parodic repetition that exposes the phantasmatic effect of abiding identity as a politically tenuous construction.[18]

In other words, we are given scripts that define who we should be and what we should do and how we should speak and dress and even think. And, we are coerced by law and custom and parenting and peer pressure to play our assigned part. Those who do not 'fit', in particular, perform out of duress – but also, usually, gladly so that we can 'pass' and so escape punishment. Yet, Butler contends, even as we – happily or not – perform what is always already expected of us, we also fail in such repetitions – and, just here, in the slippages, we may uncover the illusions and find alternatives, perhaps ones that liberate rather than confine.

The wedding clearly is one of the mechanisms that both displays and enforces who we are in terms of gender; it involves gendered performance. There is a script. It is also – and, necessarily – a place of failure, of the occasional display of how arbitrary the notions of gender to which we cling actually are. Butler turns to drag performance as one example of a place of resistance – but not a simple one. I am thinking along these same lines about same-sex weddings in relation to the Christian ritual system. In other words, all of our rites are themselves imbricated in regimes of normativity and so foster both the faithful formation of participants as disciples and the reinscription of dynamics of oppression and domination. In them (and, perhaps, in the wedding in particular), we submit to (and enact) particular norms of – among other lines that we use to divide humanity – gender, sexuality, race/ethnicity/culture and class. To be a queer body here (or, better, to queer the Body), then, involves exposing such norms through parodic performance. As Judith Butler says of Jennifer Livingston's film *Paris is Burning*, and the gay and transsexual, black and brown drag queens who are its subjects and who are known collectively as 'the children':

> *Paris is Burning* documents neither an efficacious insurrection nor a painful resubordination, but an unstable coexistence of both. The film attests to the painful pleasures of eroticizing and miming the very norms that wield their power by foreclosing the very reverse-occupations that the children nevertheless perform.
>
> This is not an appropriation of dominant culture in order to remain subordinated by its terms but an appropriation that seeks to make over the terms of domination, a making over that is itself a kind of agency, a power in and as discourse, in and as performance, which repeats in order to remake – and sometimes succeeds.[19]

The wedding, then, may be considered both a primary mechanism of larger social enforcement of naturalized gender identities, and, perhaps, also a place to foster freedom.

Given this, what I am thinking is now required of us as scholars and pastors is to consider – ritually, liturgically and theologically – the difference that the presence of explicitly queer bodies makes in our services of worship – and, for the purposes of this chapter, especially in the wedding. My hunch is that queer bodies both enrich and challenge our liturgical thinking and doing – forcing us to contend with the underlying heteronormativity in our rites and revealing new dimensions of the blessings God desires to bestow upon all of us in and through our rites. But, let us think further about bodies and the Body more generally first.

Bodies in the Wedding, the Church as Body/Bride

Bodies are central to wedding. While there are a growing number of exceptions to the rule these days, the wedding proper begins as the groom slips in from the side to the head of the aisle and awaits the bride as she processes the full length of the nave. Meanwhile the assembly stands and turns in admiration and anticipation. Even if the entire wedding party dances boisterously down the aisle to a pop song, the result is that these two stand before us. Too often they have their backs to the assembly. We have come to witness their exchange of words and symbols. The pastor should not be the centre of attention but should pivot, perhaps even descend to the floor, so the couple is highlighted. These two are our ministers, the primary sacramental signs. In them, through them, we glimpse something of divine love – in Pauline terms, an image of the love of Christ, the Bridegroom, for the church, the virgin bride (Eph. 5.21–33). Their joining is initiated here – in their promises, in the pronouncement, in the giving and receiving of rings, in the signing of documents. The joining is completed when their bodies will co-mingle and interpenetrate later in private, perhaps on honeymoon; consummation (even if we do not think it polite to discuss) culminates the wedding and commences the marriage. This is also why we feast and often dance. It is all about bodies.

And it is here that we run into problems. The new husband stands, metaphorically, in for Jesus; as Christ is the head of the church, so he is head of the woman, his wife. He is to love her, but the relationship is hier-archical, not egalitarian. Yes, his love is to be sacrificial: he, like Christ, should give up his life in order that she be presented holy and blameless. But his role is saviour; hers to be saved. His mandate is to love; hers is to submit. Here, too, the creation story is invoked: 'For this reason a man will leave his father and mother and be united to his wife and the two will become one flesh' (Eph. 5.31, quoting Gen. 2.24). Here, then, also, are 'first man' and 'first woman' – bone of bone, flesh of flesh, two out of one, companions of procreative complementarity. Arguing with the Pharisees about divorce, in one of his more absolutist moments – at least for men who would abandon their families – Jesus also quotes this same verse of the creation story to remove Moses' escape hatch (Mark 10.8 and Matt. 19.5). These are the root metaphors of the wedding. Here, conceptions of the traditional family, the valorization of gender complementarity and the construction of sexual moralities that privilege potentially procreative acts can be founded. Of course, the Bible and subsequent readings of it, and much theological reflection provide other ways of thinking about sex, relationship, family and church. But we should not be surprised that marriage and the wedding is fiercely defended as a key pillar in both ecclesial and civil orderings.

That 'this man' and 'this woman' as they stand before friends and families can embody such deep metaphors of faith is powerful indeed. The question is whether these metaphors are exclusively faithful or simply one of a number of ways to image Christian intimacy in relation to com-munity. We find some of the basic alternative approaches in Mark Jordan's collection of essays, *Authorizing Marriage?*: Dale Martin emphasizes the suspicion of marriage and family among early Christian witnesses; Mary Ann Tolbert suggests that teachings about Christian friendship rather than coupledom may be more fruitful as we reconsider faithful modes of relationship; and Eugene Rogers highlights, first, the diversity of creation – all of which has a place in the divine order and all of which requires sanctification – and then argues, second, that for the human person sancti-fication requires commitment to community and to an ascetic discipline, which can take many forms, including a same-sex relationship.[20]

Elsewhere Elizabeth Stuart focuses on baptism – looking again and anew at the debates over human sexuality from the font. She draws upon queer theory to suggest that baptism may be seen as bestowing a new sense of identity, one that relativizes all other notions of identity. Worth quoting at length, she writes:

> Through baptism human beings are transformed from being atomized individuals and taken into the very life of the Trinitarian God that is incarnated in the Church. The ontology of the baptized is radically changed, they become what might be called ecclesial persons.[21]

And, further:

> The ecclesial person is ... one in which all other identities are decon-structed and rendered non-essential, as in Gal. 3.28, 'There is no longer Jew or Greek, there is no longer slave or free, there is no longer male or female; for you are all one in Christ Jesus'. But culturally constructed identities are not abandoned, they are redeemed and given back to us as parodies of their former selves. I do not use parody in the con-ventional sense of sending up something. Linda Hutcheon defines parody as 'an extended repetition with critical difference' which has 'a hermeneutical function with both cultural and even ideological impli-cations'. Christians operate within culture that is in the process of being redeemed. It is hard if not impossible to resist the identities our culture gives to us but the Christian is obliged to live out these identities with 'critical difference', the difference being shaped by ecclesial personhood. This will often involve a deliberate subversion of identity categories. The Christian performance of maleness and femaleness will therefore be strange (and indeed throughout Christian history has often been very strange), because gender is not determinative of our relationship to God.[22]

While I agree with Andy Buechel's critique of Stuart that, despite our theological ideals, the regimes of normalization and naturalization reside nonetheless within our rites – even within baptism – and so Christians are not simply enabled and obliged to live ecclesial-ly rather than cultural-ly but also must parody the ecclesial itself, I also appreciate how Stuart pro-vides a helpful reframing of debates about the ways Christians ought to 'do' gender and sexuality.[23] She notes that our individual gender perform-ances should look strange. Further, she embeds individual members within a community that also does things strangely. Both individual Christians and the Body to which we belong is beginning to look rather queer.

Graham Ward extends this line of thinking. In his essay, 'Bodies: The Displaced Body of Jesus',[24] Ward reflects on the challenge of Jesus' maleness – the particularity of incarnation marked in circumcision, among other things. Along the way, he identifies five displacements: the transfiguration, the Eucharist, the crucifixion, the resurrection and the ascension. He argues that at each stage Jesus' male Jewish body expands and is transposed in ways that both reflect and break open our understandings of embodiment itself. In relation to the ascension, he writes:

> The ascension is the final displacement ... of the gendered body of Jesus ... [into] the multi-gendered body of the Church. A new spatial distance opens up with the ascension – a vertical transcending spatiality such as divides the uncreated God from creation. There will be no more resurrection appearances ...
>
> The logic of the ascension is birthing, not dying. The withdrawal of the body of Jesus must be understood in terms of the Logos creating a space within himself, a womb, within which (*en Christoi*) the church will expand and creation be recreated ... The body of Jesus Christ, the body of God, is permeable, transcorporeal, transpositional. Within it, all other bodies are situated and given their significance. We are all permeable, transcorporeal, transpositional.[25]

Jesus' body, the Body of Christ and the church are, then, all about bodies, too. But not discrete, essentialized bodies with stable identities and rigid boundaries; instead, we find that bodies extend across time and space, that they are interchangeable and interpenetrable. This leads us back to the wedding and its sacramental character and, to return to Butler's terms, the role that the bodies of same-sex couples may play in exposing the way weddings always already normalize and naturalize heterosexual desire and the gender binary while also appropriating such norms in order to attempt to remake them.

Same-sex Weddings as Liberating Parodies?

For some branches of the church, the wedding is sacrament; for others, it is most decidedly not. The debates are important, if not necessarily as relevant today as in the sixteenth century. What is crucial here is whether, and how, the wedding may serve ritually as a means of grace, as an occasion in which God 'condescends ... to set before us in the flesh a mirror of spiritual blessings' – as Calvin puts it in his description of 'general sacraments'.[26] Again, the couple are, in fact, themselves the primary sacramental signs here – analogous to bread broken for eating, wine poured and water enlivened by Spirit. If the wedding is sacramental, it is because two people slightly inebriated on love stand before us and make outlandish promises – not unlike the promises God makes to us, except we trust that divine love is, in the end, less fickle and more enduring. This is why the members of the couple are considered the 'ministers' in the wedding; their bodies, voices, actions embody something of divine grace. So ... what happens when the sacramental signs themselves are queer bodies? Is a so-called 'same-sex wedding', again to return to Butler's language, 'an appropriation of dominant culture in [which one remains] subordinated by its terms' or 'an appropriation that seeks to make over the terms of domination'?[27] It turns out that this is not an easy question to answer. As noted above, it seems to me there are (at least) three types of same-sex weddings: the 'traditional', the 'inclusive' and the 'reinvented'. Let us look briefly at each in turn.

The 'Traditional' Wedding as Queer

By 'traditional' I mean a ceremony in which the couple uses (perhaps with slight adaptation) a long-standing and denominationally sanctioned service designed to join 'one man and one woman'. The couple inhabits the roles of bride and groom – one in a dress or other garment that evokes the feminine in some way, and one in a suit or something else that projects masculinity. They say the traditional words and make the traditional promises: 'forsaking all others' and 'as long as we both shall live'. They, likely, seek to live happily ever after as a self-sufficient dyad in the manner of their parents or some other 'successful' married couple of their imaginations. And yet, they do all this as Adam and Steve (or, Eve and Alice). Their bodies fit only obliquely, upsetting expectations.

The couple acts, we assume, in perfectly solemn sincerity. But their 'sameness' makes parody of the reproductive complementarity that a wedding assumes. And, I am thinking, the more 'realness' they perform, the higher (or, deeper?) the parody, which makes of this wedding an occasion of 'repetition with critical difference' that can remake the institution of marriage into something into which they can – and desire to – seek entry.[28] Butler continues to dog us here, however. She notes, rather bluntly: 'Parody by itself is not subversive.'[29] There can certainly be simple repetition and so reinscription, with no critical difference to be seen. To disrupt compulsory heterosexuality, the traditional same-sex wedding must exaggerate the norms, laugh at them – the subversive laughter of a jester, the 'read' of a drag queen. As Butler notes, drag separates 'three contingent dimensions of significant corporeality: anatomical sex, gender identity, and gender performance'. She continues:

> [P]art of the pleasure, the giddiness of [drag] performance is in the recognition of the radical contingency in the relation between sex and gender in the face of cultural configurations of causal unities that are

regularly assumed to be natural and necessary. In the place of the law of heterosexual coherence, we see sex and gender denaturalized by means of a performance which avows their distinctness and dramatizes the cultural mechanism of their fabricated unity.[30]

Whether some sort of disruption is desired – rather than, say, assimilative 'equality' – will, of course, depend on the couple. Whether our desire to do the wedding the same but differently makes it so, is also a real question. We will likely always both challenge and reinscribe the norms we seek to undo if we choose a traditional form.

The 'Inclusive' Wedding as Queer

In the second, an 'inclusive service' is used. The aim is for neutrality. The members of the couple dress similarly. The 'sameness' of the bodies, costume and roles is highlighted. The gendered paradigm of the wedding is minimized. Such services are now being written and are making their way into denominational service books.[31] They are also being used by different-sex couples as well as same-sex couples. Such services are shaped by prior ideological commitments to marriage equality – both theological and ethical. The 'critical difference' in both language and actions is explicit.

The 'Order for Marriage: an inclusive version' was promulgated by the progressive denomination, the United Church of Christ, in 2006. The General Synod had voted to affirm that same-sex couples should have access to marriage on an equal basis with different-sex couples on 4 July 2005 in UCC churches (subject to local congregational decision, of course). The service promises much: 'This order has been adapted from United Church of Christ Book of Worship Order for Marriage to provide language that may be used for any marriage, regardless of gender.'[32] Emphasis is placed on entering the covenant. All mention of 'bride' and 'groom' is removed; those being married are referred to by name or as 'the couple'. While two are to become one (or, united), there is no note of reproductive complementarity nor of being fruitful and multiplying. If there is fruitfulness here, it comes in the guise of images, such as 'share your joy with others' and 'may this couple bear witness to the reality of love'. The only mention of children is of those who may exist prior to the wedding; in the 'pledges of support' section, the children may be asked, 'Will you give this new family your trust, love, and affection?'[33] The suggested vows are identical, mutual … and rather bland – so, too, the giving and receiving of symbols, such as rings. In the vows, the word 'covenant' appears in both of the two sentences; the assumption is that the relationship is lifelong – however, no mention is made of sexual exclusivity. There are two forms for the pronouncement; both include more 'charge' than announcement. The first indicates that the couple has 'united themselves in the sacred covenant of marriage'; the second, 'you are married with the blessing of Christ's church' – followed (ironically?) by a prayer of blessing.[34]

There is much good here – and much to think further about. For our purposes, I wonder if the removal of gendered language gets us very far. Perhaps it allows for greater flexibility in how gender is thought by the couple, the presider and those assembled. However, I suspect it doesn't challenge any particular individual's notions of sex, gender and sexuality; instead, it just allows for a silent proliferation of understandings. Proliferation is a goal of Butler's, as we have seen, but here the standard binary remains the ground and there is little to make it quake. Butler is always suspicious of any claim that we can escape the dominant norms and the practices that constitute them – since we have been formed so deeply in and by them. Here, questions of heteronormativity are more sidestepped than confronted. The gesture of hospitality is surely welcome, but earnestness trumps subversive parody. Since the gender and sexuality norms of the wedding run so deep, there is little promise here. In fact, of course, such rites are intended to be assimilative – welcoming the same-sex couple into the heteronormative institution rather than deconstructing it and then building something new. Perhaps after a generation or two of practising the wedding according to these more 'neutral' models we may find we think (and 'act') differently about marriage, family and community, perhaps not. At this point, I believe we should be both grateful for the effort and sceptical about the ultimate effects.

The 'Reinvented' Wedding as Queer

In the third, the ceremony is rethought and reinvented. Here, the couple's queer-ness is the starting point and the rite is built anew with this always in view. Stripped to its essentials, in my view, the Christian wedding centres on five simple acts:

1 a declaration that one intends to enter this union with a free will, without any sort of coercion or impediment;
2 the vow-making before witnesses;
3 a pronouncement that a covenant has been sealed;
4 a blessing;
5 a kiss (or some other sign of bodily consummation of all these words).[35]

Throwing out everything else we know about weddings and starting here, perhaps we can build something new. Perhaps not. Can such a marriage service confront rather than reinscribe heteronormativity? Perhaps it will, inevitably and always, do both at the same time.

I wrote such a rite years ago, before equal access to marriage was the law of the land here in the United States.[36] Still, some description of it may serve to identify some possibilities of what this sort of reconstructed rite might look like. The consent is clear and simple. While the bringing together of the betrothal and the wedding promises following Jewish patterns in the early common era leaves us with vow-like consent formulas, the idea here is simply to disallow coercion of any kind. Each partner separately declares that they come freely on this day to be wed. The vows are identical rather than complementary to emphasize mutuality and the equality of the partners. The vows, too, eschew the presumption of sexual exclusivity and allow for all manner of polyamorous configurations, not just dyads. They are also realistic about a relationship's longevity rather than assuming a parting only at the death of one or both partners, certainly excluding any notion of an eternal coupling – following Jesus' own lead (Matt. 22.30). The pronouncement confirms the promises, marking the shift into the married state, but is also flexible to reflect the intentions of this couple as they emphasize the ecclesial context or the civil or both together. The kiss is a sign of consummation; this is a relationship of embodied love, of desire for intimate communion, of erotic power generated to fuel lives devoted to love and justice for all. The blessing prayer emphasizes divine passion, mercy, strength, courage and generosity both for those being married and, through them, for all creation. Now come the rings or other symbols. They are both given and received by each partner, again highlighting mutuality and equality of all parties. The ceremony ends with a charge and benediction to those being married and to the assembly as a whole. I also add, earlier on, an opportunity for both 'given' and 'chosen' family members who are present to pledge their support of this relationship. Finally, it should be remembered that same-sex union celebrations also tend to harbour grief – since there are so often important figures who cannot accept the relationship. Still, beyond the five central actions, all these are peripheral and optional. The fabulous party that now ensues is not, however.

I make no claim to crafting a rite that is liberated from, and so liberates participants from, the heterosexual matrix. I have tried to take seriously some of the distinctive experiences and values of the LGBTQIA community. The same scepticism mentioned about 'inclusive services' still applies, however. Changing practices will change our normative expectations. But still, when (most often) two persons stand before us and join an institution by making promises, do we not all think 'wedding' – with all the baggage that word entails? And so, if it looks like a wedding and weddings function to forge and honour exclusive units of economic and emotional support that contribute to the overall stability of the social order, do such tweaks as I have made (even the most controversial ones) really get us very far? Do queer bodies who live queerly and make here queer promises remake the world or simply fit in?

Concluding Reflections

At the end of this exploration, and given our initial challenge to define what happens when queer bodies inhabit a wedding, it seems to me, what we are really asking is:

- whether any of these models of a same-sex wedding will be effectively 'queer'?
- whether any of these can resist the force of 'marriage' as an institution that normalizes and assimilates human passion?, and,
- whether instead marriage – through the wedding – will in fact domesticate queer culture?

My response, at this point, is that these can only be answered over time – perhaps a generation from now. The wedding is saturated in assumptions of compulsory heterosexuality. New approaches – whether high parody, hospitable assimilation and/or reinvention – are both necessary and will probably not get us as far in reconceiving marriage and family, community and church as we might hope. Still, each small step towards the recognition and dignifying of the myriad ways to be a human being and the myriad models of relationship that help us each to thrive is nevertheless to be encouraged and celebrated.

Second, grateful for the dignity and protections of access to legal marriage, gay and lesbian couples will continue to ask to be married by both church and state. The circle has been widened. Yet many queer folk – whether because they do not want to be a part of this institution or because they still do not fit the norms that remain – deserve dignity and protections too. The marginalized are those the church is called to welcome, to serve and to incorporate. Ecclesiologically, the queer wedding emphasizes the couple's journey forward as baptismal vocation – a space for hospitality, justice and love – not just for themselves but in a missional sense, welcoming neighbour, stranger, even enemy.[37] Marriage in the church assumes (or, should assume) that, within the Body, a special relationship emerges. Discerning the fittingness of this related pair or group within the Body, promises are made and blessings are bestowed. There is consummation and the commencement of a risky journey forward together towards the promised hope – bodies embracing bodies, bodies embraced by the larger Body, bodies yearning, and perhaps finding, intimate union with the Source of Love itself.

In the end, we are talking about the difference that different bodies make – bodies out of place. Here is a male body where a female body should be. Here is a genderfluid body where a cisgender body should be. Here are 'non-productive' or 'unfruitful' bodies where childbearing bodies should be. While these bodies, like all bodies, are already immersed in (or, even, constituted by) heterocentric and hierarchical gender binaries, still, to see the 'wrong' bodies in this central display and performance of heterosexual gender complementarity and desire is (or, should be) astonishing. In just this way, there may be parody and 'de-naturalization' of these structures – whether by 'playing it straight', by 'going neutral' or by 'beginning again'. With Butler, we may conclude that no wedding that involves a couple or group that is other than 'one man and one woman' capitulates fully to traditional scripts – there is some difference embodied here. Nor, likely, is any such ceremony a full-scale revolt against those same norms. When such a wedding reaches for 'the painful pleasure of eroticizing and miming the norms', perhaps, it is most effective as subversive parody. And certainly, such a wedding would be a lot of fun!

Notes

1 In Cook County, Illinois, USA, where I happen to live, as an example: both persons must be at least 18, must have a valid ID that states proof of age, must be able to fill out the application and pay the fee, and must have proof of divorce or a death certificate if one has divorced or been widowed within the past six weeks. That's it.

2 See my 2007, 'A Queer Fidelity: Reinventing Christian Marriage', *Theology and Sexuality* 13, no. 2: 173–88.

3 See Kenneth W. Stevenson, 1987, *To Join Together: The Rite of Marriage*, New York: Pueblo/Liturgical Press, pp. 16–29.

4 Stevenson, *To Join Together*, p. 29; see also the *Catechism of the Catholic Church*, part 2, section 2, chapter 3, article 7, http://www.vatican.va/archive/ccc_css/archive/catechism/p2s2c3a7.htm [accessed 1 June 2018].

5 See John Witte, Jr, 2012, *From Sacrament to Contract: Marriage, Religion, and Law in the Western Tradition*, 2nd edn, Louisville, KY: Presbyterian Publishing Corporation.

6 See Stephanie Coontz, 2005, *Marriage, A History: How Love Conquered Marriage*, New York: Penguin Books.

7 See Nancy Cott, 2000, *Public Vows: A History of Marriage and the Nation*, rev. edn, Cambridge, MA: Harvard University Press; the case number is *Loving v. Virginia*, 388 U.S. 1, 12 (1967).

8 Access to the majority opinion by Justice Kennedy and the several dissenting opinions can be found as a downloadable pdf document at: https://www.supremecourt.gov/opinions/14pdf/14-556_3204.pdf [accessed 26 July 2018].

9 J. L. Austin, 1962, *Doing Things with Words: The William James Lectures, 1955*, London: Oxford University Press, e.g. p. 5. He emphasized the vow – and, pointedly, the man's vow at that – as a quintessential 'performative'. While I disagree with his choice within the wedding – to my mind, 'I now pronounce you ...'

are the efficacious words in the wedding – I am struck by his focus here, and its clear entanglement in gender dynamics.

10 With apologies for the bad pun, I do want to bring to mind how embedded in popular culture are various views about romance, wedding and marriage – here, the film *There's Something about Mary*, Twentieth Century Fox Film Corporation, 1998.

11 See Ron Grimes, 2002, *Deeply into the Bone: Re-inventing Rites of Passage*, Berkeley, CA: University of California Press, p. 154.

12 I have in mind persons such as Dr James Dobson, founding president of 'Focus on the Family', a major player in the promotion of the so-called traditional family and the discouragement of all other configurations of human intimacy in the current context of early twenty-first-century political debates in the United States. See his website: www.family.org [accessed 28 July 2018].

13 The term 'Butlerian' refers, of course, to the work of Judith Butler, a leading gender/queer theorist, on how gender works to shape our individual lives and the larger social order; see, among her many works, *Gender Trouble: Feminism and the Subversion of Identity*, New York: Routledge, 1990, 1999; and *Bodies that Matter: On the Discursive Limits of 'Sex'*, New York: Routledge, 1993. We turn to some of her specific arguments below.

14 See Ron Grimes, 1995, 'Liturgical Erectitude, Liturgical Supinity', in his *Reading, Writing and Ritualizing: Ritual in Fictive, Liturgical and Public Places*, Collegeville, MN: The Pastoral Press, pp. 39–58; and Ted Jennings, 1995, 'Ritual Knowledge' in Grimes (ed.), *Readings in Ritual Studies*, Upper Saddle River, NJ: Prentice Hall, pp. 324–34.

15 I borrow the phrase from the title of Kim Long's helpful book on marriage practices in contemporary communities of faith: Kimberly Bracken Long, 2016, *From This Day Forward: Rethinking the Christian Wedding*, Louisville, KY: Westminster John Knox Press.

16 The Douglas quotes can be found in Butler, *Gender Trouble*, p. 167.

17 Butler, *Gender Trouble*, p. 178.

18 Butler, *Gender Trouble*, p. 179.

19 Judith Butler, 1999, 'Gender Is Burning: Questions of Appropriation and Subversion', which appears as chapter 20 in S. Thornham (ed.), *Feminist Film Theory: A Reader*, Edinburgh: Edinburgh University Press, pp. 381–95, at pp. 392–3.

20 See Martin's 'Familiar Idolatry and the Christian Case against Marriage', pp. 17–40; Tolbert's 'Marriage and Friendship in the Christian New Testament: Ancient Resources for Contemporary Same-sex Unions', pp. 40–51; and Rogers' 'Trinity, Marriage, and Homosexuality', pp. 151–64; all in Mark D. Jordan (ed.) with Meghan T. Sweeney and David M. Mellot, 2006, *Authorizing Marriage? Canon, Tradition and Critique in the Blessing of Same-sex Unions*, Princeton, NJ/ Oxford: Princeton University Press.

21 Elizabeth Stuart, 1999, 'Sexuality: The View from the Font (the Body and the Ecclesial Self)', *Theology and Sexuality* 11: 9–20 at 14.

22 Stuart, 'Sexuality', 16–17.

23 Andy Buechel, 2015, *That We Might Become God: The Queerness of Creedal Christianity*, Eugene, OR: Cascade Books.

24 Graham Ward, 1999, 'Bodies: The Displaced Body of Jesus Christ', in John Milbank, Catherine Pickstock and Graham Ward (eds), *Radical Orthodoxy: A New Theology*, London/New York: Routledge, pp. 163–81.

25 Ward, 'Bodies', pp. 175–6.

26 John Calvin, 1960 (originally, 1559), *Institutes of the Christian Religion*, translated by Ford Lewis Battles, John T. McNeill (ed.), Philadelphia: Westminster Press, IV.xiv.3.

27 Butler, 'Gender Is Burning', p. 393.

28 'Realness' is a category of judgement in the world of drag. One seeks to replicate the role perfectly so the artifice of performance is undetectable – and the one who succeeds best … wins. But, of course, one can only succeed when the norms of femaleness or maleness or celebrity or 'thug' or high society are known. So, as Butler points out, 'realness' both approximates and exposes the realness norm – which she also calls a symbolic norm. She writes: 'In the drag ball productions of realness, we witness and produce the phantasmatic constitution of a subject, a subject who repeats and mimes the legitimating norms by which itself has been degraded, a subject founded in the project of mastery that compels and disrupts its own repetitions. This is not a subject that stands back from its identifications and decides instrumentally how or whether to work each of them today; on the contrary the subject is the incoherent and mobilized imbrication of identifications; it is constituted in and through the iterability of its performance, a repetition that works at once to legitimate and delegitimate the realness norms by which it is produced' (Butler, 'Gender Is Burning', p. 388). As noted above, 'repetition with critical difference' is from the work of Elizabeth Stuart and serves as her translation of Butler's 'reinscription with slippage' via Linda Hutcheon; see Stuart, 'Sexuality', p. 17.

29 Butler, *Gender Trouble*, p. 175.

30 Butler, *Gender Trouble*, p. 175.

31 As one example, see Kimberly Long and David Maxwell (eds), 2015, *Inclusive Marriage Services: A Wedding Sourcebook*, Louisville, KY: Westminster John Knox Press.

32 See http://uccfiles.com/pdf/in-support-of-equal-marriage-rights-for-all-with-background.pdf for the text of the 'Equal Marriage Rites for All' resolution and http://d3n8a8pro7vhmx.cloudfront.net/unitedchurchofchrist/legacy_url/3578/323_346i_order-for-marriage-inclusive.pdf?1418427387 for the rite itself, known as the UCC Order of Marriage, an inclusive version [accessed 16 June 2018].

33 I must admit to being rather shocked to find such a question in such a rite. Children should never be asked to make a pledge in such a situation as this new relationship is not of their choosing. They cannot give free consent. They may never develop love, trust or affection for their new parent; how can they be asked to pledge such things publicly? If a new parent wants to pledge love, trust and affection to the children that is a different matter.

34 I want to express appreciation to Bryan Cones, one of the editors of this volume. He provides both a method for and a model of reading a wedding rite in the way I have begun here in his essay, '"With all due respect, I ain't his husband": Gender, Sexuality, and Theology in The Episcopal Church's Rites of Partnership' (unpublished).

35 This is echoed in the preface to the UCC Order for Marriage, an inclusive version, even as that document sets out a detailed rite. It directs that the couple be counselled prior to the service about 'the Christian understanding of the marriage relationship', which is, then, summarized as: 'The essence of marriage is a covenanted commitment that has its foundation in the faithfulness of God's love. The marriage ceremony is the glad occasion on which two people unite in the mutual exchange of covenant promises. The one presiding acts as an official representative of the church and gives the marriage the church's blessing. The congregation joins in affirming the

marriage and in offering support and thanksgiving for the new family.' See *Book of Worship*, 2012, "Order for Marriage," Cleveland, OH: United Church of Christ, pp. 323–46, at p. 323.

36 My 'same-sex union' ceremony was created during the denomination-wide liturgical project, Worshipping into God's Future, but did not make the final cut for publication and remained unpublished. It appears below as Appendix 1.

37 For a more traditional path to some of these same conclusions, see Long, *From This Day Forward*.

6

I Had to Do It for My Son:
The Story of a Same-Sex Wedding

FRANK C. SENN

On 6 October 2016, in New York City, I officiated at the same-sex wedding of my son Nicholas and his partner Benjamin. Even as I was officiating, I couldn't believe that I was doing this. Nor could friends and colleagues believe that I did this. Some were thrilled; others were confused; a few were angry. This essay is about putting together a liturgy that was performed in a secular site to solemnize a same-sex covenant relationship for which few models exist. It was the first time I officiated at a same-sex wedding and probably also the last since I am a retired pastor. But I felt I had to do this wedding for my son.

Like all marriage liturgies, this one was tailored to the couple involved and their families. It was a liturgy at the margins of church and society, and that's why it is described in this book. But the story of how I came to be the officiant is as important as describing the order of service and the homily for the occasion because clergy who officiate at same-sex weddings may still be putting themselves out on a limb with their ecclesiastical supervisors and colleagues. So this essay will be to a great extent autobiographical.

I will not get into general issues of homosexuality or gay identity; space precludes that. I will just say that I have two gay sons. I don't know why they are gay, and I cannot solve the controversy over whether homosexuality is inborn or learned. I can only accept their self-identity. I know it wasn't easy for either of them to 'come out' to their parents, especially since I was known to be a pretty orthodox Lutheran pastor. My wife and I tried to be supportive of our sons even while I continued to teach, as I was obliged to do by my ordination vows, the traditional Christian understanding of marriage from the pulpit and in the confirmation classes that they both attended.

I will get into some exegetical and theological issues, although not deeply given the limitations of space. My purpose in raising these issues is only to lay the groundwork for explaining how I came to the point – as a pastor, theologian and father – at which I was willing to offer my services to officiate at a same-sex wedding.

Again because of limitations of space, I will simply presume the whole cultural backdrop of the gay liberation movement. It has been a backdrop throughout my entire ministry. I was ordained to the Holy Ministry of the Word and the Sacraments on 29 June 1969, the feast day of Saints Peter and Paul, one day after the police raid on the Stonewall Inn, a gay club located in New York City's Greenwich Village. This raid was part of a systematic harassment of homosexuals by the police in New York City, and this time a riot broke out that lasted six days. In these riots, it is claimed, the gay liberation movement was born.

However, it is important to note that the gay liberation movement included Christians who pressed to gain acceptance of gays and lesbians within their churches. At first, they simply wanted an explicit welcome in congregations. Increasingly, they focused on the ordination of practising gays and lesbians because if homosexual ministers could be accepted, so could homosexual members. Mainline churches did not preclude the ordination of homosexuals as long as they were celibate. But standards of expectations precluded clergy living in a sexual relationship outside of marriage. That would include gay and lesbian clergy. In instances where clergy did live in a relationship outside of marriage, including gay and lesbian clergy, they were removed from the ministry, including in my 'liberal' Evangelical Lutheran Church in America (ELCA).

Since churches did not approve of sexual partnerships outside of marriage, especially for the clergy, this inevitably raised the issue of same-sex marriage. Marriage laws in the United States come under the 50 states; churches and other religious groups cannot just marry people. Marriages without a state licence would have no legal standing. This required lobbying to get state legislatures to approve of same-sex unions or marriages.

The idea of same-sex marriage was 'out there' already by the 1970s because the Universal Fellowship of Metropolitan Community Churches, a conservative Pentecostal fellowship founded by Troy Perry in 1968 that ministered to gays and lesbians, promoted it. Perry also taught that homosexuals are what they are because that's how God made them (the essentialist view). He enlisted authorities more scholarly than himself to reconcile these views with the traditional biblical texts that many believe taught God's condemnation of homosexuality.[1] Perry's teaching was picked up by gay and lesbian Christians in other churches. Thus, a theological debate over homosexuality entered the churches' assemblies and conventions. Homosexuals claimed that they should be accepted because this is how God made them.

Furthermore, as the idea of gay marriage picked up steam in the 1980s and 1990s, it was promoted by conservative gays such as Andrew

Sullivan, Jonathan Rauch and Bruce Bawer. The goal of getting gay men in particular to settle down and take care of each other was really a conservative goal of containing unbridled sexual freedom, which they argued had led to the AIDS epidemic. Also, integrating gays into general society by marriage would be good for everyone. Of course, not everyone was convinced, including many gays who saw marriage as a bourgeois institution. Andrew Sullivan edited a very comprehensive anthology of writings on *Same-Sex Marriage Pro and Con* that defined the state of the issues up to 2004.[2]

My Exposure to Gay Life and Love

I had little awareness of homosexuality until I was in college. Hartwick was a small private liberal arts college in upstate New York somewhat immune from the social-cultural caldron of New York City. I knew only one gay person – a fraternity brother who 'came out' during my senior year.

My own first awareness of the gay culture came from reading John Rechy's *City of Night*[3] in the summer of 1966. Quite frankly, it was a real eye-opener. The book had been a *New York Times* bestseller when it was published in 1963. I re-read it after its fiftieth anniversary of publication and was impressed anew by the sheer force of the narratives. My original impression of the 'youngman's' narrative was reinforced. In addition to the seaminess of the scenes Rechy described, I thought the novel conveyed a sense of alienation and loneliness among the denizens of the urban nights who furtively sought 'scores' and tried to avoid the police.

The summer I read *City of Night* I was working on the student work crew of the Lutheran School of Theology at Chicago as we cleaned up and painted apartments in Chicago's Hyde Park community that had been bought by the seminary in preparation for students to move in when this academic institution, a merger of several Midwestern Lutheran seminaries, relocated across 55th Street from the University of Chicago. My first and only gay encounter occurred when a fellow seminarian came on to me that summer after a night of eating pub food and drinking beer at the end of a workweek. I was tired and ready to leave that scene and go back to my apartment in one of the seminary-owned buildings.

One of my fellow seminarian friends on the work crew, who stayed in his parents' home in the suburbs during the summer, came back with me to use the toilet before driving back to the suburbs. I changed out of the clothes I had been painting in all day and put on a pair of shorts and sat on the bed. (The apartment was sparsely furnished.) He sat down next me and we began a conversation when suddenly he rolled over on top of me, kissing me on the lips and chest, his hands roving all over my body, telling me over and over: 'don't be afraid, I love you'. Fortunately, this awkward situation quickly came to an end when the doorbell rang and the others arrived from the pub. My friend darted into the bathroom to freshen up and then excused himself and left.

The next day he sought me out to discuss what had happened the night before, insisting that he really loved me. I tried to smooth over the situation by telling him that we had both been drinking, and I apologized if I had done anything to encourage his assault on my body. But I emphasized that I couldn't reciprocate his love the way he wanted me to. I told him I wasn't angry (although I had been freaked out) and affirmed that we should still be friends. So we were for the rest of the summer. But his desire for my love made me realize that gay men have the same romantic feelings as heterosexual men. This was a different kind of situation than the scenes of hustlers looking for scores as described in *City of Night*. I held on to these two ideas: that homosexuals may be lonely people and that they have a human need to connect with someone in a genuinely romantic and loving way just as heterosexual people do.

'Reconciled in Christ' at Christ the Mediator

In the years that followed, I was aware of a gay presence in some of the places in which I lived as well as the gay activism in society and increasingly in church assemblies. But I did not have to deal with these issues directly until I became pastor of Christ the Mediator Lutheran Church on the near south side of Chicago in 1981. Christ the Mediator was a mostly African American congregation, but there were also white persons, bi-racial couples, and gays and lesbians in the congregation. This was the height of the AIDS epidemic, and I conducted the funerals of two gay African American brothers who died of AIDS. One funeral occurred on a Saturday when a blood drive was being held in the church's fellowship hall. Some members expressed concerns about the use of the chalice in Holy Communion in this very liturgical parish. I did my own research to write an article for the worship office of the Lutheran Church in America about AIDS and the common communion cup as well as to assuage the fears in the congregation of contracting the AIDS virus from drinking out of the common cup. I did research in the library of the nearby Michael Reese Hospital (no longer in existence) and the Howard Brown Clinic, which served gay men, many of whom had contracted the AIDS virus.[4]

Our church building was sometimes a meeting site for Lutherans Concerned, a gay and lesbian organization devoted to getting more congregations to intentionally welcome gays and lesbians. Bill, one of the members of Christ the Mediator who was active in Lutherans Concerned, asked if the congregation could vote on becoming a 'Reconciled in Christ' congregation. He felt that we could set an example for other congregations in Chicago and Illinois. He also felt that the church needed to be a place where gays and lesbians felt both affirmed and safe. One night he took me and a church council member on a tour of gay bars and clubs in Chicago to make the point that gays felt more welcome in this kind of place than in many churches.

The proposal did not go through without resistance from some members on biblical grounds. I also needed to do my own exegetical study. I focused primarily on biblical passages that were used to say that homosexuals would go to hell unless they abstained from homosexual practices. A recently published book offering a theological approach to sexuality provided some hermeneutics for approaching these biblical texts.[5] The Pauline texts (Rom. 1.18–32 as well as 1 Cor. 6.9) were seen primarily in the context of idolatry in civil society generally (Romans) and perhaps cult prostitution (in 1 Corinthians). Cult prostitution would square with the condemnation of same-sex acts in Leviticus 18.22 and 20.13 as 'abominations', the term usually reserved for Canaanite fertility cults (which often led to sexual orgies). I reported these interpretations in the discussions.

I also pointed out that the terms 'homosexuality/heterosexuality' came out of the social sciences and could not be used to translate any biblical words, especially in 1 Corinthians 6.9. To do so would be an anachronism and possibly not an accurate description in terms of homosexuality as we use that term today to describe a same-sex attraction. St Paul uses the specific words *malakoi*, which suggests someone taking the submissive role in sex (perhaps a male prostitute), and *arsenokoitai*, which suggests someone taking the dominant role (usually referred to as a 'sodomite'). *Arsenokoitai* is a neologism, which means it is a unique word. By it, Paul could have been referring back to Leviticus 18.22 and to behaviour – lying with a male as with a woman – which is called an abomination. 'Abomination' usually refers to the activities of pagan cults in the Old Testament. The whole rubric over Leviticus 18 is 'You shall not do as they do in the land of Egypt, where you lived, or as they do in the land of Canaan, to which I am bringing you' (18.3, NRSV). I didn't know whether in 1 Corinthians 6.9 Paul was referring to cult prostitution. But pederasty would cover both terms (both submissive and aggressive roles). It had been a cultural practice for centuries in ancient Greece for men to become mentors to boys and initiate the boy into sexuality. There are explicit drawings of pederastic relationships on ancient Greek urns. I didn't show the pictures to members of the congregation. But I agreed that those who did such things would not inherit the kingdom of God.

St Paul's discussion of sexual aberrations in Romans 1 is also set in the context of a discussion of idolatry. The sexual practices Paul describes are a result of worshipping the creature rather than the Creator. The sexual aberrations described by Paul illustrate the disorder that results. But it is important to understand that the term 'nature' in Romans 1 (*physis*) is not used in a biological sense but in a cultural sense. When Paul used the same term 'nature' in 1 Corinthians 11.14 to suggest that it is degrading for men to wear long hair, this is not some timeless truth based on biology, especially since biologically our hair would continue to grow unless we cut it. So in Romans 1.26–27, when Paul speaks about men and women exchanging natural sexual intercourse for unnatural, he is referring to cultural mores. It might mean, for example, that when women give up natural intercourse for unnatural they are being sexually aggressive rather than submissive; and when men commit 'shameless acts with men' someone has to take the submissive or female role. Both of these role reversals would be repugnant to traditional Roman mores. By speaking of 'exchanging' sexual practices, Paul would be implying that those whom we today would call heterosexual were adopting what we would call 'homosexual' practices.[6] Paul's readers could also well imagine the 'degrading passions' that were caught up in the well-known sexual debaucheries of the imperial courts of Caligula and Nero. So the fact that Paul refers to male-on-male sex does not mean that he is discussing homosexuality as it is understood today as a same-sex attraction. It is an expression of lust, not of self-giving love. I suggested that it would be difficult to say that this passage categorically condemns all male-on-male sex unless one was also willing to say that it categorically condemns an aggressive female role in sexual intercourse. Moreover, after a long list of 'every kind of wickedness' in Romans 1.29–30, in addition to the sexual aberrations mentioned in 1.26–27, St Paul goes on to say in 2.1, 'you have no excuse, whoever you are, when you judge others; for in passing judgment on another you condemn yourself, because you, the judge, are doing the very same things'. The point the apostle is leading up to in 3.23 is that 'all have sinned and fall short of the glory of God; they are now justified by his grace as a gift, through the redemption that is in Christ Jesus' (NRSV). Homosexuals are sinners like everyone else, but not because they are homosexuals.

I also pointed out that the major Protestant theologian Karl Barth regarded homosexuality as 'a phenomenon of perversion, decadence and decay'.[7] He held to the biblical interpretation of homosexual acts as idolatrous because the homosexual person is seeking a reflection of himself or herself in same-sex attraction. Nevertheless, he came to the conclusion that while homosexual *acts* must be condemned as contrary to the divine purpose of human sexuality, homosexual *persons* must not be condemned because no one is beyond the scope of God's grace. This is the theological basis of the motto 'hate the sin, but love the sinner'. Lutherans are people who err on the side of grace rather than the side of the law. So this argument may in itself have been enough for the congregation to vote overwhelmingly to become a 'Reconciled in Christ' congregation.

But I also read Helmut Thielicke's *The Ethics of Sex*. This German Lutheran theologian who was rector of the University of Hamburg and preacher at St Michael's Church in Hamburg had criticized Barth for his exclusion of natural anthropology in his ethics. In *The Ethics of Sex*, Thielicke agreed with Barth's position that homosexuality is a 'perversion … [which] is in every case *not* in accord with the order of creation'.[8] But he went beyond Barth in recognizing that homosexuality is not a condition that is easily changed. Furthermore, it is a predisposition that should not be depreciated any more than any other dispositions that afflict fallen humanity. If the predisposition cannot be changed, then homosexuals should structure their sexual relations 'in an ethically responsible way'.[9] By implication, Thielicke's recommendation implies an adult, fully committed relationship.

One of the events that took place after the vote was a house blessing when Bill and his partner Dennis together moved into a new apartment. I joked with Bill that I couldn't legally marry him and Dennis (same-sex marriage was not legal in 1985), but blessing their home certainly implied a blessing of their domestic relationship.

My Resistance to Same-Sex Marriage

Nevertheless, while I saw the biblical passages as less categorically condemnatory of homosexuality than was assumed by many, I didn't see same-sex marriage as a possibility in our society or as a practice that should be endorsed by the church. The biblical teaching on marriage as a union of man and woman with the blessing of offspring (God willing) is well established in the church's teaching and practice. I would say further that humankind created male and female in the image of God with the possibility of a third (and more) implies that what Pope John Paul II would call 'the spousal meaning of the Body' is a reflection of God the Holy Trinity.[10] The whole point of the pope's catecheses was to shore up the doctrine of marriage, which was seen in a state of crisis in the Western world as a result of the sexual revolution beginning in the 1960s.

In the mid 1990s I was involved in founding an inter-Lutheran pastoral society and ministerium, the Society of the Holy Trinity (founded 1997). The purpose of the Society was to inculcate through its Rule a confessional Lutheran understanding and practice of ministry and support pastors in living out their ordination vows. The Society was one response to the crisis of faith in North American Lutheran churches, and it can be located among several confessional movements that emerged in mainline Protestant churches in the United States and Canada at that time. While a number of critical issues of faith were identified in the Founding Statement, the movement towards blessing same-sex unions in some of the churches was not one of them. The sexuality issue affecting many Protestant clergy at the time was marital infidelity and divorce. Hence, Chapter II of the Rule, 'A Life of Obedience to Jesus', included: 'Be chaste and pure, faithful in marriage and celibate in singleness, according to the norm of Scripture and the tradition of the Church.'

In my own personal timeline my oldest son, Andrew, had 'come out' as gay just a few years before the founding of the Society and my second son, Nicholas, also 'came out' at this time. There was nothing in the Rule that was opposed to homosexuality, and we actually had a few gay members. Thus, there was no reason to subscribe to the Rule of the Society just because one was opposed to the 'gay agenda'. But since the members tended to be theologically orthodox and many of them conservative on social issues, practices like same-sex unions came up in informal discussions during retreats. The leadership of the Society has consistently discouraged discussion of ecclesiastical controversies in retreats; it is not edifying. The Society was not founded to 'take back' the Lutheran churches but to renew the Lutheran ordained ministry.

As Senior of the Society I had to lead the Leadership Council in drafting 'A Pastoral Statement on Blessing Same-Sex Unions' in response to a request for teaching on the subject from our Canadian members when Canada's high court made same-sex marriage legal. I agreed with the pastoral statement we produced that the Holy Spirit was not teaching anything new in the churches; that the biblical teaching on marriage needed to be upheld; that God's blessing cannot be given in situations in which there is no clear command and promise of God; and that churches and pastors could in conscience resist any pressure by the state to perform same-sex unions on the basis of obeying God rather than human authority (Acts 5.29). Pastoral statements in the Society are developed as guidance to members; they are not adopted by the Society as official positions.

In 2009, ELCA adopted 'A Social Statement on Human Sexuality, Gift and Trust'. Social statements must be adopted by two-thirds vote of the Churchwide Assembly and they represent the most authoritative teachings of this church. On the contentious issue of homosexuality, the statement recognized that there are several different approaches to ministering to homosexuality that are conscientiously held in 'this church' and that no common agreement could be found. Instead the statement identified four positions held by members 'on the basis of conscience-bound belief' and out of concern for the neighbour and the community. The first position holds that 'same-gender sexual behavior is sinful, contrary to biblical teaching and their understanding of natural law'. Persons in same-gender relationships should be called to repentance and encouraged to live a celibate lifestyle. The second position holds that while even lifelong, monogamous homosexual relationships 'may be lived out with mutuality and care, they do not believe that the neighbor or community are best served by publicly recognizing such relationships as traditional marriage'. The third and fourth positions are prefaced by the statement: 'On the basis of conscience-bound belief, some are convinced that the scriptural witness does not address the context of sexual orientation and lifelong loving and committed relationships that we experience today.' The third position does not equate same-gender relationships with marriage but suggests that such lifelong, monogamous relationships or covenant unions may be supported by the community and surrounded with prayer. The fourth position holds 'that the neighbor and community are best served when same-gender relationships are lived out with lifelong and monogamous commitments that are held to the same rigorous standards, sexual ethics, and status as heterosexual marriage. They surround such couples and their lifelong commitments with prayer to live in ways that glorify God.'[11]

The ELCA statement did not outrightly endorse same-sex marriage; in fact, by the end of 2009 only seven states had authorized same-sex marriage either by court decision or legislative action. It should also be noted that this Churchwide Assembly also amended the standards of ministry by simple majority vote to allow the ordination of persons living in 'publicly accountable, lifelong, monogamous, same-gender relationships'.[12] Congregations were under no obligation to call pastors living in same-gender relationships. And the 'bound conscience' was supposed to be honoured and respected by all. But many conservative pastors felt that their conscience was not respected. Claiming that this was the last straw in a church that did not take the authority of the Bible seriously, several hundred pastors and congregations withdrew from the ELCA over the next year, most to form the new North American Lutheran Church, others to associate with Lutheran Congregations in Mission for Christ, and a few to join the Lutheran Church–Missouri Synod.

Why I Decided to Officiate at Nick's and Ben's Wedding

During my tenure as Senior of the Society of the Holy Trinity our second son, Nicholas, and then our oldest son, Andrew, married their male partners. My wife, Mary, and I did not attend either wedding, although we later helped to host receptions for them. We both felt bad about not being able to provide parental support at their weddings. Nick married

Kenny from California just after the State of California allowed same-sex marriage (and they wanted to get married before same-sex marriage could be rescinded by a ballot proposition). It was a quick decision, and my wife and I were not able to attend at short notice. Andrew married his partner Edward just after the Commonwealth of Pennsylvania legalized same-sex marriage. Theirs was a private service in First Presbyterian Church, where Andrew serves as organist and choir director. In the meantime, Nick and Kenny divorced. Nick later found a loving relationship in another partner, Ben, and they determined to be married. In talking with my son about their wedding plans, I offered to officiate if they were not able to find someone since he had no idea who could officiate. Even my wife, Mary, was surprised at the precipitousness of my offer. Naturally, Nick and Ben were willing to accept my services.

It wasn't a totally impromptu offer because Nick and Ben had been talking about their plans for some time before the event was formally announced, and I had had time to think about it. First of all, by virtue of the US Supreme Court's decision in *Obergefell v. Hodges* on 26 June 2015, same-sex marriage became the law of the land. Second, I thought Nick needed my support. He needed my affirmation of what he was doing in his relationship with Ben after sitting through sermons in which I was critical of the gay agenda. I thought it would also be reaffirming for Andrew and Edward to see me officiate since I hadn't been present at their wedding. I could have asked the ELCA bishop of Metropolitan New York to find a pastor to officiate, but that pastor would have no relationship with Nick and Ben. Moreover, if it was thought wrong to officiate at a same-sex wedding, why would I ask another pastor to do it? Third, the families of both Nick and Ben are church people (Ben's father is a Catholic deacon), but Ben and Nick are unchurched. I thought their families also needed some pastoral support on this occasion. I felt that I could pull together some thoughts in a homily that would be helpful to everyone concerned, including this father of one of the grooms.

I had my own kind of 'coming out' experience before the wedding. I read the book by Mark Achtemeier, which had just come out in a second edition in 2014, and found myself agreeing with the same 'change of heart'[13] described by the author. Achtemeier is a Presbyterian theologian who had led the fight in the Presbyterian Church (USA) to uphold the 'traditional' teaching of marriage and oppose homosexual practice. But he became acquainted with several same-sex couples who were living in marriages that were just as loving as straight couples he knew. I had the same experience, except that one of the loving same-sex couples I knew was my oldest son, Andrew, and his husband, Edward. With Achtemeier as a guide, I once again went through all the Scripture texts that had been used against same-sex marriage and concluded that they deal with specific sexual activities that can't be used to condemn the kind of same-sex marital relationships we are experiencing today. Attempted gang rape in Sodom, pederasty in ancient Greece, debauchery in the Roman imperial court, male cult prostitution might have all involved male-to-male sex, but not necessarily same-sex orientation much less same-sex relationships based on mutual love. Achtemeier went even further than I am prepared to go. In an act of constructive theology, he proposed on the basis of God's covenant relationship with his people and the gospel message of Jesus Christ that the Bible could be used to actually support same-sex marriage as a loving, committed, lifelong monogamous relationship. For me, I wouldn't go that far because I don't think the Bible addresses the situation of loving, lifelong committed same-sex relationships. On this, as on some other issues facing the modern church, such as the ordination of women, the Bible is silent. Appealing to an old Lutheran principle, I concluded that what is neither commanded nor forbidden by a clear word of Scripture must be left free to the church's pastoral discretion. Realizing that this is what I really believe in my heart was my own 'coming out' experience.

Putting Together a Suitable Liturgy

Once I decided I would officiate at my son's wedding, I had to become a marriage officiant licensed by the City of New York. This was accomplished by sending to the City Clerk of the City of New York a copy of the page in the ELCA Yearbook showing that I was listed in the roster of ordained ministers and paying $15.00. I received a Certificate of Marriage Officiant Registration and a sheet detailing my officiant responsibilities.

The wedding would be on a Thursday night because the venue, a restaurant in Brooklyn, would be available (and cheaper). The venue for the liturgy would be the outside courtyard. Adjacent buildings and a brick wall on the street side provided privacy. The gathering and liturgy would be in the courtyard. Then the guests would move inside the restaurant for drinks and refreshments and the wedding dinner. Formal photos would all be taken before the liturgy so as not to hold up the dinner service.

Ben especially didn't want a liturgy that was too 'churchy'. On the other hand, the families of Nick and Ben were church people (Lutheran and Roman Catholic) and they wanted something that seemed like a real wedding liturgy. There weren't many models of a same-sex marriage service. The only one I knew had been prepared by The Episcopal Church under the title, 'The Witnessing and Blessing of a Lifelong Covenant'.[14] I used this liturgy as a template, removing words that presumed a church context but borrowing words that seemed appropriate. There would not be a nuptial blessing since a Lutheran pastor cannot pronounce God's blessing when Scripture provides none. But we would pray for God's grace in the lives of Ben and Nick.

Nick's organist brother Andrew would provide music on a large keyboard. Nick's sister, Emily (a singer), would sing a song. Ben's sister would read the lesson. The boys settled on one reading from 1 Corinthians 13. I would have been happy to involve Ben's father, a Catholic deacon, but we didn't want to compromise his situation. I decided not to wear any vestments since this liturgy was not a service of the church. It was under no sponsorship by any church. It was a civil ceremony in which we included Christian prayer and a Bible reading. But I put on a black clergy shirt and collar for the liturgy and changed to a white shirt and tie for the dinner to indicate changing my role from officiant to father. (See Appendix 2 for the Order of Service.)

The Homily

I also had to figure out what to say to Nick and Ben and their families – and to myself – in the homily. I decided to appeal to Martin Luther's doctrine of the orders of creation as a theological basis for this marriage under the category of 'household' (the economic order).[15] I felt that all people need to be loved by another (going back to the insight of my early gay encounter). My parental concern (and the concern of all the parents) was that Nick and Ben should each have someone in their life to whom they are committed and who would be committed to them.

Texts: Genesis 2.18; 1 Corinthians 13
I always said I wouldn't be the family chaplain for weddings; I'm the father. But today there was no bride to walk down the aisle, so I was available. And I'm happy about that, because there are some things I'd like to share with you. But preparing for this wedding also gave me an opportunity to work through some thoughts in my own mind since yours is not marriage in the biblical sense of a man and a woman becoming one flesh and by God's will producing a third – the kind of weddings I've been used to officiating during my pastoral career.

Let me start back in the time of beginnings. The Lord God decided that it wasn't good for Adam to be alone. So he created Eve. And together they procreated more Adams and Eves – and Abels and Cains. It wasn't all good in that first family. But the important thing I want to bring out from that story is that we humans aren't meant to be alone. We are meant to find fulfilment in another.

That's the text I kept thinking about as I prepared for this wedding.

The Lord God didn't think it was good for Adam to be alone. Most humans will find fulfilment in and wed someone of the opposite sex. Some will live in singleness but find fulfilment in family, friends or even a religious community of celibates. But celibacy isn't for everyone. Some are attracted to persons of the same sex, for reasons that remain a mystery. And parents, who desire their children to find someone to love and care for them, have been especially concerned about who their gay children will find to love and care for them after we can no longer do so.

Tami and Bob [Ben's parents], and Mary and I have 'accompanied' you, Ben and Nick, all through your lives. We brought you into the world and kept you safe in childhood and navigated with you the landmines of adolescence and saw you transition into capable and productive adults. We are happy that you have found and were attracted to each other and now intend to wed each other. The laws of our nation now provide for that possibility. It's your civil right. A recognizable place has been made for you in society.

Martin Luther spoke of the orders of creation: the church, or spiritual institution; the household, or economic institution; and the state, or institution of government. Sometimes he spoke of that second institution as the estate of marriage. But he clearly meant the household, and we understand marriage to be establishing a new household. That's why so many wedding gifts are household items. Religion has invoked God's blessing on the household and government has a responsibility to protect households.

You guys are establishing a household. It is a recognized institution in our society. But that doesn't mean that everyone is in agreement with the law or comfortable with your status as husband and husband. You don't change hearts or minds by changing the law. So on top of all the other issues of married life, you may have to deal with this one at some time and place.

You are not lacking support. Those of us who are here today intend by our presence to support you in this step you are taking. For some of us, this is our first experience of a same-sex wedding. It's my first experience of one. We've had a same-sex couple in our family in Andrew and Edward, but your mother and I weren't at their wedding. I can tell the Bauer family that there may be some awkwardness as you get used to the fact that Ben and Nick are not just boyfriends but husband and husband. But, then, it's not easy to accept any son- and daughter-in-law, is it? Family dynamics are family dynamics, whether same-sex or opposite-sex.

But Ben and Nick, since you intend to get married, what I would say to any couple applies to you. You're making a commitment to be exclusive to each other – to forsake all other entangling relationships and be faithful to your spouse. Monogamy seems to be the end result of human sexual evolution. Even the Bible arrived at this conclusion only over a long period of time. Some patriarchs and kings had multiple wives. Monogamy is asking a lot, as indicated by the rate of marital breakups in our society. And it will work only if your relationship is bonded in love.

What do we mean when we say that we love someone? Greek gives us three words for our one English word 'love'. There's *philia*, or brotherly love or friendship. There's *eros*, or erotic love or passion. But then there's the love St Paul talked about in our reading: *agape*, or self-giving love. It's the kind of love marriage requires to make it work.

Your first step toward this day was becoming friends. The kind of sharing of interests and experiences that friends enjoy will continue in marriage. But marriage is more than friendship. You have found passion as you have grown in your relationship, and that will continue. But marriage is more than passion. Marriage is about caring for someone else through the best of times and the worst of times. The traditional marriage vows speak of 'for richer or poorer, in sickness and in health'. In the marriage relationship we have to 'bear all things, believe all things, hope all things, endure all things', as we heard in the reading from 1 Corinthians 13.

That's not easy for us, because our human tendency (a condition of our fall, if I may say so) is to be turned in on ourselves, to be focused on our own needs, our own hopes, our own desires. *Agape* love requires that we get over ourselves and live for the other. The reality is that we need help to do that.

That's where grace comes in. It's the help God gives to make our relationships work – whether we ask for it or not. Grace is the sheer givenness of providence by which the world and the orders of creation are preserved.

God gives grace because he does not think it's good for the man to be alone. We need someone who will be there for us. God is also there for you, Nick and Ben. He has given you each other. We pray that you will be enfolded in God's grace – his unearned loving-kindness – all the days of your lives. And we hope they will be many. Amen.

The Consequences of My Actions

This was only one wedding out of hundreds I've performed over 45 years of pastoral ministry, but it was the only one with consequences for the officiant thanks to Facebook. Photos of the wedding were posted as they were being taken, and many of my friends and colleagues saw my involvement in the wedding. When I returned home, I received a phone call asking me to withdraw from giving an address at a theological conference to which I had been invited because participants would hear about my involvement in a same-sex wedding and that might deflect the purpose of the conference. I was no longer the senior of my pastoral society, but it was reported to me that many members of the Society were confused and some even angered by my action. How could I do what our pastoral statement counselled not to do? It didn't carry any weight that it was a civil ceremony not sponsored by a congregation.

The Leadership Council of the Society has since revised the Statement on Blessing Same-Sex Unions to eliminate the 'loophole' that seemingly allowed me to claim that I was not in disagreement with the Statement by stating that pastors don't cease being pastors when they officiate at a wedding outside of the church building. I agree with this. Even in retirement and not engaged in active pastoral ministry, I am still an ordained minister who could be called upon for service as long as I am able. But I disagree that I was acting contrary to the word of God when the word of God does not clearly address this situation.[16]

On the other hand, many other colleagues and lay people were pleasantly surprised by what I did and have been very supportive. Some members of the Society told me personally that while they wouldn't have done this, they understood the needs of my family situation. A few gave me credit for acting pastorally in that situation. One wrote to me and thanked me for the homily (which I posted on my blog) as a model for what to say in such a situation.

I cannot say that what I did was absolutely right. But it's what I had to do for my son. If I sinned, I 'sinned boldly' (as Luther said). And I don't regret it.

Reflections on the Church's Ministry to Same-Sex Couples

What should the churches do now that the laws of the state allow legal recognition of same-sex couples? Some churches have clearly defined positions that marriage is only between a man and a woman, and they will expect their ordained ministers to uphold their teachings from the pulpit and in pastoral practice. I believe that churches need to continue teaching the biblical understanding of marriage as a conjugal union between a man and a woman as an arrangement God clearly blesses. But I also think that in the light of the new situation in which same-sex marriage is a legal right even those churches that do not countenance same-sex unions will have to decide what kind of pastoral care they will provide for their gay and lesbian congregants.

Pope Francis has spoken of 'accompanying' those who live in morally ambiguous ethical situations, including homosexual church members. On the very day of Gay Pride festivals and parades in many cities around the world in June 2016, the pope said to reporters on board his return flight to Rome from Armenia, 'I repeat what the Catechism of the Catholic Church says: that they must not be discriminated against, that they must be respected and accompanied pastorally.'[17]

What would this 'accompaniment' look like for pastors who could not officiate at a same-sex wedding? Attend state-sanctioned same-sex weddings of church members as a guest? Before I officiated at the wedding of my son and son-in-law, I received a letter from a Lutheran pastor with a list of sample excuses a pastor could use to decline an invitation to attend a same-sex wedding of a parishioner, a friend or a relative. In his view, I should not have even attended my son's wedding much less officiated at it. I've known parents who have stayed away from their child's wedding for various reasons. It does not make for a good relationship with the new family. While reconciliation is always possible in the future, parents should want to be supportive of their children at this most momentous occasion in their lives whether they are in agreement with the marriage or not.

Why would it be important for the church to reach out to include homosexuals (as well as transgender persons and other marginalized people) in its life and fellowship? First of all, because homosexuals are sinners like all other human beings who have fallen short of the glory of God and live in a broken world with broken relationships. They with all people need to hear the gospel of Jesus Christ, which announces forgiveness of sins and enacts reconciliation.

Secondly, the experiences of brokenness in the lives of gay men turn out to be especially acute. Michael Hobbs, in an article in the *Huffington Post Highline*, brings together research that shows that mental health issues, physical health issues, sexual addiction, erectile dysfunction, rates of substance abuse and suicide are higher among gay men than in other groups in society. This is after all the strides that have been made in gay rights in North American and Western European societies.[18]

Gay men have embodied their sense of marginality in society in general and in male society in particular. They grew up being perpetually wary of how others would perceive them and react to them. Not all gay youths grew up in the kind of supportive family and community my sons grew up in. Many gay men have body image issues. They have striven to be perceived as 'masculine' and have bent their bodies to emulate 'masculine' characteristics, however understood. They internalized feelings of marginality from their youth and have found that these feelings are aggravated rather than lessened by living in a gay ghetto. Hobbes reports from one of his respondents:

The word I hear from Paul, from everyone, is 're-traumatized'. You grow up with this loneliness, accumulating all this baggage, and then you arrive in the Castro or Chelsea or Boystown thinking you'll finally be accepted for who you are. And then you realize that *everyone else here has baggage, too.* All of a sudden it's not your gayness that gets you rejected. It's your weight, or your income, or your race. 'The bullied kids of our youth', Paul says, 'grew up and became bullies themselves'.

My impressions on reading this article reminded me of my reaction to reading Rechy's *City of Night* more than 50 years ago: homosexuals are often lonely people, even in a crowd of other homosexuals. They are, as Hobbes said in his title, 'Together Alone'. My response is: they need the support of a loving community made up of all sorts of people who will accept them as they are. This was true at the time Christ the Mediator became a 'Reconciled in Christ' congregation; it is true now even though same-sex marriage is legally available.

How would gay individuals and same-sex couples be included in the life of a congregation or parish? Would their marriage and personal needs be included in the thanksgivings and intercessions of the assembly in public worship? If a same-sex couple has children, would their children be publicly baptized and their parental role recognized? Would gay, lesbian or transgender members of a congregation be invited to serve in all areas of congregational life? I think these are ways in which we accompany gay and other marginalized persons, whether our church discipline allows us to officiate at same-sex weddings or not. Gay people must be explicitly invited to know that they are hospitably welcomed.

Marginalization continues even when rites of same-sex marriage are performed. For those pastors whose denominations allow clergy to offici-ate at same-sex weddings, the question arises as to what rite is available for such celebrations. The content of the traditional order for marriage that references a conjugal union is not appropriate for same-sex weddings. Nor, as I said above, is a nuptial blessing that applies God's promise appropriate. What kind of prayer for grace will be composed? When con-structing a marriage liturgy, in addition to the legal parts required by the state, we are free to add specifically Christian ritual elements such as songs and hymns, Scripture readings, homily, expressions of love and commitment, prayers, and perhaps the Eucharist. Choosing appropriate liturgical material and biblical readings requires ritual competence and pastoral sensitivity.

In this essay, I have told the story of one same-sex wedding that was celebrated in a secular venue rather than a church building and with some churched and many unchurched people in attendance. I suspect that for some time to come all same-sex weddings are going to be liturgies celebrated at the margins of church and society with a wide mixture of people in attendance. This will require creativity and experimentation until a suitable liturgical order gains wide acceptance and the clergy become more practised at officiating at same-sex weddings.

Notes

1 R. Stephen Warner, 2005, *A Church of Our Own: Disestablishment and Diversity in American Religion*, New Brunswick, NJ/London: Rutgers University Press, pp. 183–208; originally published as R. Stephen Warner, 1995, 'The Metropolitan Community Churches and the Gay Agenda: The Power of Pentecostalism and Essentialism', in Mary Jo Neitz and Marion S. Goldman (eds), *Sex, Lies, and Sanctity: Religion and Deviance in Contemporary North America*, Greenwich, CT: AJI Press, pp. 81–103.

2 Andrew Sullivan (ed.), 1997, 2004, *Same-Sex Marriage Pro and Con*, with an Introduction and a new Preface, New York: Random House, Vintage Books.

3 John Rechy, 1963, *City of Night*, New York: Grove Books.

4 Frank C. Senn, 1999, *A Stewardship of the Mysteries*, New York/Mahwah, NJ: Paulist Press, pp. 138–54; originally published as Frank C. Senn, 1983, 'The Cup of Salvation: Take and Drink', *Lutheran Forum* 20: 221–7.

5 James B. Nelson, 1978, *Embodiment: An Approach to Sexuality and Christian Theology*, Minneapolis: Augsburg Publishing House, pp. 181–8.

6 John J. McNeill, SJ, 1976, *The Church and the Homosexual*, Kansas City: Sheed, Andrews and McMeel, p. 55.

7 Karl Barth, 1961, *Church Dogmatics*, Vol. III/4, ed. G. W. Bromiley and T. F. Torrance, Edinburgh: T&T Clark, p. 166.

8 Helmut Thielicke, 1964, *The Ethics of Sex*, translated by John V. Doberstein, New York: Harper and Row, p. 282.

9 Thielicke, *Ethics*, p. 283.

10 John Paul II, 2006, *Male and Female He Created Them: A Theology of the Body*, translation, introduction and index by Michael Waldstein, Boston: Pauline Books and Media. The pope's catecheses were delivered at his Wednesday audiences from 5 September 1979 to 28 November 1984. He did not address issues of homosexuality.

11 http://download.elca.org/ELCA%20Resource%20Repository/SexualitySS. pdf [accessed 27 July 2018], pp. 20–1.

12 http://download.elca.org/ELCA%20Resource%20Repository/Candidacy_ Manual_2012.pdf?_ga=1.137348656.1866600449.1401298335 [accessed 27 July 2018].

13 Mark Achtemeier, 2014, 2015, *The Bible's Yes to Same-Sex Marriage: An Evangelical's Change of Heart*, new edition with study guide, Louisville, KY: Westminster John Knox Press.

14 http://www.episcopalchurchsc.org/uploads/1/2/9/8/12989303/lifelong_ covenant_liturgy.pdf [accessed 27 July 2018]. Ruth A. Meyers, 2014, '"I Will Bless You and You Will Be a Blessing": Liturgy and Theology for Blessing Same-Sex Couples in The Episcopal Church', *Studia Liturgica* 44, nos. 1–2: 197–210, describes the process by which this provisional rite was developed and authorized and the issues it sought to address, especially the authority of Scripture and whether this liturgy is a marriage service. My adaptation of it is included in Appendix 2.

15 On Luther's understanding of the three estates of church, government and household, see Vitor Westhelle, 2009, 'Power and Politics in Luther's Theology', in Christine Helmer (ed.), *The Global Luther: A Theologian for Modern Times*, Minneapolis: Fortress Press, pp. 287–93.

16 Same-sex marriage is an issue analogous to the ordination of women for which Scripture is inconclusive. See the study of The Lutheran Council in the United States, 1970, 'The Ordination of Women' as a model for an inter-church study of same-sex marriage: http://www.womenpriests.org/related/lutheran2.asp

17 http://www.ncregister.com/daily-news/pope-francis-church-must-accompany-gays-not-discriminate/#ixzz4Da8cKdT6 [accessed 27 July 2018].

18 See Michael Hobbes, 2 March 2017, 'Together Alone: The Epidemic of Gay Loneliness', https://highline.huffingtonpost.com/articles/en/gay-loneliness/ [accessed 27 July 2018].

PART 3

Liturgy in Migration:
People, Culture and Language

7

Liturgy, Language and Diaspora: Some Reflections on Inclusion as Integration by a Migratory Liturgical Magpie

KRISTINE SUNA-KORO

Inclusion is a tricky business. On the one hand, it elicits an 'enough already' roll of the eyes. Hasn't all that's worth saying already been said in all disciplines and from ever more assiduously scrutinized minority perspectives? Aren't low-tech or high-tech 'welcome to X church' signs dotting urban and suburban streets in North America? Doesn't almost every church website and app feature a blazing 'welcome' banner? On the other hand, as the debates of what it means to include/exclude sprawl over an ever more expansive arena of life and worship and as we delve into yet more subtle expressions of the empowerment/disempowerment dynamics involving race, gender, ethnicity, ability, age, sexuality, class and so on, it is too soon to claim 'mission accomplished'. Even as we are more aware of the limits/pitfalls of the notion of inclusion itself, the desire to move 'beyond' it might just be a bit too hasty. Moving 'beyond' too hurriedly is to overlook and devalue the experiences of those who live with a sense of alienation and non-recognition despite the almost ubiquitous rhetoric of welcome. When it comes to people living, thinking, acting, feeling and worshipping from seemingly ever more intricately and jaggedly configured minority positions (not necessarily marginal or sub-altern by default in all possible contexts), there remains a lot of unfinished business to discern, evaluate and transform.

At least one thing is clear. As we wrap up the second decade of the twenty-first century, voices from black, Latinx, as well as varieties of feminist, womanist, liberationist, Asian, postcolonial, decolonial, mulatto, queer and mujerista perspectives have compelled – albeit sporadically and often grudgingly – the liturgical mainstream/malestream to put inclusion issues on the radar screen in churches and theological education. Even if the inclusion conundrum is dismissed as theologically irrelevant or outright impious in some ecclesiastical circles, the questions of whose rites, whose bodies, whose language, whose traditions, whose cultural conventions, whose aesthetics, whose scriptural hermeneutics, whose moral values and whose political commitments take precedence, make meaning and exert authority in worship – and how – are no longer impossible to ignore.

How, then, do we include what, we realize, has undeservedly been left unnoticed, carelessly ignored all along or intentionally rendered invisible? How can we render our communities of worship inclusive not because (especially in the Euro-Atlantic cultural milieu) inclusion might somehow be the last-ditch effort to stop the trend of steadily dwindling parish membership in virtually all mainline Western Christian denominations but because the incarnational grammar of salvation calls forth a performative liturgical embodiment of the graced dignity of human variety? When does inclusion risk being nothing more than a utilitarian strategy for institutional or cultural, or ethno-racial self-preservation? When does inclusion function hegemonically and condescendingly despite the ubiquitous mild-mannered rhetoric of welcome coming from pulpits, greeters, road signs and newsletters? When does inclusion require taking a long and hard look at how majorities and minorities navigate the tricky politics of recognition and affirmation in a theologically sound and pastorally responsible way?

It is impossible to address all the above pertinent concerns in my brief comments here beyond flagging them as indispensable for further exploration. And there is a multitude of 'we' – a multitude of worship traditions and communities across the globe where all of these questions resonate differently. Different answers will need to be found in response to different needs and circumstances. My objectives here must be necessarily limited. First, I offer a few reflections on the fluid patterns of interaction among majority and minority groups in the context of diasporic experience of worship in a Latvian Lutheran church in North America. I will proceed from the perspective of what Christopher Baker has proposed as 'a local performative theology' that is 'locally rooted, yet understands the nature of the global forces impinging on its locality'.[1] Second, in light of reflecting on what postcolonial theorists Françoise Lionnet and Shu-mei Shih have somewhat elusively called 'minor transnationalism',[2] I offer a few suggestions about the priorities of a postcolonial liturgical praxis of recognition and integration.

Liturgical Diasporas and Their Fluid Majorities/Minorities: A Latvian-American Experience

All majorities and minorities are inescapably contextual and situational. Moreover, all identities and subjectivities are, to a greater or lesser extent, and more or less consciously, fluid and braided from multiple strands of human experience and history. They are embedded in various racially, economically, sexually, linguistically, generationally and culturally inscribed lifeworlds. Migratory experience and diasporic existence among overlapping, intertwining and competing cultures, languages and allegiances engender hyphenated identities that are hybrid *par excellence*. Such a hybridity renders a unique (not better or more omniscient, though) sensibility that the postcolonial thinker Edward W. Said and many after him have variously described as being otherwise than 'purely one thing'[3] and indwelling more than one place, and hence speaking of God and to God 'from more than one place'.[4] And those of us who live and move diasporically among several semiotic lifeworlds in contrapuntal ways[5] may also find ourselves inter-abiding, paradoxically and sometimes quite ironically, in both majority and minority positions in various arenas.

In diaspora, language – or more precisely, languages – matter. Migrant and diasporic life is marked by the phenomenon of 'code switching', or the process of fluctuating from one language to another and back in a way that simultaneously adheres to the grammar rules and cultural underpinnings of two or more languages, which is recognized as a pivotal tenet of identity for diasporic persons. It is the subject of endless jokes as well as heated intra-diasporic and trans-diasporic battles about identity. As the diasporic Latvian Lutheran experience in the United States shows, to reflect on majority/minority dynamic and the intricacies of inclusion/exclusion calls for paying attention to very complex spaces of worship where identities and subject positions can be surprisingly fluid, multi-layered – and ambivalent.

To contextualize briefly but (hopefully) thickly enough: the ethnic Latvian immigrant community in the United States dates back to the time of migratory crescendo in American history at the end of the nineteenth century. Attempting to shake off intertwined deprivations under the colonial Russian czarist regime and what amounted to the sunset era of German colonial apartheid in the late nineteenth century, Latvians not only came to the United States with hopes for freedom and opportunity but also sought out compatriots to establish their own ethnic churches in the 1890s in cities such as Philadelphia and Boston. The clampdown on immigration, especially from Eastern Europe, and the hardly fought for independence for Latvia in 1918 as it emerged from the carnage of World

War I and the Russian revolutions decreased the numbers of Latvian immigrants in the 1920s and 1930s.

But that trend was spectacularly and tragically reversed when the next calamity struck. The Soviets occupied Latvia and unleashed the Stalinist terror and deportations to Siberia (1940–1). Soon thereafter, the Nazi occupation arrived during World War II. Towards the end of the war, a mass exodus of Latvians took place ahead of the advancing Red Army. After the war was over, many thousands of Latvian DPs ('displaced persons') were welcomed to resettle in the United States, Canada and other Western countries as refugees.

Today, the Latvian Evangelical Lutheran Church in America (LELCA) consists of former war refugees, three generations of their descendants as well as less numerous Latvian immigrants who arrived for various reasons after the collapse of the Soviet Union in the 1990s.[6] The congregation I focus on – the Latvian Evangelical Lutheran Church of St John, which I served as a pastor in Philadelphia, Pennsylvania – is part of this ecclesial body. My observations about the variations of diasporic liturgical inclusion are rooted, primarily but not exclusively, in the worship life of this community where the primary language in worship remains Latvian.

Like it or lump it, hybridization is inevitable. With increasing regularity (and with much chagrin of the traditionalists), second- and third-generation Latvians married Americans from various ethnic backgrounds. At best, those spouses learnt some very rudimentary Latvian. Younger generations became less and less proficient in the language of their cultural heritage. Some joke about speaking 'Latv-Ish' (a kind of 'pidgin' of Latvian and American English). Some now even speak 'Sp-Latv-Ish' as a member of my former church once remarked about her children's experience while living trilingually in Puerto Rico.

Amidst all this actual cultural-linguistic hybridity, the church and its worship has been a virtually intractable bastion of ethno-linguistic purity and avowed traditionalism. Sunday worship – hymns, sermon, prayers, Scripture readings – proceed exclusively in Latvian in most LELCA churches. The shift towards using English at first was slowly accepted for occasional services like funerals (consider the spouses, grandchildren, colleagues and neighbours!), weddings (it helps to understand what one is promising in marriage, right?) and baptisms (what about our extended families?). Meanwhile the non-Latvian speaking American spouses stoically sat through the Sunday worship services without the possibility of deeper engagement.

Some 'American'[7] stalwarts who officially joined the congregation due to their Latvian spouse's church affiliation supported it financially and came to worship with their families at least for Christmas, Easter and the ever-popular youth confirmation services. Some even served on committees! A few cracked jokes about how it must have felt for many Roman Catholics before the Vatican II liturgical reforms when the absolute majority of worshippers didn't know Latin and yet attended the Mass regularly. Even well into the first decade of the twenty-first century pastors were required to submit the statistics of church weddings to the LELCA's Executive Council by breaking it down into categories of how many *latvieši* ('Latvians') married *sveštautieši* ('foreigners'). Note that by 'foreigners' the statistics data categorization meant Americans or Canadians: *they* were considered 'foreigners' based on what their native language was according to the Latvian diasporic identity politics.

Eventually, however, my growing pastoral unease about preaching the word that these majority-turned-minority worshippers stood no chance of understanding at all, while their participation in liturgy was superficial at best, resonated with a quietly emerging sense in the community that the time for change had come. Despite pushback behind the scenes, we decided to experiment with worshipping in English.

Diasporic imaginary of hybridity in theological method and liturgical praxis always speaks of and to God from 'more than one place'. This is the 'locality' from which I formed a Sunday service rite that included elements from American, Swedish and German Lutheran liturgical traditions as well as material inspired by the Anglican/Episcopal *Book of Common Prayer* reflecting the ecumenical thrust of the Porvoo Communion. Liturgical material from *A New Zealand Prayerbook / He Karakia Mihinare o Aotearoa* added a focus on justice and solidarity that was – and still is – sorely lacking in the scripted rites of the diasporic Latvian Lutheran community. All of these traditions of worship are practised in countries where the worldwide Latvian diaspora is present. The hybrid rite aspired to honour and integrate the treasures of the various traditions through liturgical texts, gestures and music with flexibility and variation depending on the liturgical seasons. It also performatively acknowledged the postcolonial awareness that, as HyeRan Kim-Cragg summarizes, 'the Eucharist carries a hybrid identity whose elements and traditions are mixed and whose practices intermingle with the current traditions and subvert old traditions while at the same time adopting and creating new ones, refusing to settle into one unified text or practice'.[8] The rite was, indeed, the handiwork of a diasporic liturgical 'magpie', to borrow a mischievous description of the Archbishop of Canterbury, Justin Welby. Welby joked in an interview with *Daily Telegraph* that he is 'a spiritual magpie'[9] who goes after liturgical, theological and spiritual elements from many traditions that are life-giving to him. Diasporic 'magpies' don't intentionally seek out diversity for diversity's sake. It happens organically before any self-scrutiny sets in. Migratory liturgical spirituality is always already more than one thing; it is connected to more than one location; it draws from more than one already inter-culturated tradition; and it dips into more than one language. Indeed, as a magpie, it 'poaches' from different traditions and drinks from wherever the living water of grace and wisdom is to be found.

Music, always so central for Latvian worship,[10] was chosen to include mostly metric and melodious hymns that all, young and old, could sing with ease even if they couldn't read the scores. Hymns and service music intentionally reflected a variety of cultural heritage to make the liturgy more welcoming to as many as possible including a surprising group of worshippers who arrived totally unexpected (more about that later). The eucharistic rite, Scripture readings, the creed, prayers and the hymn texts were available in large-print bulletins considering the high number of older worshippers and the general unfamiliarity with the new hybrid order of worship. The church newsletter with the liturgical calendar described it as 'the English service'. Suddenly, alongside those who would come every Sunday, come hell or high water, quite a few previously 'inactive' church members whose Latvian was not too splendid showed up to check out 'the English service' with their family and friends! To this day, 'the English service' takes place a few times a year and remains firmly embedded in the church's liturgical calendar.

And then another group of unexpected worshippers showed up – a small group of German immigrants started to frequent 'the English service'. However, these were German Americans with an Eastern European twist: they were Baltic Germans (*Deutschbalten* or *Baltendeutsche*) and their spouses who ended up immigrating to the United States in the aftermath of World War II. As small children, they had spent their early years in Latvia before the war, only to be 'repatriated' to Germany after Adolf Hitler's Nazi party came to power in 1933. Some could actually still speak some sentences in Latvian, although it was not their native language as a diasporic minority in Latvia. The Baltic German community were the descendants of the ethnic German colonists who effectively ruled what is today's Latvia for several centuries after the eastern crusades in the Middle Ages. Historically speaking, the relations between the Latvian and ethnic German communities in the early postcolonial period between the World Wars were filled with tensions, considering the colonial subjugation of indigenous Latvians and the legacy of apartheid-like serfdom that had lasted until the nineteenth century under the imperialistic umbrella of czarist Russia.

Fast-forward to early twenty-first century: during the sunset years of their lives, however, the interest in making connections with the country where they were born and the culture that many now remembered with a certain nostalgia helped engender a complex liturgical assembly. Most, but not all, were cisgender Euro-American men and women. The immigration status of those present varied from citizens and naturalized citizens with dual or more citizenships to people in between various visa statuses but also the people with immigration violations of various kinds. Most of us prayed with an accent and sang hymns with an accent alongside the group of 'native' American English speakers of various ethnic backgrounds and various confessional creeds who now, in this setting, comprised a minority – but finally at home, so to say, in their native language! After worship services, many partook in the indispensable coffee hour savouring scrumptious Latvian pastries during which not only variously accented English and 'Latv-Ish' but now also German and 'Germ-Ish' was spoken. The postcolonial ambivalence percolated just under the surface as we all polished off the cake while many ageing worshippers carefully danced around the tensions of history to listen to one another's memories and life stories from the war time.

All over that, however, hovered a feeling that something new, strange and unpredictable had happened. Through a confessionally and culturally hybrid rite, this liturgical assembly blended together several linguistic, ethnic, cultural minorities into one hybrid ecclesial body. The hybrid liturgical space facilitated encountering otherness through shared participation in a eucharistic rite that did not belong exclusively to one single denominational or cultural tradition even though this time, it all transpired in what was for the most of us our second, third or fourth language. In a sense, this liturgical space was now foreign for everyone albeit differently. We were all caught, as Gloria Anzaldua puts it, in the hybridity of *nepantla* – a borderland – 'in between cultures and [could] simultaneously be insiders, outsiders, and other-siders'.[11]

Praying, Singing and Confessing from More Than One Place

As Anzaldua argues, 'the body is the ground of thought ... [writing is] about being in your body'.[12] The brief reflection on the Latvian-American-German experience of navigating cultural-linguistic difference through a pastoral 'theology of blurred encounters'[13] offered one example of addressing the ever-tricky conundrum of inclusion through liturgical performance of hybridity. In that case, the diasporic appropriation of the language of majority – English (albeit with a good dose of accents) – facilitated the more lateral interaction among various minorities in the shared space of hybrid liturgy. However, this is only one way to negotiate difference, inclusion and exclusion. In the concluding part of this chapter, I would like to offer a few other observations that suggest a contrast to the first example while also resonating with postcolonial liturgical sensibility while remaining rooted in the existential actualities of diasporic life and worship.

Postcolonial analyses of culture, history and politics have ordinarily probed the widest array of structures of dominance. When it comes to the majority/minority dynamic, such a slant of enquiry has often been 'framed vertically' as Lionnet and Shih put it, while 'we forget to look sideways to lateral networks that are not readily apparent'.[14] Instead of exclusively gravitating towards the critique of sociopolitical, cultural, economic, racial and religious binaries that enshrine the logic of domination and exploitative asymmetries in the global postcolony, it is worth paying attention to what Lionnet and Shih call a 'transnationalism from below' or 'minor transnationalism'.[15] From this perspective, the attention shifts to the exploration of 'the complex and multiple forms of cultural expressions of minorities and diasporic peoples' to emphasize their 'micropractices of transnationality'.[16] Such minor transnationalism acknowledges the complexity and ambiguity of cultures and communities that live in the liminal and hybrid borderlands of diaspora, be they dominant or marginal. The point is that across these transnational and trans-diasporic terrains of encounter and interaction, the centre, as it were, can be decentred laterally or 'sideways' to discover new apertures recognizing and honouring otherness as well as engaging diversity in a more subtle and transformative way. If so, what might such decentring micropractices reveal in the arena of liturgy?

Above all, there are, as it were, many mansions in the communal spaces and subjective identity positions for both majorities and minorities. In diasporic contexts, everyone is more than 'purely one thing' – more than just a simplified 'majority' or 'minority'. Rather, a more multilateral imaginary of identity is needed for cognitive, ethical and pastoral recognition of the degree of complexity that hybrid lives and souls bring to prayer and worship. Both majority and minority status can be perplexingly and even conflictually multilateral and fluid. In diasporic spaces it may well be one's ethnicity, language and history of immigration that, counterintuitively, determine one's 'nativeness' or 'foreignness' in quite a quirky way, as the Latvian example illustrates. That is not to say, however, that a multilateral imaginary of identity triumphantly solves the systemic and mutilating effects of endemic institutionalized injustice in church communities around the principal vectors of disempowerment: race and gender. The postcolonial hybridity and the intersecting complexities it engenders do not play out across an idyllic and equitable terrain of realized eschatology of peace and justice. What a decentring micropractice of transnationality can foster is a commitment for worship assemblies to become aware of the hybridities and complexities that permeate the lives of those who in their communities, by choice or by force, live glocally. That is, they dwell in more than one culture, race, language ethnicity – all the time. The fruit of such committed and effortful awareness is a more attentive and more realistic way of relating to otherness and difference.

Furthermore, individuals in migrant diasporas perennially struggle with finding a liturgical home where they can truly belong. The canonized structures of majority/minority dynamic along the either/or axis of identity are becoming increasingly inadequate to comprehend and categorize the hybrid overlaps of race, ethnicity, gender, class, as well as the 'magpie-like' religious imaginary and worship practices of migratory lifeworlds. That being said, sometimes diasporic communities of faith themselves are far from hospitable. Some become self-ghettoized to the extent that they end up being the most inhospitable worship spaces for those who fall outside the diasporic benchmarks of gender roles, sexual orientation, immigration status, class and sectarian politics of identity. Time is ripe for a more intersectional self-scrutiny when it comes to naming others from both majoritarian and minoritarian positions inside and outside of diaspora. In particular, when it comes to naming minorities by majorities – but also among variously empowered minorities themselves – categories are to be used vigilantly and cautiously since, as Namsoon Kang has argued, 'the place from which the human exercises power is often a hidden place ... especially if the power is hidden under the canopy of the "Divine"'.[17] What matters most, from a postcolonial perspective, is to intentionally transform the logic of domination which, as Kang elucidates, tends to robotically reproduce the reductive and alienating juxtapositions of 'superior–inferior, normal–abnormal, inclusion–exclusion, neighbor–stranger, orthodoxy–heterodoxy, redemption–condemnation' while overlooking the 'greatest commission of *planetary-neighborly-love* ... ' and '*trans-boundary-solidarity*'.[18]

No worship community, 'native' or diasporic, exists pristinely and innocently beyond or outside the contested arenas of human strife despite the often self-serving deployment of the adage 'we are in the world but not of the world'. Nevertheless, the diasporic quest – of which any person who identifies as not 'purely one thing' racially, ethnically or sexually, might have an inkling even if they have not migrated – always gravitates, as the African American Jewish philosopher Jacqueline Scott puts it, 'toward a place where I can bring all of me'.[19]

In this era of unprecedented forced planetary migrations and convoluted globalization, it is important to recognize in Western liturgical contexts that the multiple (and even seemingly contradictory!) belonging of more and more persons who fall into various situationally and contextually shaped majorities/minorities calls for careful attention to and examination of local practices of liturgical hospitality. Liturgical hospitality is not just about a superficial invitation to encounter Christ in a 'one-size-fits-all' (i.e. assimilation) way. Liturgical hospitality worth its salt requires a praxis, indeed, an attentive and informed ethics of recognition. Such praxis calls for the willingness and readiness to learn about, welcome and honour at least some parts of the 'all of me' that people living out of one or more minoritarian locations bring to the sanctuary but that may otherwise remain invisible and therefore feel worthless. There is no space to offer here a comprehensive catalogue of micropractices of trans-nationality which can facilitate welcoming strangers in a less hegemonic way. What I would like to underscore from my diasporic theological and liturgical location is the role of language as one of the central elements of liturgical praxis of recognition and hospitality.

A recent (2017) study of outreach and integration programmes in American Roman Catholic institutions by the Center of Migration Studies (CMS) shows what most migrants and diasporic individuals already vis-cerally know. Namely, the survey data shows that when asked to list programmes and services that most strongly advanced immigrant integra-tion, parish and school respondents emphasized bilingual and bicultural Mass.[20] This finding is extremely relevant from a liturgical point of view: the impact of bilingual and bicultural worship (i.e. Mass in the Catholic context) once more shows the crucial importance of recognizing how the use of minority languages – in some cases multiple minorities' languages – allows for life-giving and spiritually fulfilling integration. Note, not inclusion as assimilation, but integration – a two (or more) way street or reciprocity even if it is asymmetrical in power and impact!

Hopefully, at this point in history, the presence of sizeable minority groups in any worship community should have already sparked initiatives that proactively and substantially invite worship services in other than the dominant language. If not, the 2017 CMS study comprises a good argument to consider doing so despite the pastoral challenges and cul-tural tensions that bi- or multilingual worship can often present. Many churches, however, don't have one or more large and clearly visible cultural and linguistic minorities. Yet, it does not mean that the cultural-linguistic hospitality in worship is an automatic non-issue. For example, the pastoral leadership might be aware that there are several individuals or smaller groups of diasporic worshippers whose native language is dif-ferent or if there are multiple generations of migrant families participating in worship. If so, why not have at least one of the intercessory prayers said in those languages? Why not have a Scripture reading, at least now and then, in a language that will resonate in a unique spiritual intimacy of the homeland that they left behind for those who usually worship in the language that is not their mother tongue? What can be more genuinely inviting and affirming for worshippers who identify as cultural minorities, even if for a brief moment and on some occasions, than a targeted and culturally accurate recognition of their presence, their belonging and their full spiritual 'citizenship' in a community by making space for elements of the service in their language? For those whose native tongue is not the ever more dominant English, the recognition of their language as a fundamental tenet of their cultural and spiritual identity often matters more than the native speakers of English (who often don't need to learn any other language to be understood or survive) realize. While they can speak their mind unfettered virtually all over the world almost as if 'at home', the gesture of making an effort to welcome those who don't have such a privilege, due to their native language's minor status and displacement through migration, heralds a very special level of respect.

Such a liturgical hospitality requires explicit and context-specific gestures, not just generic pronouncements that 'all are welcome here'. It almost goes without saying, but what about making an intentional effort to incorporate music or sacral art from cultures actually represented in the assembly? What about including a hymn or stanza in a hymn in one or several languages spoken at homes of parishioners? Or liturgical dance if that is what is meaningful for cultures present in the worship? Or making an effort to pray for events and needs in the homelands of migrant worshippers? Or intentionally including sermon illustrations that are drawn from the cultural resources of minority worshippers instead of catering exclusively to the presumed majority? Some churches might even discover that their membership arcs towards what sociologists in the United States call the 'majority of minorities' – a spectrum of minorities who all together actually constitute a majority vis-à-vis one single cultural, racial, ethnic or linguistic unit.

In Cincinnati, Ohio, where I currently live, there is a large Evangelical Lutheran Church in America (ELCA) congregation that at least on Pentecost Sunday includes the reading of Acts 2 in several languages besides English. How thrilling to tune into the words of Scripture actually talking about people from various Jewish diasporas hearing the good news in their primary languages while being in a communal worship that rendered that Pentecost so resonant with what the assembly was actually experiencing now. I presume that for the majority of monolingual Anglo-Americans present this might have been a bit of a bewildering moment. Although my native Latvian was not spoken, as a diasporic 'magpie', I knew a few others that were and in which I felt at home at least to some degree. Somehow, the carousel of languages in the exuberant Pentecost services made (even) me feel seen and heard before God in a deeper and more complete way although I was only a 'guest' in the tongues that I had acquired in the course of my migratory life. This was indeed a liturgical performance of minor transnationalism: various minority languages and imaginative worlds intersected to bring the good news home in a way that no translation ever can. The Scripture resonated in the beautiful sanctuary with such outspoken multilingual affirmation of the hallowed richness of God's creation and the Spirit's power to uplift our fundamental equality before God through an inclusive polyphony – even if for a brief blurred moment of surprise and joy. Integration, or the deep end of inclusion, of course goes beyond such moments even though it builds on them as transformative gateways for the evangelical welcome to become genuinely enfleshed to embrace the precious diversity of creation on more than one Sunday.

From the Inclusion of Blurred Encounters Towards Integration

To be sure, on this side of the eschaton this polyphony is incomplete, imperfect, episodic and asymmetrical. Not all tensions are miraculously resolved and not all injustices wrought by the logic of dominance swiftly undone by the micropractice of decentring transnationality through reciting a few verses of the Bible in languages that only certain minorities can fully understand. Yet, the willingness of the majority – or the minority holding the power in some cases – to become a stranger on one's own home turf, even if for a moment, and to let others be more of themselves on that turf signals a willingness to welcome and honour difference in the Pentecost spirit of humble eschatological anticipation. There are plenty of churches that never do anything like this even though their pastors and lay leaders know that there are people from various countries and cultures worshipping among them every Sunday. What can kindle the Pentecost spirit in our assemblies is a commitment to cultivate, through liturgy, what Miroslav Volf has memorably called the 'catholic personality': it is a 'personality enriched by otherness, a personality which is what it is only because multiple others have been reflected in it in a particular way. The distance from my own culture that results from being born by the Spirit creates a fissure in me through which others can come in.'[21] Approaching worship from a dual vantage point, 'with one foot planted in their own culture and the other in God's future', individual Christians and liturgical assemblies can better discern how to 'perceive and judge the self and the other not simply on their own terms but in the light of God's new world – a world in which a great multitude "from every nation, from all tribes and peoples and languages" is gathered "before the throne and before the Lamb" (Rev. 7.9; 5.9, NRSV)'.[22]

Inclusion is a tricky business for all of us – diasporic 'magpies' and those solidly rooted in one culture, one language or one liturgical tradition alike. Liturgical micropractices of minor transnationalism that decentre entrenched perceptions of majority/minority and exclusion/inclusion make space, however imperfectly, to recognize and honour the histories and experiences of surprisingly fluid, hybrid and intersectional majorities and minorities that are far less uniform than they appear to a careless out-sider. Above all, only such sustained micropractices of transnationalism that stagger on despite setbacks and gaffes can reach towards the 'holy grail' of inclusion – integration. Integration occurs when the sporadic and imperfect acts of inclusion acquire an ongoing and sustained quality to be able to form a habit of making space for multifaceted recognition of minoritarian others where their agency and identity can flourish under less alienating conditions. Integration is more than just passively allowing them (if at all) to carve out pockets where they can be seen without trying to 'pass' for the majority, internally or externally, and where their voices can be heard not just at the Pentecost service.

The micropractices of transnationalism – however shaped by the nexus of intersecting differences of those who worship together in any particular assembly – constitute an opening for more intentional discernment and transformative contemplation of what Christian discipleship means, ecclesiastically and liturgically, in our increasingly polarized, tribalized and fragmented world. How, indeed, ought we to 'welcome one another, therefore, just as Christ has welcomed you, for the glory of God' (Rom. 15.7, NRSV)? What might it mean and demand from us all and what might it look/sound like if our Christian worship assemblies really cared about envisioning and enacting liturgical spaces to integrate those who are 'not purely one thing', where they can bring if not yet 'all of me' then at least more of the hybrid 'me' in full stretch before God?

Notes

1 Christopher Baker, 2007, *The Hybrid Church in the City: Third Space Think-ing*, Abingdon/New York: Ashgate. Baker explains that 'by "locally rooted" I mean that [theology] listens carefully to the experiences of those sharing a particular globalized locality, as well as having an overview and understanding of the history of that locality and the experiences, memories and ways of belonging that have shaped it in the past and brought it to the present moment' (p. 126).

2 Françoise Lionnet and Shu-mei Shih (eds), 2005, *Minor Transnationalism*, Durham, NC/London: Duke University Press.

3 Edward W. Said, 1994, *Culture and Imperialism*, New York: Vintage Books, Random House, p. 336.

4 Nancy E. Bedford, 2005, 'To Speak of God from More than One Place: Theo-logical Reflections from the Experience of Migration', in Ivan Petrella (ed.), *Latin American Liberation Theology: The Next Generation*, Maryknoll, NY: Orbis Books, p. 104.

5 The contrapuntality of postcolonial and diasporic/exilic experience was memorably explored by Edward Said. Building on Said's work, I have elsewhere offered a more in-depth analysis of the ways and means of diasporic sensibilities and their hybrid subjectivity, imagination and theological method as contrapuntal in postcolonial contexts in Kristine Suna-Koro, 2017, *In Counterpoint: Diaspora, Postcoloniality, and Sacramental Theology*, Eugene, OR: Pickwick. See Parts I and II.

6 For more information regarding the ethnic Latvian Lutheran community, see Kristine Suna-Koro, 2015, 'Journeying Before God with a Divided Heart: Theological Virtues in Light of Postcolonial Migrations of Latvian Lutherans', in Allen G. Jorgenson, Hussam S. Timani and Alexander Y. Hwang (eds), *Strangers in This World: Multireligious Reflections on Immigration*, Minneapolis, MN: Fortress Press, pp. 155–73.

7 In North America, it remains a standard habit up to this day to refer to the non-Latvians as 'Americans' or 'Canadians' based on ethnicity even though, at this point in history, the absolute majority of the Latvian church membership themselves are not only naturalized citizens but have actually been born in the United States or Canada.

8 HyeRan Kim-Cragg, 2016, 'Postcolonial Practices on Eucharist', in Kwok Pui-lan and Stephen Burns (eds), *Postcolonial Practice of Ministry: Leadership, Liturgy, and Interfaith Engagement*, Lanham, MD: Lexington Books, p. 80.

9 Charles Moore, 12 July 2013, 'Archbishop Justin Welby: "I was embarrassed. It was like getting measles"', *Daily Telegraph*.

10 On the pivotal role of music in Latvian spirituality in the context of a postcolonial diasporic perspective, see Kristine Suna-Koro, 2011, 'Not With One Voice: The Counterpoint of Life, Diaspora, Women, Theology, and Writing', in Emily A. Holmes and Wendy Farley (eds), *Women, Writing, Theology: Transforming a Tradition of Exclusion*, Waco, TX: Baylor University Press, pp. 207–32.

11 Gloria E. Anzaldua, 2015, *Light in the Darkness: Luz en lo oscuro: Rewriting Identity, Spirituality, Reality*, ed. Analouise Keating, Durham, NC/London: Duke University Press, 2015, p. 71.

12 Anzaldua, *Light in the Darkness*, p. 5.

13 Baker, *The Hybrid Church*, p. 137.

14 Lionnet and Shih, *Minor Transnationalism*, p. 1.

15 Lionnet and Shih, *Minor Transnationalism*, pp. 5–6.

16 Lionnet and Shih, *Minor Transnationalism*, p. 7.

17 Namsoon Kang, 2011, 'Constructing Postcolonial Mission in World Christianity: Mission as Radical Affirmation of the World', in Desmond van der Water (ed.), *Postcolonial Mission: Power and Partnership in World Christianity*, Upland, CA: Sopher Press, p. 116.

18 Kang, 'Constructing Postcolonial Mission', pp. 125, 124. Italics in the original.

19 Jacqueline Scott, 2012, 'Toward a Place Where I Can Bring All of Me: Identity Formation and Philosophy', in George Yancey (ed.), *Reframing the Practice of Philosophy: Bodies of Color, Bodies of Knowledge*, Albany, NY: State University of New York Press, p. 203.

20 Donald Kerwin and Kyle Barron, 2017, 'Building Structures of Solidarity and Instruments of Justice: The Catholic Immigrant Integration Surveys', http://cmsny.org/publications/ciiisurveysreport/

21 Miroslav Volf, 1996, *Exclusion and Embrace: A Theological Exploration of Identity, Otherness, and Reconciliation*, Nashville, TN: Abingdon Press, p. 51.

22 Volf, *Exclusion and Embrace*, p. 53.

8

Liturgy's Missional Character:
Trusting Truth in Real Bodies of
Culture and Tradition

BRUCE T. MORRILL, SJ

Liturgy, Mystery and Mission

One way to ground the necessary pastoral-theological work of theorizing and practising liturgical worship attuned to difference is boldly to embrace a seemingly anodyne principle reaching back to ancient Christianity: the purpose of the church's *leitourgia* is the glorification of God and the sanctification of people. One finds the principle operative, if not explicitly stated, in the homilies, mystagogies and euchologies of the early Christian period, in the medieval Western theology of such luminaries as Aquinas (himself drawing on those ancient sources), in the work of the modern liturgical movement as well as such seminal texts as Schillebeeckx's *Christ the Sacrament of the Encounter with God*,[1] and in what would prove to be the guiding document for liturgical reform and renewal across multiple global ecclesial bodies, Vatican II's Constitution on the Sacred Liturgy. An early paragraph in the Constitution states succinctly one of its first chapter's 'General Principles', that the liturgy is 'this great work wherein God is perfectly glorified and men are sanctified'.[2] But might not such a principle risk being a sort of boilerplate warm-up for the more substantial, detailed doctrine to follow? Would it not seem obvious that human acts of divine worship are for the purpose of glorifying the divinity, with adulation of the Deity comprising the holiness of the humans so engaged? I open by problematizing this principle because it has proved so problematic in history, that is, problematic in the actual ways the church's rites (or public worship) have functioned ancillary to, if not often supportive of, powers contradictory to the divine power that is the Spirit of God, the God of Christ Jesus, the resurrected crucified one.

In the realms of earthly monarchies, civil governments, athletics and entertainment industries, to glorify is to exalt the great, those powerful of force or fear, the skilled, the beautiful, the talented, such that the glorified are barely approachable. Spaces protected for the glorious – daises, podiums, red carpets, stadium playing fields – comprise the sacred, set aside from the ordinary. Social-scientific (sometimes philosophical) study of religion has, of course, identified the sacred in a similar fashion, as a realm set apart from the mundane world, establishing, in typical modern fashion, the universal category 'religion' with its own form of dualism: the sacred versus the profane. For Christianity, in fact, the phenomenon reaches centuries back into Christendom, with emperor (or czar) and patriarch, king and bishop (or, for many centuries, the two combined in the papacy), not only exercising government but functioning as symbols of great power, answerable to nobody – nobody except God 'above', in a manner inaccessible to the laity 'below'. Derivations of this phenomenon persist across Catholicism, Orthodoxy and, yes, Protestantism, whereby people in their desire for autonomy to exercise profane or 'real-world' power readily attribute glorious status to the leadership in their churches. God is in his heaven, and his vicar or minister acts and speaks on his behalf for us on this spot of earth. With the sacred duly secured, we can go about our profane business (words, transactions, organizations, relationships) in society. Sanctity resides in the sacred precinct of the church, whether altar or pulpit or religious-vowed cloister or, in the case of colonial mission-aries (a phenomenon persisting to this day), in faraway places fraught with sufficient hardships or dangers to acquire a certain sacrality (a space of dread and wonder) of their own.

The notion of the sacred is, nonetheless, apposite to Christianity, even as applied to personages or places, but only if situated in a sacramental relationship to the one who alone is holy, the Creator, the Life-Giver, who is also the Saviour, the Redeemer. Sacramentality is not just the asser-tion that creation is shot through with the presence of the divine, making everything indiscriminately holy or, more likely, leaving humans to iden-tify by their own lights what or who is sufficiently glorious so as to be recognized as a manifestation of the divine. No, for Christian faith, the sacramental only comes to light by means of the biblical word, revealing the particular, radical *difference* of the God revealed in Christ Jesus. This is the God of all creation who glorifies in saving slaves, whose glory is revealed through prophetic signs and acts delivering a people as good as dead into a covenantal life, a divine–human bond symbolized as parent to child, mother to baby, husband to wife, lover to beloved.

The vast difference between this God and worldly measures of glory, Christians believe, came to its paradoxical apotheosis in the person of Jesus, the Galilean prophet whose death by imperial execution (with certain religious collusion) the Gospel of John identifies as the hour of glory, the revelation of the full, creation-wide scope of divine redemption from death (and its minion, sin). Divine glory and human salvation, then, are so intimately, inextricably joined that sanctity (holiness) is not grasped as sacredness but, rather, is revealed through mystery, Christ Jesus' paschal mystery of death and resurrection, the source of life flowing from the side of his dead body into the sacramental body of the church.[3] But this is the church in its members, disciples-called-friends upon whom the resurrected Christ breathes the Spirit, empowering them to participate in the mystery of a love stronger than death, a life-giving way, an itinerary lighted by (sacramental) moments of truth. Mystery, then, rather than the sacred, better bespeaks the biblical Christian belief in divine glory and human sanctification as two sides of the same coin, the single token given as the way, the truth and the life. Truth thereby comes along a long arch of human history.[4] Faith is trusting in God, in the God who trusts the long arch of truth stretching through individuals' lives and a world's history punctuated with sacramental moments, glimpses of the promised new heavens and new earth. Christian time is at once bounded in our corporality and stretching into a dimension we variably call heaven or the reign of God or the communion of saints or the new creation.

While most intensely identified with Jesus' death and resurrection, the theology of the paschal mystery entails the entire scope of his passage through horrific death into a new life form, raised bodily by the Spirit and ascended to God's right hand, sending that same Spirit as power animating the church's earthly mission until he returns. The paschal mystery, then, is not a matter of theatrically re-enacting past events but, rather, of the ongoing history (or human story) whereby the Spirit who raised Jesus from the dead adopts sons and daughters, anoints disciples and friends, to carry on the redemptive mission inaugurated in Christ. Early baptismal instruction called the church a 'temple built of living stones', converting the image of a literal sacred site or building into a metaphorical symbol of the entire Christian life as worship of God. God was glorified in Jesus' life-giving mission unto death. Those baptized in the power of his divine Spirit glorify God by having a share (*koinonia*, communion, participation) in that mission of fostering life in abundance, deliverance from sin, healing and reconciliation among individuals and social bodies, crossing humanly drawn lines of division to embrace difference.

Christian holiness, then, is a comprehensive way of bodily life, that is, a life-ethic that seeks the presence of the unseen God through Christ-like availability to serving and being served in whatever life-spaces. The presence of that totally other one (God) is not readily or steadily detected in the throes of life. Hence the church's liturgy, the ritual work (*leitourgia*) whereby God's people perceive more clearly, over and again, the mystery of God's glory in humanity's salvation, deepened and renewed through participation in proclaimed word and sacramental signs. The members of a liturgical assembly bring precisely their bodies to the celebration, their daily life (ethics) as persons engaged in the social and cosmic corporeal-ity of the human story being written in history. By participating in the traditional body of the church's sacramental worship, we submit to the mystery of God revealed in the crucified and resurrected Jesus, a God who comes to us in and through the shared bodily medium – in all its differ-ences – of our human knowing, suffering and loving. In bodily difference does the God of Jesus become really present to our lives, even as that sacramental ecclesial presence always recedes in its coming, sending us in the Spirit to discover the Word as living and active in us and our world. Mystery entails mission, God's mission amidst the human race.

Still, as indicated at this essay's outset, the liturgy's mission as an empowering call to all believers for participation in the saving, sanctify-ing, redeeming mystery that is the work of Christ's Spirit in the world has been occluded by alternative ideologies of the sacred, distorting the service of God as members of Christ's Body into 'attending services' offered by a sacred clergy. It is this problem that gave rise in recent decades to certain theologians constructing a 'missional' ecclesiology, the principles of which have further inspired some Protestant and Anglican liturgical theo-logians to argue for 'missional worship' or 'liturgy as mission'. Episcopal theologian Ruth Meyers has summarized the key insight to this practical ecclesiology in the assertion that the church is not the primary subject of mission, rather, God is. The church does not receive faith and then go out on missions, rather, God is the one on a mission for the life of the world. The church, in its members, shares in that mission through liturgical proc-lamation and ethical enactment, with these constituting the very way they encounter the God of Christ Jesus.

By means of this missional concept, Meyers resolves the disheartening, if not scandalous, struggle for so many mainline Christians to perceive the intrinsic relationship between liturgy and ethics in a manner not unlike the paschal-mystery theology I introduced above:

> Through the Spirit, God calls together a community whose identity is rooted in the mission of God, a community that participates in God's mission, embodying God's healing, reconciling, and saving love for the world, and proclaiming the good news of God's reign.
>
> When worship *is* mission, the assembly embodies and inhabits wor-ship in such a way that ritual texts and patterns come alive, for people today, through speaking and singing, in symbols and actions. Such worship turns outward, for the sake of the world. It is true liturgy, in the deepest sense of the word: work for the common good, a public service. Responding to God's self-offering, the people of God offer praise and proclamation and prayer on behalf of all creation ... Always more than what appears on the surface, worship uses basic elements of

everyday life – water, bread, wine, oil. Through the purposeful action of the assembly in their encounter with God, these common things reveal the mystery of God.[5]

The divine mystery, I would underline, is boundless love for a humanity created in its image and likeness, saving and raising up each person-body through a communal body of tradition that itself only remains vital through creative interaction with the wider social-cultural bodies wherein people are 'hearers of the word'.[6]

As the biblical word of God instructs through Paul's writing, Christian holiness is a matter of our 'bodies' (entire lives) comprising our 'spiritual worship'. For this to be so requires that the faithful 'discern what is the will of God – what is good and acceptable and perfect' (Rom. 12.1–2). On that point of discernment, this chapter turns to narrative, the only theological method adequate to the particularity inherent to the reflection, decision and actions practised by believers in their cultural-ecclesial contexts. By means of narrative drawing on my pastoral experience in Yup'ik Eskimo communities in western Alaska, I shall demonstrate how reflection on participation in a profoundly different, seemingly marginal ecclesial setting can offer insights into the missional character and potential of liturgical ministry.

Living Pastoral Liturgy with the Real People

The following first-person narrative is one that, to use a colloquialism from American university culture, 'flips' the conventional colonial (or colonizing) notion of mission or missionary work in Christianity. Mine is the story of a white American Jesuit priest-professor having found himself called to service among the Yup'ik people through the intervention of one of their elders I happened to meet in the summer of 2000. Nearly two decades earlier, freshly graduated from a liberal arts college, I gave a year's service in the Jesuit Volunteer Corps as a youth minister and catechist in a Yup'ik village on the Yukon River Delta. Thereafter I returned to New England to enter the Jesuit novitiate of that province, inaugurating a decade of formation to priestly ordination, followed by doctoral studies and then a tenure-track faculty position at Boston College. Summer of 2000 was my first time back in Alaska since 1982, and among several reasons for the trip was my desire to visit an older Yup'ik woman who had been a good friend to me. Unusually lacking in immediate family, she had moved from the Bering Seacoast to Anchorage, where she lived in an elderly Native housing complex.

One Sunday, I accompanied my elder-friend to Mass at the Alaska

Native Regional Hospital where, before concluding the service, the age-ing Jesuit celebrant exhorted young and middle-aged parents amidst the packed chapel to answer the need for catechism teachers. He asked the elders in the assembly who for many years had taught the children in their villages to stand, as he challenged the younger adults to emulate the elders. After the Mass, my friend introduced me to an elder (whose deceased brother, it turned out, I had known). My friend explained that I was a Jesuit priest from far-off Boston, to which the woman, in the authoritative manner befitting a Yup'ik elder, turned to me and said: 'Then why aren't you helping as our priest? You heard Father. He is one of just a few Jesuits left here. You come work in the villages.' Speechless, I was relieved to hear my friend quickly respond, 'No, no, he teaches the other ones who go out and work.' Undeterred, the elder returned to me, 'Okay, then I want you to send us three of them.'

While I took genuine delight in that interaction with the elder, I knew only too well that my efforts to 'promote vocations' to what was still called the Alaskan Mission had meagre prospects. Far more significant, however, proved to be her direct challenge to me when, soon afterward, I made an eight-day silent retreat at the Jesuit spirituality centre in the nearby foothills of the Chugach Range. With the help of the Jesuit guiding my retreat, I discerned the call to go out to the villages to the degree my primary academic vocation would allow. Before summer's end, the Jesuit superior of the western Alaskan Mission had arranged for my serving at Christmas in the community of Chevak, one of three villages (with no connecting roads) a middle-aged Jesuit moved among as pastor. Those two weeks proved such a good start that I decided to spend seven weeks of the following summer there, forging relationships. Over the next decade, I made one and sometimes two long trips per year from Boston to the Central Bering Seacoast (whereas my current position at Vanderbilt only affords my going every few years). Without lapsing into pious prose, I can report that through many experiences across a handful of villages (Chevak proving to be my base) I have found myself repeatedly convinced that my ministry of word and sacrament, of listening and learning and accompaniment, with those Real People (English translation for the word 'Yup'ik') has been anything but the work of a missionary bringing God to a faraway land. No, I have been invited into encountering Christ amidst the faith lives of a people struggling to negotiate between the world of their ancestors, the Catholicism of the elders but also the institutional church, and the commercial-cultural, economic and bureaucratic forces of late-modernity.

During my early years in Chevak, one of the sharpest points of tension for my pastoral work amidst the Yup'ik people's world of colliding cul-tures was the sacrament of baptism. In the course of my 2001 summer stay, I received a succession of requests by young women for the baptism of their toddlers. In asking why they were seeking the sacrament for their children now, I gradually learnt that the deacon, a Yup'ik elder away at his family's seasonal tent camp, did not favour requests for infant baptism from unwed parents, replying that they first needed to enter the sacrament of matrimony and then get their family in order. The Code of Canon Law does not require such but, rather, only that both parents (if available) approve of their child receiving the sacrament and that the minister see evidence the child will be raised in the faith. I found myself in a difficult pastoral bind. I knew that multigenerational, extended families actively participate in the rearing of children (with elders traditionally being the ones to teach beliefs, virtues, ways of wisdom); thus, the latter criterion was not in question. Nor, it turned out, was the former, as fathers (sometimes responding from other villages) readily agreed with the mothers that their children should be baptized. Canon law made me sympathetic to these young people's requests for their children's baptisms, but I thought it wise to reserve my knowledge of it while trying to get advice to prevent my causing disruption to local pastoral practice.

One of the mothers challenged me in private conversation as to whether I, the white priest, was passing judgement on the worthiness of the children and their families. My concern, rather, was not to usurp the leadership of the deacon, whom I could not reach at his campsite on the tundra. I did, however, phone the regional pastor, who expressed familiarity with this type of scenario and did not object to my performing the rites. And so I did during the remaining Sunday Masses, while also glad that before my departure the deacon returned so that I could tell him directly what had transpired. Within the next couple of years, the diocesan chancery office clarified policy concerning visiting priests, including that deacons (in parishes that have them) should approve and oversee any requests for baptisms. From that point, I recall being engaged in but a few baptisms in Chevak and neighbouring Hooper Bay, whose parish at that time also had a Yup'ik deacon. Both of those elders were among the first group of Native married men chosen by their local people in the 1970s for training by the Jesuits and ordination by the Bishop of Fairbanks. I admired and enjoyed working with each of them, learning as best I could to wait on their words when, in my contrasting cultural mode, I was quick to ask questions seeking immediate answers.

The elder deacons embodied the Yup'ik ways with time: patient speaking and listening to the teachings and stories of their culture (one of the very last in North America to be reached by 'outsiders'),[7] repetitive practice of subsistence, hunting, household, spiritual and artistic practices, waiting upon the arrival of others, whether that be migratory creatures, seasonal plants, favourable changes in weather allowing for travel, or the slow but steady arrival of community members to a gathering of whatever sort. Truth's mediation over long arcs of time, which I attributed above to Christian sacramental tradition grounded in the incarnational paschal mystery, resonates profoundly with primordial Yup'ik tradition. An overview of their tradition, very brief due to the page limits of this chapter, is essential for interpreting the rest of my tale of ministry to baptism.

The historical arc of the presence of European and American Jesuits and various religious sisters from the late 1880s up to the 1960s entailed no small measure of what academics now characterize as colonialism, including the condemnation of the people's spiritual beliefs about their natural environment, various personal mores and their masked dancing traditions. Still, as various elders have explained to me over the years, the biblical message of one God who is Creator, Sustainer and Redeemer of all instantly found and continues to bear resonance with the Yup'ik belief in *Agayun*, the overarching and all-pervading source of life in the world. The Yup'ik world is deeply spirit-animated, with *Agayun* empowering episodic and sustained connections across creation. The Yup'ik symbolically perpetuate their cosmology and anthropology with circles, whether in carvings and woven crafts, standing together in prayer or sitting at such gatherings as dances. Traditional dance masks are ringed with hoops connecting symbols for animals, birds, fish and humans. The stories told in the dances bespeak myriad connections, ancient to recent, between creatures (human and others). An exemplary practical teaching is that if a man is lazy or mean to his family then a seal will observe this and not give himself up to him in the hunt. A virtuous hunter, having killed a seal, will immediately address the creature in gratitude and apologetic explanation that he needs to feed his people.

Much of this I learnt as guest of various men's evening-long sweat baths, the popular remnant of fire baths practised in the *gasgi* (men's communal house) of old. Men retold for my benefit stories of how whales of the sea can morph into wolves of the land, and vice versa, or eyewitness accounts of phantom figures shape-shifting or vanishing on the tundra. The most insightful, reflective among them explained how the message of the divine Father sending his Son in human form to teach and heal and give his very life for the salvation of all readily resonated with Yup'ik beliefs and ways. For nearly a century, the people quietly maintained their own traditions in tandem with the teachings, rituals and discipline of Catholicism but in such a way as not to mix them directly in church. Only with Vatican II and subsequent papal endorsement of inculturation have recent generations of priests and nuns sought to facilitate an integration of Yup'ik spirituality and symbolism with Catholic teaching and ritual. The results have been mixed. Consistent with their customary reverence for past elders (both their own and the church's), many older people proved resistant to modifying the strict symbolic boundaries set by earlier missionaries, while with increasing speed the younger generations have become indifferent to, if not rejecting of, Catholicism and even much of Yup'ik tradition. Now approaching their final years, the elders, many of whom three decades ago successfully led the cause for indigenous land, educational and other village rights, were reaching consensus that the contemporary shape of Catholicism comprised the last, best hope for perpetuating the similar values and related customs of Yup'ik heritage.

Indeed, I have continuously observed how, whereas regular Sunday services draw only a small percentage of the village population, Christmas Midnight Mass and the hours-long, elaborate Easter Vigil attract a packed house. People of all ages love the Vigil's opening service of fire and paschal light, joining creation and redemption, succeeded by readings spanning from Genesis through the prophecies of life-giving water and revitalizing Spirit to the resurrection gospel, followed by the blessing of water with baptismal renewal, and finally the eucharistic service. The night gets noisy with restless toddlers and children, gets hot and stuffy with people crowded into pews, on the floor and along the walls, and yet all are there through the joyous kiss of peace, which for practical reasons is saved for the very end. Everyone moves about to shake hands with all others, making the lengthy concluding gesture an exuberant enactment of the Yup'ik circle of life, a genuine instance of liturgical inculturation.[8] That exchange of the peace of the risen Christ is a far cry from earlier generations' silent witnessing of Mass on bended knee, and yet it exudes God's glory in human sanctification, holiness in the wholeness of the assembled body, despite all pains and struggles and losses, as Real People on their beloved land.

My baptismal experience in Chevak, nonetheless, comes full circle with Easter Sunday morning Masses in 2005 and 2007. In the first of those Holy Weeks, the deacon told me there would be a young couple bringing their baby for baptism on Easter. He explained that annual morning Mass was the occasion on which Father Fox, storied pastor to the region in the 1930s and 1940s, would baptize all the babies born in the previous several months. I was delighted that the community and I would have such a sacramental sign of the risen Christ – an actual baptism – to enhance the celebration. I preached a homily centred on the Holy Spirit as the power of God that incarnated his Son, anointed him in his baptism in the Jordan River and raised him from the dead. That same Spirit would now come upon the water in the white plastic, five-gallon bucket positioned by the paschal candle, I explained, as I called forward the young parents, baby and godparents. Feeling a sense of space and freedom – the permission of the people and the deacon, really – I took my time expounding on the significance of each symbolic step of the rite. Asking them the child's name, I acknowledged how among the several names given each Yup'ik baby is that of the most recently deceased person in the community, marking a continuity in spirits. As deacon, parents and godparents signed the cross on her tiny forehead, I instructed all to do this constantly with their children, a blessing they are empowered to give. And so forth.

Two things from my gradual experience in the villages motivated my approach. First, early on I had experienced how ineffective a pre-baptismal session with the parents and godparents consistently proved to be. It felt utterly artificial, and for the men, downright uncomfortable. But I knew, secondly, that the people's love of family as well as of ritual meant that once assembled, they were willing to spend as much time as necessary in the Mass. And so, I did not hold back as I catechized through the full complement of baptismal symbols, maximizing people's roles therein. I was consciously imitating the paschal mystagogy of the ancient church, drawing connections between symbols and the life of faith. Eyes and body language, attentive silence, and eager participation by the parents, godparents and wider families seemed evidence of a successful pastoral liturgy.

My hunch that the deacon (and, most likely, the people in conversation with him) held a similar view found confirmation when I was once more assigned to Chevak for Holy Week two years later. Upon my arrival, one of the first things the deacon wanted to tell me was that there would be lots of baptisms on Easter morning. I smiled at the prospect, realizing that the Yup'ik use the word 'lots' to indicate abundant generosity. Still, I could not have imagined the number of babies that morning would grow to 21! Knowing time was not an issue, that the people assembled to enter fully into the sacramental-ritual moment, I performed the symbols and spoke words of instruction and encouragement in a Mass that lasted two and a half hours. As the full church emptied afterwards, the deacon, his eyes sparkling in the subdued Yup'ik way of expressing joy, declared to me: 'Father Fox was here today. You had the spirit of Father Fox.' Very late that night, as I was packing for the next days' series of flights home, a knock sounded at the door. The primary leader of the Eskimo dancing (*yuraq*) presented me with a splendid mask he had crafted. You could have knocked me over with one of the feathers emanating from its circumference. Liturgy's gospel mission is an act of faith, of trust in truth's long mediations through generations, of hope amidst colliding cultures, of love renewed for lives of mutual service.

Notes

1 Edward Schillebeeckx, 1963, *Christ the Sacrament of the Encounter with God*, London: Sheed & Ward.

2 Constitution on the Sacred Liturgy, *Sacrosanctum Concilium*, Second Vatican Council, 1963, no. 7, http://www.vatican.va/archive/hist_councils/ii_vatican_council/documents/vat-ii_const_19631204_sacrosanctum-concilium_en.html.o

3 Constitution on the Sacred Liturgy, no. 5.

4 See, Jean-Louis Souletie, 2008, 'The Social Sciences and Christian Theology After Chauvet', in Philippe Bordeyne and Bruce T. Morrill (eds), *Sacraments: Revelation of the Humanity of God: Engaging the Fundamental Theology of Louis-Marie Chauvet*, Collegeville, MN: Liturgical Press, p. 195.

5 Ruth A. Meyers, 2014, *Missional Worship, Worshipful Mission: Gathering as God's People, Going Out in God's Name*, Grand Rapids, MI: Eerdmans, pp. 35–6.

6 For a brief overview of this fundamental concept in Karl Rahner's theology, arguing for how humans are by nature oriented to God's self-communication in the context of their lives, see William Madges, 2017, 'The Human Person: Fundamentally Open to the Transcendent', in Michael Daley and Dianne Bergant (eds), *Take & Read: Christian Writers Reflect on Life's Most Influential Books*, Berkeley, CA: Apocryphile Press, pp. 117–21.

7 See Ann Fienup-Riordan, 2005, 'Elders Spoke and Young People Listened', in *Wise Words of the Yup'ik People: We Talk to You Because We Love You*, translated from the Yup'ik by Alice Rearden, Lincoln, NE: Bison Books, pp. 1–43.

8 See Anscar J. Chupungco, 1998, 'Liturgy and Inculturation', in Anscar J. Chupungco (ed.), *Handbook for Liturgical Studies: Volume II: Fundamental Liturgy*, Collegeville, MN: Liturgical Press, pp. 337–75.

9

'beyond words, gestures and spaces – evoking and imagining liturgical contra*dictions*'

MICHAEL JAGESSAR

the shortest route to the future is always one that involves the *deepened understanding* of the past.[1]

'in this country you have an accent ... hate in this place is as restrained as the landscape'.[2]

I am yet to read of a Christian assembly confessing that its liturgical texts, rituals and practice exclude. 'Welcome' and good intentions of 'inclusion' of all sorts of diversity abound across notice boards, motivation for working groups on liturgical revision and mission statements of ecclesial communities. The reality, though, is that many still feel excluded and/ or experience exclusion. Even though privileged, I can recount numerous occasions of exclusion as an ethnic minority and as a 'multiple religious belonger'. The most telling bit, however, is that the exclusion may also come from people who may look like me, may have similar (not same) minority experiences or may hold so-called liberal and transgressive theological views.

In *Wikipedia and the Politics of Openness*, Nathaniel Tkacz[3] addresses one of the myths of technology's participatory potential: openness. The author argues that openness is a political project that obscures its own inner workings by sweeping power differentials and inequality under an apolitical rug. So, a project that proclaims itself 'open' can sidestep questions of power and agency even when it's clear that such issues remain. 'Openness' may contain the seeds of its own closure, especially given its reliance on a neoliberal market framework. What starts out as open and inclusive gets quickly hijacked by profit. The point for this essay is that hierarchy, power and privilege do not disappear even in so-called open and inclusive spaces. Exclusionary habits are so radically entrenched that good intentions on diversity and difference largely fail to undo the 'majoritarian norms' (such as whiteness, maleness, abled-bodiedness, heteronormative narratives and unhelpful binaries) that constitute liturgical practice and every part of our ecclesial life together. Heteronormativity in almost everything associated with Christian assembly continues to rule supremely.

In my work, theological writings and ministry practices (largely around inclusion and diversity content themes), I used to hold the view that 'minority-ness' serves the purpose of the dominant majority class if we continue to situate ourselves on marginal and peripheral places and if we remain locked in that place, on the periphery (real or imagined). In my own ecclesial community, I have tried to counter this by working with minority groups and privileged traitors from the 'majority enclave' to bring the connecting and intersecting discourses 'centre' stage on and around the common table at the heart of the church's life. The change I envisioned is yet to happen. Exclusion seems to thrive even more intensely. That dominant 'table-space' or 'centre' continues to find ingenious ways to hijack, co-opt and re-baptize 'minority-ness', to keep its own power and maintain its privilege, while giving the impression of an experience of total conversion towards a 'heaven on earth inclusion' landscape, life together embodying all the difference of the community. 'Majoritarian norms' and their agents find it extremely difficult to create space for difference around that common table.

The evidence around me is that the underlying architecture remains intact with token gestures to minority voices or to difference, drinking unwittingly from the cup of privileged salvation and falling prey to the many avatars of its alluring stupor. Power and privilege are often a no-go area, and convenient ways are found to allow these to remain intact through entitlement to rights and resources, knowledge production, comfort and attention, access to space, and deference. Even minorities are sucked into this pattern – while showing that the system is inclusive, that is *almost*.

The whole edifice and architecture needs to implode. I am now not sure that moving from periphery to centre offers abundant life for all. Centre is so 'fucked-up' (to draw on street parlance) that we lose integrity and authenticity. We may be comforted by significant parts of our gospel narrative, which underscores that the one who offers such abundance of overflowing generosity remained on the margins and got nailed outside the city. The verdict is still out as to how much of the 'old and inherited' is necessary or of value in the reconstructing of the new.

What follows here is a plea to evoke and imagine participatory and subversive spaces that will contribute to the implosion of the dominant liturgical edifice. While I can understand 'de-centring' of the dominant, with 'difference' assuming a central place, I am more inclined to instinctively follow my Caribbean plural heritages. I have learnt from this heritage about multiplicity, opacity and the rejection of oppositions between 'familiar' and 'other', or the one between 'centre' and 'periphery'. Rather than a reversal of the centre–periphery model, I prefer to play with its deconstruction.

Foremost questions for me are: In what ways can peripheral liturgical texts, gestures and spaces continue to contribute to and speed up this process of implosion (beyond margins and centres)? What shape should our interrogation take? What are some of the inherited liturgical deposits (texts, gestures, space, etc.) that underpin the 'majoritarian norms' of this architecture that we reinscribe? In what practical ways can Christian assemblies reflect multiple expressions of human difference that embody generosity, openness and abundance? At what point are we able to recognize (or dump) liturgical practices that are neither reflective of the ways of the divine nor capable of evoking transcendence? Can the re-conception of centre and periphery or marginal edges deliver liturgical texts, gestures and space from exclusionary captivity? Will bringing to the centre human difference undo exclusionary habits?

'in this country / I have not become British / but my island has become wider'[4]

I once came across a London Underground advertisement that reads: 'on first impression I may seem conservative'. After reading this essay, it would be possible to replace 'conservative' with a variety of other descriptors! First impressions can be deceptive in a world of complex identities. So, let me partially undress myself in your company – as it may help locate my thoughts. I am a complex Caribbean Diasporan traveller – accidentally landing on these shores and largely welcomed by some friendly natives. While I am a minority in a majority context in the UK, I am also privileged within my minority context. Though polio has left me scarred from a very young age, I am identified as able-bodied! My faith/spirituality has been informed and shaped by impulses from multiple religious and cultural traditions living in the fullness of two or three simultaneously. My God-talk (theology) is done within the rich world of diversity, identities, hybridity, impurity, many-one-ness, contradictions, fluidity and 'tidalectics' (ebb and flow), Anansi-ism (Caribbean saint and trickster figure) – with all the exciting possibilities and challenges these offer.

I found a home in what used to be a dissenting, non-conforming and minority heritage in the United Reformed Church (URC). As a minority church in three nations and dependencies, the URC wrestles with identity issues, diversity and inclusion in all sorts of ways. While we may have lost our non-conforming vigour, we have not given up on good intentions of creating spaces to give agency to all sorts of minorities. It is easier to 'talk the talk' than walk it. Though I was elected moderator of our General Assembly (2012–14), it did not mean that belonging was reconfigured to include the difference and culturally shaped giftings I brought to the table. One had to largely fit into a white-male-extroverted-heterosexual-able-bodied-English-cultural framework. To find a place in church as a minority is somehow to be generally complicit with the dominant ethos! I was invited centre stage but within the dominant group's terms of engagement. Everything about me, including my words, thoughts and accents were alien around that table. The most terrifying thing about it all is that I found myself being co-opted into spaces that I could not identify with, so becoming a 'black version' of the system. I have learnt not underestimate the power, hold and allure of the dehumanizing majoritarian norms. In that leadership role, my mind and integrity got 'screwed'. I had to find solace outside 'church', control my rapid weight loss and constantly manage my sanity/wellbeing in a variety of ways. Writing became part of my coping strategy.

My personal 'experience' of human difference in ecclesial assemblies of the URC and among ecumenical partners in the UK is captured by the Caribbean poet Kei Miller in the heading of this section: in many ways liturgical words, gestures and spaces continue to make me feel marginal while my world (island) has become broader. Is the problem because 'difference' is not yet co-opted as taking centre space in our liturgical/worship acts? I am now not sure that this is what I wish or that it will serve to displace the dominant mindset and some of the inherited deposits and practices that need expunging. Perhaps in seeking to evoke and imagine the participation of all that moves us 'beyond' while living with the contra*dictions*, I have reached a point where 'centre and periphery' continue to be the game of the privileged majority. I yearn for a space where the host and guest will be the manifold manifestations of a God who is vulnerable and grows with me.

'my grandmother only worshipped in tents. She believed / something was arrogant in stone and in cement ...'[5]

My grandmothers were Muslim (maternal) and Hindu (paternal). Their faith and faithfulness were practised outside fortress edifices. From them I have received multiple religious and spiritual blessings. I suspect that in Michelle Voss Roberts's categorization of models of Multiple Religious Belonging, I would be placed in the categories of popular ritual participation and hybrid identities on the borders of traditions and cultures.[6] Growing up in a context where my grandparents, parents and siblings on both sides were/are practising Hindus, Muslims and Christians, religion was the most observable fact of daily life. Religious diversity was a given in that very plural community in Guyana. My faith and spirituality have been informed and shaped by impulses from these religious traditions. I can see this in my own confidence to draw freely from various religious texts, to embrace diversity and to identify as a multiple 'belonger'. I have no choice but to live in the fullness of two or three simultaneously, much to the fear of 'mono' mindsets and less than generous orthodoxy of purists. With such an inheritance, one brings to their engagement a dialogical identity with no fixed and defining limitations. I am enabled to understand my own faith with a confidence that at the same time demands that I understand it differently.

Current liturgical practices (words, symbols and gestures) are unable to cater for 'multiple belongers'. I think that the default mode of liturgical practices heads in the direction of 'drawing the line at God' that 'shallows' the divine. Our liturgies are unable to grasp multiplicity in One though we deploy our inherited trinitarian formula with ease. Look closer at the rite of baptism or conversion, for instance. Where in our liturgies do we represent conversion as a continuous movement into a deeper experience of the divine, rather than a leaving of something behind? Inheritors of 'multiple religious socialization' do not necessarily despise or hate the religious traditions they have 'moved' from. I am certainly more at home in the Christian tradition, but not necessarily in opposition of what I have moved from. That would amount to denial, self-hate and erasure of too much of what is part and parcel of who I am.

Over the years, I practised theological self-control, reorientation of conscience and the development of 'multiple religious citizenship', with a commitment to the Jesus Way, open to the maverick movement of God's Spirit. Ecclesial and religious traditions are yet to find a theology to touch and embrace people with multiple religious identities and experiences – travellers, not cemented long-term boarders. Will new liturgies help us to reframe our theology of conversion and salvation? The fundamental challenge remains: the inherited theological understanding that insists that conversion must include a total divesting of oneself from one's cultural, religious and historical past. To erase a people's worldview from their consciousness seems insidious to me and a betrayal of incarnation. We should not underestimate the ways in which conversion has messed up the social and cultural identity of a person. Our liturgical imaging of a new creation in Christ, washing away of the old self and putting on a new identity must be radically reframed. Liturgical practices should evoke or point to rather than catechize or invest in arrogant exactitudes as in our baptismal liturgies.

'what is language but a sound we christen?'[7]

The reading and hearing of God's word has been and is an integral part of Christian worship. Early worshipping communities seemingly could not get enough of hearing Scripture. In one of the earliest descriptions of Christian worship (Justin Martyr, AD 155) we read that 'the memoirs of the apostles or the writings of the prophets are read, as long as time permits'. By the beginning of the seventh century, a listing of suggested Scripture readings for each worship service (known as a lectionary) had been established. The Reformers of the sixteenth century sought to keep Scripture at the heart of the church's life and worship. It was a clear expectation that when the word was read, God was again speaking to the gathered community. 'Words' – Scripture or our own words – are integral to worship in the Reformed tradition and the church. In the URC, we ordain people as 'ministers of the Word and Sacraments', yet there is little doubt which of the two is more prominent.

Our liturgies depend on words, imageries and symbols. We would largely agree that language is a human construct and that as such it is both limited and provisional. We may not, however, readily agree that we are chained by our limited use of words largely dictated by what we hold to as T/tradition. Drawing from the French theorist Roland Barthes who speaks of 'readerly' and 'writerly' texts, we can see that worship is based around a 'closed' readerly text (wordy sermons, Scripture readings, pastoral prayers, liturgies) delivered to a congregation in rows facing one direction (even in our newer arrangements), with (in the Reformed tradition) the most minimal of liturgical symbols and crafted to avoid incongruities and ambiguities or the audience going their own interpretative ways.[8] There is an attempt to control listening, discerning and speaking. Evoking is too risky, and so we end up with a diet of wordy junk food. Marilyn McEntyre's critique and warning may serve to highlight this point. Writing in *Caring for Words in a Culture of Lies*,[9] McEntyre compares language today like processed food nicely packaged with all its nutrients removed. Committed to 'words' though, she makes a case for 'loving words' if we are to challenge the prevailing culture of lies around us.

A culture of lies is not new in God-talk. Such has been with us in much of the writings of our inherited ecclesial habits, practices and theologies. 'Centering marginal communities' in liturgical theology, rites, symbols and practice, McEntyre's thesis that any vision and striving after a common good and any shape towards an inclusive beloved community must be related to our ability to care for words, is what we need to note. Words and language, however, are a matter of more than 'bad English' or the musicality of metaphors and hyperboles. It is the ability to deploy truth-telling that is elusive, counters institutional control, pushes the boundaries of conventional syntax, is relational, and flickers. And to trust that it is like drinking saltwater (you are thirsty for more).

While McEntyre's concern is the practice of precision, clarity and exactness in what we write and say, I would contend that it is precisely our obsession around precision in liturgical craft that continues to impoverish the diversity of our life together. Precision leads to closure on the divine or experiences of the sacred rather than risk evoking that will take us into unknown zones (de-centre all). But we can take from McEntyre that there may be an urgent need of 'clarifying where there is confusion; naming where there is evasion; correcting where there is error; fine-tuning where there is imprecision; satirizing where there is folly; changing the terms when the terms falsify'.[10]

One may reasonably contend that some of the fiercest ecclesial debates can be pared down to issues around identity and what shapes us through the dominance of words. Thus, we should not give light attention to the role of words and language in identity re/shaping for Christian communities. And our ideal emphasis/vision on full and active participation of all, where 'comprehensibility and speakability have become key concerns in the provision of all liturgical texts',[11] ought to make us wary of privilege and power. For questions remain about reading abilities, participation of those from oral cultures, language and other ways of experiencing the numinous/holy besides the medium of word and speech.

'straight lines on a map are decisions / made by men who knew nothing / of mountains or lakes or the spread / of aunts and uncles, or of language'[12]

In an online essay Marina Warner observes the following:

> When the Chinese artist Ai Weiwei dropped a 2,000-year-old ceramic vase and filmed the act of destruction (*Dropping a Han Dynasty Urn*, 1995), he was making an analogous claim: that when your liberties and your survival are endangered by state oppression, there are higher values than respecting centuries-old heritage. Privileging an artefact over the liberty of the human spirit is tantamount to worshipping false gods, to which the only riposte is an act of irreversible profanation.[13]

Liturgical theology and practices need an act of irreversible profanation that would bring about a radical change of mindset. Moving from the margins to the centre will not do.

I recall a conversation I had with Stephen Burns as we gladly received the announcement of the first female bishop for the Church of England. At some point during this conversation, Stephen remarked to me that he would rather a 'feminist bishop than a woman bishop'. That thought has stayed with me. Can I honestly say that a black Archbishop of York, a black moderator of the General Assembly of the URC or a black president of the Methodist Church made any difference to the 'operational ethos and theologies' of our respective ecclesial traditions, much less the worship life of these communities? Has an LGBTIQ leader in one of our 'established churches' brought in the change we all dream of? What changes, with them taking centre stage in the life of the church, do we see in liturgical theology and practice? I have seen little evidence that minorities are able to advance without being willing and able to imitate the status quo and embrace a white-male and heteronormative model of leadership and success.

The challenge and opportunity before us is the entrenched depth of our inherited deposit of faith, which is largely male-shaped-embodied and heteronormative. To overturn some of these sacred golden calves is daunting as we have to confront power, our own privilege and all the ambiguities we embody. Mary Beard in *Women and Power: A Manifesto* wrestles with 'just how embedded in Western culture are the mechanisms that silence women, that refuse to take them seriously and that sever them from the centres of power'.[14] Her point is that because the prejudice is so ingrained we need to contemplate 'how can we make ourselves more aware of the processes and prejudices that make us not listen to her'.[15] Beard sees a need to dig deeper, 'to go back to some first principles about the nature of spoken authority, about what constitutes it, and how we have learnt to hear authority where we do ... thinking more about fault-lines and fractures that underlie dominant male discourse'.[16] Her substantive point is that if marginal voices are not perceived to be able to take a place within the structures of power – to disrupt and renegotiate belonging – then it is power that needs to be redefined rather than the marginalized groups being redefined.[17] For it seems that the pivot around which all meaning is being constructed remains power and privilege.

My experience over the years in diversity–intercultural–racial justice awareness across the ecumenical landscape of the UK would endorse the reality of this entrenchment. Whiteness, maleness, straightness, meritocracy, the myth of a level playing field, fear and insecurity continue to rule. Despite the resources deployed, the good intentions demonstrated and all sorts of policies in place, we continue to experience a shrinking space when it comes to generosity.

'even God's limbs had to be torn before the world could sing ...'[18]

When we talk about centring marginalized communities, it's important to keep in mind that such communities are not homogeneous. For instance, queer, trans and gender-variant communities are likely to have different needs and priorities in different contexts. It's also important to keep in mind that even within such communities, there are privileged and sub-ordinated identities. For instance, white, cis folks carry privilege in queer communities; trans and gender-variant people of colour face compounded systems of oppression and inequalities.

In the context of 'beloved civil community', is it a liberal fantasy to imagine that there was and will ever be a space where all will participate equally?[19] Some contend that to suggest such a possibility is to ignore 'the politics and institutional biases of the public and private arenas in which different actors jostle for space, and in which a diverse range of political spaces are constantly being closed down and opened-up'.[20] This is not helped by the totalizing of the experiences of marginalized groups.[21] Structures find it convenient to dispel the intersecting dynamics of exclusion and play off marginalized groups by prioritizing injustices, resulting in 'oversimplifying the problem and misidentifying the potential solutions, and also erasure and appropriation of racial and gender justice struggles'.[22]

My experience across the UK is that those who gatekeep mainstream discourse and its space will co-opt and dictate the terms of engagement of minority/marginalized groups. At the same time, those that are call-ing for more radical and critical engagement face being delegitimized, replaced by more moderate and 'white-male' voices even though they may embody and speak from minority perspectives. In effect, the status quo engineers a crisis of solidarity. So protests such as 'Black Lives Matter' are quickly being delegitimized; Muslims are demonized under the pretence of a state of emergency; environmental activists are criminalized; whistle-blowers have to seek sanctuary in consulates; and justice movements find themselves caught between conservative and radical elements. What is happening here is that a privileged elite group that represents the status quo will do all within its reach to deal with any threat to its power base and privilege which feeds pernicious norms. The centre's tactic is to regu-late 'enabling environments' for minorities to deal with any transgressive liturgical input that would disrupt the ecclesial deposits that they continue to benefit from.

Once ecclesial communities are tied to the current neoliberal capitalist framework, they will find ways to deploy authoritarian habits, delegiti-mizing spaces where real change is possible. Are ecclesial communities, as Robin Myers asks, 'toxic beyond redemption' and should they be allowed to die to release Jesus? A good question when we honestly wrestle with what 'church' has turned into: an economic enterprise where grace is commodified, the thief passes as orthodoxy itself and none will give up their power base.[23]

'love is how our skin breaks against each other, / how we bleed into each other; how we heal'.[24]

The 2015 film *Look Who's Back*[25] is no laughing matter. What is striking is how close the film is to the truth of our reality. The largely positive reaction to Hitler from sensible people is a sobering reminder of the current growth of far-right politics, populism and how easily intelligent people are duped. What is it that feeds such latent prejudices and fear of differences? Where is it coming from? Hope in the future lies in a 'deepened understanding of the past', as Aimé Césaire puts it in my opening quote.

Notwithstanding the plethora of good intentions, the fear of differences continues and exclusion happens. We struggle to internalize 'welcome' as a habit and live it out. Is it because we are yet to bring 'difference centre stage'? I would not wish to dismiss this as a way forward. But after 20 years with this struggle in the UK, I am cynical that such a strategy will change much. The 'other' and his/her/their presence can be easily objectified when seen as the one to be incorporated around a 'table' (itself already a compromised and insider symbol) where belonging simply means: 'you join us', become like one of us and leave all your 'cultural and other trappings at the door'. Welcome in such a context then means coming to 'our' party around 'our rules'. Welcome, inclusion and openness do contain seeds of their own closure, especially if hierarchy, power and privilege do not disappear in our so-called welcoming, open and inclusive spaces.

I often think of the Seer's call (Rev. 18.4) to 'come out of her, my people' akin to the Rastafarian's call to 'come out of Babylon and the shitstem' as the appropriate tactic. The question is: Can we, citizens of two or more kingdoms, with complex allegiances ever totally be divested from the reach of 'empire'? I am not sure. What I am sure about is the need to come out and re-enter with a different tactic! Centre and periphery will have to go in allowing Jesus and the way of full life for all to be 'host, guest and stranger' simultaneously. Perhaps, we may then be in a better place to at least understand that 'we are all in need', that all need to be inconvenienced (especially insiders). Are we able to get out of our own way and seek not what we want but what needs changing around us?

Notes

1 Aimé Césaire, 2010 [1956], 'Culture and Colonization', *Social Text* 28, no. 2: 127–44 at 130.

2 Kei Miller, 2007, 'How We Became Pirates', in *There Is an Anger that Moves*, Manchester: Carcanet Press, p. 9.

3 Nathaniel Tkacz, 2015, *Wikipedia and the Politics of Openness*, Chicago/London: University of Chicago Press.

4 Miller, 'How quickly you grow', in *There Is an Anger*, p. 16.

5 Miller, 'Tangent a', in *There Is an Anger*, p. 24.

6 Michelle Voss Roberts, 2010, 'Religious Belonging and the Multiple', *Journal of Feminist Studies in Religion* 26, no. 1: 43–62.

7 Miller, 'Speaking in tongues', in *There Is an Anger*, p. 33.

8 See Susan Leigh Foster, 1985, 'Reading Dancing: Gestures Towards a Semiotics of Dance', PhD dissertation, University of California–Santa Cruz, pp. 76–7, 202–9; Frank Senn, 1983, *Christian Worship and Its Cultural Setting*, Philadelphia: Fortress Press; Catherine Bell, 1997, *Ritual: Perspectives and Dimensions*, New York/Oxford: Oxford University Press.

9 Marilyn McEntyre, 2009, *Caring for Words in a Culture of Lies*, Grand Rapids, MI: Eerdmans.

10 McEntyre, *Caring for Words*, p. 59.

11 Juliette Day, 2013, 'Language', in Juliette Day and Benjamin Gordon-Taylor (eds), *The Study of Liturgy and Worship*, London: SPCK, p. 66.

12 Miller, 'The Broken', in *There Is an Anger*, p. 49.

13 Marina Warner, 25 September 2015, 'Falling Idols: Public Monuments, Islamic State and Contesting the Story of the Past', *Frieze.Com*, https://frieze.com/article/falling-idols [accessed 26 July 2018].

14 Mary Beard, 2017, *Women and Power: A Manifesto*, London: Profile Books, p. xi.

15 Beard, *Women and Power*, p. 34.

16 Beard, *Women and Power*, pp. 40–1.

17 Beard, *Women and Power*, p. 83.

18 Miller, 'The Broken', in *There Is an Anger*, p. 47.

19 Ben Hayes, Frank Barat, Isabelle Geuskens, Nick Buxton, Fiona Dove, Francesco Martone, Hannah Twomey and Semanur Karaman, April 2017, 'On Shrinking Space: A Framing Paper', Amsterdam: Transnational Institute, https://www.awid.org/publications/shrinking-space-framing-paper [accessed 26 July 2018], p. 1.

20 Hayes et al., 'On Shrinking Space', p. 6.

21 Hayes et al., 'On Shrinking Space', p. 6.

22 Hayes et al., 'On Shrinking Space', p. 6.

23 Robin Meyers, 2009, *Saving Jesus from the Church: How to Stop Worshipping Christ and Start Following Jesus*, San Francisco: HarperOne, p. 10.

24 Miller, 'The Broken', in *There Is an Anger*, p. 49.

25 This film is based on the bestselling novel (2012) with the same name by Timur Vermes.

PART 4

Liturgy and Mission in the World

10

'All Are Welcome?': A Sermon[1]

TERESA BERGER

'All Are Welcome'[2] – so we sang in our opening hymn for this worship service. The hymn is among the most popular contemporary hymns, at least in English-speaking congregations in the United States. And its message is repeated not only in song but also in worship bulletins and church signs that enthusiastically proclaim, sometimes with accompanying visuals such as a rainbow flag, 'All Are Welcome'. The message is a posture of radical inclusion, and far be it from me to question the deepest truth of the claim. But like other sweeping claims – 'All lives matter' – this one too demands probing.

Our Gospel reading for today, Matthew 18.1–4 (NRSV), encourages such probing because it puts pressure on claims of radical inclusion. If one wanted to put Jesus' saying in this passage in a nutshell, it might be rendered thus: 'Some are more welcome than others.' Or, more pointed still: 'Unless you turn around, you will not enter the kingdom of heaven.' Jesus even uses a solemn 'Amen'-pronouncement here, for emphasis. In a way, he is saying, 'Unless you turn around, you will not be welcome in the reign of God.'

This is a stark claim, and one that would not sing well as an opening in a worship service. But Matthew is actually kind to the disciples in the way in which he depicts them in the opening of chapter 18 of his Gospel. The Gospel of Mark, which also includes this story, introduces it by depicting the disciples as arguing among themselves about who is the greatest (Mark 9.34). They fall into an embarrassed silence when Jesus asks what they were arguing about. Matthew, on the other hand, simply has the disciples muse – somewhat innocently? – 'hmmm, we wonder who might be the greatest in God's reign?' In both Gospels, however, Jesus' response strikes the same note: if you want to be great, turn to smallness. And for visual emphasis, Jesus places a child in the midst of the disciples.

Much ink has been spilled on the meaning of the term *paidion* – 'child' – here (and elsewhere in the Gospels). Never mind that interpreters over almost two millennia have gone for a 'nice' or 'ideal' child; even with that, interpretations have ranged broadly indeed: from the child as a symbol of prepubescent purity and sweet innocence, to infantile humility and trust, to happy and worry-free dependence. In recent decades, with growing emphasis on the social location of New Testament texts, the focus has shifted to the low social status of children in the ancient world: namely, children were insignificant and without legal standing. It is no coincidence that the word/s for child can also be used to mean 'slave'.

But whatever the precise meaning of 'child' here is, the conversation between the disciples and Jesus in this Gospel passage clearly turns around notions of hierarchy and difference, with Jesus turning upside down established notions of status. The lowly will be the highest. The first will be last. The last will be first.

What to make of this Gospel, for us today? Let me suggest one possible lens. I think this text confronts us with rivalling ways of self-identifying and ways of naming ourselves – our chosen markers of difference, if you will. Jesus is presented with one particular marker of difference (which also sits on top of a social hierarchy): 'the greatest'. He challenges his disciples to claim a different marker, in the opposite direction of the 'greatest', namely the smallest, a child.

For the disciples, this must have been a familiar note in many ways. They had already encountered Jesus as one who proclaims and embodies a reign of God that topples the mighty from their thrones and lifts up the lowly; where the rich are sent empty away and the hungry are fed; where the poor in spirit enter God's reign; where the way to life opens in dying.

Did this memory of Jesus' proclamation put an end to the disciples arranging themselves by markers of difference and status? No. The second reading in our worship service today, Galatians 3.27f., makes clear that issues of naming differences continued to trouble the early Christian communities. The apostle Paul, in his letter to the Galatians, had to remind a divided community, over and against specific markers of difference, that they were all baptized into Christ. And therefore, Paul claims, there is 'neither Jew nor Greek, there is neither slave nor free person, there is not male and female; for you are all one in Christ Jesus'. Paul names differences here according to some basic binaries of his time and culture: Jew versus Greek, slave versus free, man and woman. He leaves other important binaries invisible, however, such as young and old, and rich and poor. Furthermore, he occludes in his list markers of difference that would soften the stated binaries, for example, eunuchs and persons with intersex conditions. All this really goes to say is that naming differences – never mind honouring or subverting them – is a complicated task indeed. The differences we choose to name, after all, are never innocent; they always both highlight and occlude.

Here are a couple of examples from my own experience. When I first came to the United States many years ago, I was confronted with ways of naming differences and marking one's identity that were utterly foreign to me. There was one particular moment that crystallized this feeling for me. I had to fill in a form that wanted to know my 'race'. Coming from Germany, this seemed an exceedingly dangerous category to fit human beings into. Even worse was the fact that I could find nothing on the list of possible categories that resembled anything I knew about myself. When a friend informed me that I should check 'Caucasian', I protested loudly: what on earth did I have to do with a mountain range in the then-Soviet Union? Soon, however, I started to teach in this context, and acknowledging one's social location was a fashionable way to begin. In my case, the race–class–gender narrative went something like this: I am white, and originally from Europe; I am a woman; I was raised in an upper middle-class context and educated in European universities. Now fast-forward to today. None of these markers of difference have really changed, but how to name them has morphed, and other ways of self-identifying have emerged. For example, the 'woman' I am might be described as cisgender. Just as important to me now is to acknowledge the fact that I reside in the traditional homelands of the indigenous Quinnipiac peoples. And, taking to heart the recent book *Watershed Discipleship*,[3] I should note that I live in the Quinnipiac River watershed of southern Connecticut. In short, naming my markers of difference is an ever-changing task.

What does all this have to do with our Gospel text for today, and with Christian faith and worship in our time? I cannot help but wonder whether the complexity of adequately naming differences is one of the reasons for the popularity of Marty Haugen's hymn 'All Are Welcome'. The inclusivity and elasticity of the 'all' allows some communities to envision a rainbow flag while singing, and others to welcome an undocumented immigrant asking for sanctuary. On the other side of the spectrum might be welcome for a pregnant woman carrying a severely disabled child in her womb who is determined to carry her unborn child to term because 'all are welcome' – the born and the unborn. Who would deny her a claim on this radical inclusivity?

The latter example already gestures towards the differences we all inscribe, in one way or another, into the 'all'. Think of the song 'For Everyone Born, a Place at the Table'[4] (I simply note that there doesn't seem to be a place for the 'unborn'). In one of the verses, there is the following line: 'For just and unjust, a place at the table, abuser, abused, with need to forgive ...' I am not so sure about that (radical? or simply facile?) inclusion of 'abuser and abused' in one breath. But one thing I am sure about: the struggle over differences is not easily settled, in worship as in the rest of life.

Maybe a final look back to the Gospel for today can help. In contradistinction once again to the Gospel of Mark, Matthew begins his Gospel not with Jesus' entry into public ministry but rather with Jesus' genealogy, birth and earliest days. In other words, Matthew begins his Gospel with Jesus as child. This child Jesus is four things for Matthew: the human face of God in our midst; exceedingly vulnerable (a newborn, a refugee); threatened with death – and not just the high infant mortality of his time but violent death by a ruling elite (Herod); and finally, a child who only lives because others commit to sheltering his life. Those committed to sheltering his life included his mother, his adoptive father Joseph and some wise visitors. This is the child that opens Matthew's Gospel.

When Jesus puts a child in the midst of the disciples and tells them to become children in order to enter God's reign, he might just be inviting them to model their life on his: to enter the world, not by their own power but God's, to become small signs of God's presence on the margins of power, safeguarded by God's promise and the courage of friends.

When we take upon ourselves to sing 'All Are Welcome', we do well to remember this: just like none of us can actually succeed in making ourselves small as a child, so 'welcoming all' exceeds even the highest of our human abilities. Certainly, welcoming all demands more than a purely human capacity to be 'nice', and even more than our own struggle to welcome a diversity of voices – rather than merely those diversities we ourselves favour, or our own particular community already presents us with. The power behind the invitation 'all are welcome' has to be God's. So yes, all are welcome. All are welcome to turn, to live the gospel and to seek to enter God's reign. Ultimately, we dare to sing, because this is *God's* invitation, not one of our own making.

Notes

1 This sermon was preached at Yale Divinity School's Marquand Chapel during a regular morning service in the Fall of 2017.

2 Marty Haugen, 1994, Chicago: GIA Publications.

3 Ched Myers, 2016, *Watershed Discipleship*, Eugene, OR: Cascade Books.

4 Shirley Erena Murray, 1998, 'A Place at the Table', Carol Stream, IL: Hope Publishing Co.

11

Preaching in an Age of Disaffiliation: Respecting Dissent While Keeping the Faith

EDWARD FOLEY, OFM CAP

Introduction

In his popular study of the universe entitled *The Whole Shebang*, Timothy Ferris laments what he calls the 'sadness' of maps. This sadness arises from the fact that, despite the best intentions of those who craft them, all maps are imperfect since they 'represent the territory under investigation more economically than does the territory itself, they inevitably contain less information',[1] thus being more *exclusive* than *inclusive*. Second, maps introduce distortion, as they are two-dimensional guides to a three-dimensional reality.

There is a similar 'sadness' about titles, whether those of movies or theological essays. While intended to elicit interest or provoke curiosity, they – like maps – are necessarily exclusive and introduce distortion. Thus, the title of this essay is both a pastoral provocation and at least a distorted if not inaccurate caricature of both the current age and the nature of preaching.

While one could characterize the current age from the perspective of dominant culture United States as a time of religious disaffiliation, this characterization is also inaccurate. In my own church (Roman Catholic), the group we are bleeding the most is 18- to 35-year-olds. However, many are not actually leaving their spiritual homes or religiously disaffiliating. As Kate Devries pointedly noted in a response to the 'Catholics Come Home' movement, you cannot invite young adults 'home' to a church that for many was never really their home in the first place.[2] Young adults are not leaving home; rather, many are simply abandoning the religious affiliation of their parents that many presumed would be their home, but never was.

Disaffiliation is one aspect of this era of spiritual fluidity that renders preaching within a faith tradition challenging. Maybe the topic is better served by migrating to the more porous framework of liquidity.

Our Liquid World

In his celebrated 2000 publication, Zygmunt Bauman christened the current era one of 'liquid modernity'.[3] While previous historical periods have witnessed cycles of sometimes-radical disintegration and renewal, Bauman argues that current modernity is different. Whereas the 'solids' of a previous era were deconstructed but then replaced by new solids, in this modernity melting solids are not being displaced by new and improved ones. Rather, the state of commerce, relationships, society and even self-identity are characterized by liquidity, deregulation, liberalization and 'flexibilization': constantly poised for change.[4]

The Christian churches have recently experienced waves of such liquidity in multiple and shocking ways. One such tsunami that hit the Roman Catholic Church in the United States was the 2007 Religious Landscape Study from the Pew Forum on Religion and Public Life, which noted that roughly one in ten adults in the United States were former Roman Catholics; if they gathered together as a new 'church' they would be the third largest Christian denomination in the United States.[5] A parallel tidal wave that hit virtually all US religious institutions was the recognition that almost 15 per cent of all adults in the United States had no religious affiliation. That number has grown so quickly that in 2014 Pew reported that 'the number of Americans who do not identify with any religion continues to grow at a rapid pace. One-fifth of the US public – *and a third of adults under 30* – are religiously unaffiliated today.'[6]

An even more telling sign of religious liquidity is the degree of disaffiliation occurring among those who still identify with some religious body and even frequent our sanctuaries with some regularity. Already in 1985 Andrew Greeley documented the widespread phenomenon of 'cafeteria Catholicism', i.e. adherents who pick and choose among the teachings and practices of the church they wish to hold or observe.[7] A stark example is Greeley's 2010 report that demonstrated only 7 per cent of Roman Catholics in Chicago at that time accepted what Greeley called 'the 5 big rules', i.e. the church's stance against abortion, against birth control, against divorce, against gay marriage and for infallibility.[8]

Another frame for considering this phenomenon in Roman Catholicism is secular or cultural Catholicism. Tom Beaudoin actually believes that the majority of US Catholics today can be characterized as secular or cultural Catholics. By these terms, Beaudoin refers

> to those with a Catholic heritage ... who cannot find Catholicism central to the everyday project of their lives ... Secular Catholics are typically baptized Catholics who, by the time of adulthood, find themselves having to deal somehow with their Catholicism, and do so as

an irremediable aspect of their identity ... Secular Catholics find their Catholicism existentially 'in play' at some level that cannot be dispensed with, but do not or cannot make of it a regular and central set of explicit and conscious practices.[9]

A pointed example of cultural Catholicism was the published comment of Illinois appellate judge Sheila O'Brien: 'Would someone in Rome formally excommunicate me, please? I want to be excommunicated by the Roman Catholic Church because walking away will break my heart.'[10] A similar sentiment was expressed by Kate Henley Averett, who wrote, 'I'm sure I believed ... that I could remain a Catholic despite the institutional Church, but ... This place has become too foreign to me, and I can no longer call it home. And I'm so, so sad about that. My heart is so heavy it feels like it's crushing me.'[11]

German sociologist Ulrich Beck, celebrated for writing about the emergence of 'a risk society',[12] argued that one of the more challenging frameworks operative in such a society is what he calls 'zombie concepts'. Zombies are the living-dead, and a zombie concept[13] is a social concept that is increasingly impotent (or dead) – such as social class and family – but a concept that scholars yet keep alive to describe the growing fiction of traditional social institutions.[14] While such zombie concepts have lost their 'explanatory power', according to Beck, they are still powerful in that they legitimize practices, actions and explanations. So the question: Is the very idea of liturgical preaching – as well as the worship that provides its context – developing into a zombie concept that is increasingly impotent in its impact except maybe for legitimizing the role of the preacher?

Zombie categories emerged in the framework of Beck's larger work on reflexive modernization, which among other things calls into question the production and reproduction of knowledge between the laity and the experts. Beck argues that, in many cases, 'lay people were probably much more knowledgeable ([or] aware) about what was going on around them than the experts ... charged with responding to challenges faced by society'.[15]

The implications of Beck's work for religious institutions and key practices of those institutions such as preaching are critical. In this epoch of liquid society and liquid faith, he challenges us not to allow churches, mosques or synagogues to become zombie institutions, whose central energies go towards legitimizing practices, beliefs or religious power structures. He also prods us to theologize from the bottom up, recognizing the agency and expertise of what he calls 'lay people' rather than instinctively relying upon the insights and analysis of the so-called experts. Yet here's the Beckian rub: if those who attend the preaching event are increasingly liquid in their faith, cafeterial in their creed and polydoxical in their spirituality, how do we honour their practical and embodied intelligence about religion, God or worship? How do we respect them as subjects of religious knowing without turning potentially zombie faith communities into arenas of free-believing or self-constructed religion?

While some contemporary thinkers do not believe that religion can make much of a contribution in this liquid era, Beck believes otherwise, positing that religion can be a useful tool in the contemporary project of 'realistic cosmopolitanism'. While acknowledging the destructive capacity of religiously inspired violence – both past and present – he opines:

> it is hardly possible to overstate the potential of the religions as cosmopolitan actors – not only because of their ability to mobilize billions of human beings across barriers of nation and class, but because they exercise a powerful influence on the way people see themselves and their relationship to the world. Above all, they represent a resource of legitimation in a battle for the dignity of human beings in a civilization at risk of destroying itself. Thus, what is on the agenda is the competence and readiness of the world religions to assume the role of spokespeople and champions on issues affecting humankind: climate change, the plight of the poor and excluded and, not least, the dignity of ethnic, national and religious others.[16]

Beck has given us a credible path forward for rethinking worship and the preaching that punctuates it in this liquid age. Maybe the call is no more preaching from the inside out, idealizing our religious community as a 'light to the nations', or worship as 'mission-sending' whose trajectory only moves in one direction: from organ or altar or bema or prayer rug to the world. Maybe this is a pivotal moment to re-envision preaching and its worship context in a distinctively Johannine mode: in service to a world where God's Spirit already and constantly broods, embracing anew Karl Rahner's contention that the liturgy of the world, not the liturgy of church, mosque or synagogue is primary.[17] This is a liturgical recalibration that fashions liturgical preaching which is not only attentive to the spiritual needs of our coreligionists, but transmutes into public theology responding to a world threatened with environmental risks and the growing marginalization of the poor.

Preaching as Public Theology

In my own tradition, preaching is construed in multiple ways, almost exclusively envisioned as a clerical enterprise. Burke and Doyle summarize the canonical view of Roman Catholic preaching as 'a graced moment in which those mandated by the Church present, explain, persuade and empower the listeners to envelop themselves in God's word and, thereby, to believe'.[18] After Vatican II, Roman Catholic seminarians were frequently taught that the four basic types of preaching were evangelization, catechesis, *didaskalia* and the homily, with only the latter being properly liturgical.

Disproportionately influential was the 1982 document *Fulfilled in Your Hearing*, which defined the homily as 'a scriptural interpretation of human existence which enables the community to recognize God's active presence, to respond to that presence in faith through liturgical word and gesture, and beyond the liturgical assembly, through a life lived in conformity with the Gospel'.[19] Devoid of what David Tracy calls the 'analogical imagination', its emphasis on preaching Scripture sounds oddly Protestant to these Roman Catholic ears. Even more zombiesque is its centripetal focus on the spiritual development and evangelical living only of believers, possibly camouflaging an underlying subtext concerned with promoting church membership.

While an understandable strategy for maintaining institutions in an age of solids – when defections from one faith community to another were only calculated in terms of erosion and diminishment – this preaching trajectory seems less useful in this heightened fluid environment. More fertile, from my perspective, is the homiletic stepchild known as public theology.

Martin Marty defined public theology as an effort to interpret the life of a people in the light of a transcendent reference. The goal of public theology is not helping individuals reflect upon their personal relationship with God, nor evangelization bent on corralling new adherents, but instead is theologizing concerned with influencing and shaping 'civil, social and political life from a theological point of view'.[20] Marty has persuaded me to reconsider the nature of preaching and worship no longer as what I would caricature as an in-house strategy for engineering the salvation of its adherents and the collateral fiscal and political support of its participants. Rather, preaching in this liquid age seems better conceived as a form of public ritualizing: a creedal enactment announcing essential beliefs and values not only in full view of society but, even more so, for the sake of that society. This is preaching retuned not for maintaining and expanding the body of adherents, but for promoting the common good.

Three major objections to this reframed approach to preaching spring to mind. First, it seems to abandon what might be considered the religious community's 'spiritual base'. On the other hand, maybe preaching as public theology is not so much an abandonment of the base as an effort to prod them into the lived evangelization that Pope Francis contends is the responsibility of every Christian.[21] Francis voiced his concern about the laity, especially those that take up various forms of ministry, because their ecclesial involvement is 'not reflected in a greater penetration of Christian values in the social, political and economic sectors ... [and seems devoid of] a real commitment to applying the Gospel to the transformation of society'.[22] From a missiological perspective, the church does not exist to serve itself but to contribute to the *missio Dei* and the inbreaking of God's reign throughout the world.[23] Preaching recalibrated as public theology more properly serves that purpose.

Second, while preaching to the disaffiliated seems like preaching to a phantom assembly, given the state of cafeteria religiosity, polydoxy and deconversion in this country, are not many of our assemblies already peppered with pew-dwellers of variegated interest and commitment? That equation tilts even more towards the so-called 'nones' on holydays become holidays such as Christmas and Easter. And then ponder all of those occasional services – especially the weddings and funerals, but also the baptisms and bar mitzvahs – attended by a whole panoply of believers and seekers. Isn't every funeral, especially of the young, an exercise in kaleido-scopic believing? Even the obsequies for an octogenarian grandmother convene in a unique and unrepeatable way not only the disaffiliated from her own offspring, but grandchildren with their Buddhist partners, sup-ported by their Sikh friends and humanist co-workers.

Third, preachers are not called to abandon their tradition when preaching in this public mode, but are respectfully called to exploit the pluriformity of resources within our traditions that extend an invitation of common ground to the hearers. While admittedly as much construct-ing as utilizing what was handed on to him (cf. 1 Cor. 11.23), Paul offers one model for this in his celebrated preaching at the Areopagus (Acts 17.22–31). Paul had done his homework. His speech indicates that he understood the local philosophies and was quite knowledgeable about Greek and Roman gods.[24] While he sprinkles his speech with citations from familiar Greek sources and even employs conventional patterns of Greco-Roman rhetoric, he does not water down the gospel message but contextualizes it in order to make it more palatable to his Athenian audience.[25]

Rather than rhetorically circling the wagons, this disquisitional approach is more resonant with what Pope Francis and others have envisioned as the creation of a 'new Areopagus' – a fresh incarnation of the court of the Gentiles, special places of encounter 'where believers and non-believers are able to engage in dialogue about fundamental issues ... and about the search for transcendence'.[26] Francis believes that engaging the unaffiliated and agnostics is critical, as he deems them 'precious allies' especially 'in the commitment to defending human dignity, in building peaceful co-existence between peoples and in protecting creation'.[27] This is Beck redux, religion as cosmopolitan actor, representing 'a resource of legitimation in a battle for the dignity of human beings in a civilization at risk of destroying itself'.[28]

The Strategic Move

One key theological step towards shaping such centrifugal preaching that nurtures dialogue without abandoning one's base faith community or foundational religious traditions is the cultivation of a positive theological anthropology. It is difficult to extend an invitation to common ground if I intuit that the ground that I inhabit is fundamentally graced, while that of my invitees is essentially corrupt. Such a rift is too wide for the mutuality this endeavour requires. A positive theological anthropology is not one that ignores sin, error or corruption. Paul did not gloss over the pervasive idolatry of ancient Athens on that Areopagan outcropping, yet he also approached his hearers respectfully, going so far as to acknowledge that, in every respect, they were very religious (Acts 17.22).

Leading with a favourable view of humanity is not only strategically important but also theologically critical, since Catholic Christian traditions affirm that eternal transcendence assumed humanity, and in doing so divinity testified to the fundamentally graced nature of all humanity. In the words of Leonardo Boff, the Word made flesh not only introduced something new – such as resurrection – but also fundamentally revealed the holiness of all people and things.[29] Thus, the mystery of incarnation is neither spent nor confined to the only-begotten but continues in the being and bones of every woman and man.[30]

If there is wisdom in the maxim that grace builds on nature, then the preaching event – at least for Christians – must be incarnational, grounded in the very humanity that all people have in common, and which the Dalai Lama pointedly notes is the only thing that has the potential to unite us all.[31] Similarly Pope Francis consistently emphasizes the significance, even primacy of humanity in the evangelizing process,[32] which requires keeping 'an ear to the people' and developing the ability to link sacred texts 'to a human situation, to an experience which cries out for the light of God's word'.[33]

This is preaching reimagined as an exercise in Christian humanism, a framework that has gained increasing currency, particularly within Roman Catholicism. In 2009, Benedict XVI proposed that 'Christian humanism' was an appropriate stance in response to the economic policies of this globalized age.[34] Decades before, Paul VI spoke about our life newly enhanced through incarnation, through which it acquires 'a transcendent humanism'; on that theological foundation he called for a 'new humanism that will guarantee authentic human development'.[35] This 'full-bodied humanism', in Paul's view, leads to the fulfilment of the whole person and every person, yet also points the way towards God.[36] More recently, on multiple occasions, Pope Francis has called for a 'new' and 'renewed' humanism in Christ.[37]

The preaching strategy that arises from this anthropological turn is not one that commences with insider beliefs or in-house rules, which exact too high a toll from seekers or visitors. Rather than declaring some christo-logical or trinitarian imperative, my task is first to engage the depth of people's humanity through concrete interface with some current event or social reality that resonates across the believing spectrum of the assembled. There are sufficient illustrations of racism, sexism, nativism and violence bombarding the airwaves for eliciting just anger, narrative empathy and basic compassion across a wide swathe of hearers. On a more positive note, there is such an abundance of beauty and goodness, hospitality, and sheer humanity afoot in our communities that those who take a more appreciative approach have a myriad of launching points as well.

Leading with the human condition, in all of its joys and griefs – espe-cially in narrative mode[38] – is the strategy that I have adopted for preaching in this age of disaffiliation. My reasons for the narrative turn are legion. Anthropologists have well documented the importance of storytelling for the emergence of cultures, and social scientists have explained that storytelling is a fundamental way that human beings communicate them-selves and their world to others.[39] Recently neuroscientists have taken this narrative insight and amplified it through stunning scientific findings. By employing magnetic resonance imaging, scientists have demonstrated that vivid storytelling can light up as many as seven different parts of the brain, in comparison to what happens when only information is communicated.

Professor Paul Zak of Claremont Graduate University pushes even fur-ther. In the past decade, his lab discovered that the chemical in the brain oxytocin is key to signalling that another person or situation is 'safe'. 'It motivates cooperation with others ... by enhancing the sense of empathy, our ability to experience others' emotions.'[40] He further reports that com-pelling human stories consistently prod the brain to produce oxytocin, effectively engage listeners and motivate them to respond empathetically.

This neuroscience corroborates an insight from philosopher Richard Kearney, who argues that an empathetic imagination is a *narrative imagin-ation*. The failure of the narrative imagination, according to Kearney, makes possible genocides and atrocities. He concludes, 'if we possess narrative sympathy – enabling us to see the world from the other's point of view – we cannot kill. If we do not, we cannot love.'[41]

Recovering *Leitourgia*

Using a sometimes-flawed philological argument, it is common to explain the nature of liturgy through the mistranslation of the Greek words *laos* and *ergon* rendering liturgy as 'the work of the people'. That suggests that worship, in Christian terms, is a semi-Pelagian enterprise that largely ignores the theological tenet that liturgy is something that God does in Christ through the Spirit. If we ponder the original usage in ancient Greece, *leitourgia* was not simply work that people did, but a public work accomplished – especially by the privileged and powerful – on behalf of ordinary folk, such as sponsoring a festival, commissioning a play, underwriting sporting events or leading a diplomatic delegation to another city-state. Consequently, *leitourgia* is best translated not as 'the work of the people', but rather 'work for the people'.

From an Areopagan perspective, the 'people' for whom this work is done are not simply the baptized but the whole people of God, including those non-theistic 'precious allies' of whom Pope Francis spoke. If Christianity exists not simply in service of its own mission – a surefire formula for becoming a zombie institution – but in service of God's mission to the world, then it seems right and just that my tradition's preaching and ritualizing, praying and singing, processing and communing must also be in mission to that same world.

Notes

1 Timothy Ferris, 1998, *The Whole Shebang: A State-of-the-Universe(s) Report*, New York: Touchstone, p. 71.

2 Katherine DeVries, 2007, 'New Evangelization and Young Adult Catholics: Movement toward a Renewal of Faith', unpublished D.Min. thesis-project, Chicago: Catholic Theological Union, p. 175.

3 Zygmunt Bauman, 2000, *Liquid Modernity*, Cambridge, UK: Polity; in subsequent years with the same publisher he produced, among other works, *Liquid Love* (2003), *Liquid Life* (2005), *Liquid Fear* (2006), and *Liquid Times* (2006).

4 Bauman, *Liquid Modernity*, p. 3.

5 Pew Research Forum on Religion and Public Life, 25 February 2008, *US Religious Landscape Survey: Religious Affiliation: Diverse and Dynamic*, http://www.pewtrusts.org/en/research-and-analysis/reports/2008/02/25/us-religious-landscape-survey-religious-affiliation [accessed 2 June 2017].

6 Pew Research Religion & Public Life Project, 9 October 2012, '"Nones" on the Rise', http://www.pewforum.org/2012/10/09/nones-on-the-rise/ [accessed 15 February 2017], emphasis mine.

7 Andrew Greeley, 1985, 'Cafeteria Catholicism: Do You Have to Eat Everything on Your Plate?' *U.S. Catholic* 50, no. 1: 18–25.

8 Andrew Greeley, 2010, *Chicago Catholics and the Struggles Within Their Church*, Piscataway, NJ: Transaction Publishers.

9 Tom Beaudoin, 2011, 'Secular Catholicism and Practical Theology', *International Journal of Practical Theology* 15: 22–37, at 24.

10 Sheila O'Brien, 4 August 2010, 'Excommunicate Me, Please', *Chicago Tribune*, http://articles.chicagotribune.com/2010-08-04/news/ct-oped-0804-excommunicate-20100804_1_excommunication-bishops-hierarchy [accessed 3 July 2017].

11 Kate Henley Averett, 2014, 'The Stories We Tell', in Christine Firer Hinz and J. Patrick Hornbeck (eds), *More than a Monologue: Sexual Diversity and the Catholic Church*, New York: Fordham University Press, pp. 143–9 at p. 148.

12 See Beck, 1992 [1986], *Risk Society: Towards a New Modernity*, London: Sage Publications.

13 Ulrich Beck, 2002, 'The Cosmopolitan Society and Its Enemies', *Theory, Culture and Society* 19, nos. 1–2: 14–18.

14 See the useful summary in Paul W. Chan, 2013, 'A Zombie Existence: Exploring Ulrich Beck's Zombie Categories and Construction Management Research', in S. D. Smith and D. D. Ahiago-Dagbui (eds), *Proceedings of the 29th Annual ARCOM Conference*, Reading, UK, pp. 1059–69.

15 Chan, 'A Zombie Existence', p. 1063.

16 Ulrich Beck, 2010, *A God of One's Own: Religion's Capacity for Peace and Potential for Violence*, trans. R. Livingstone, Cambridge, UK: Polity, p. 198; also, see Simon Speck, 2013, 'Ulrich Beck's "Reflective Faith": Individualization, Religion and the Desecularization of Reflexive Modernity', *Sociology* 47, no. 1: 157–72.

17 See Karl Rahner, 1976, 'Considerations on the Active Role of the Person in the Sacramental Event', in *Theological Investigations XIV: Ecclesiology, Questions in the Church, The Church in the World*, trans. David Bourke, New York: Seabury Press, p. 169; for a further expansion, see Michael Skelley, 1991, *The Liturgy of the World: Karl Rahner's Theology of Worship*, Collegeville, MN: Liturgical Press.

18 John Burke and Thomas Doyle, 1986, *The Homilist's Guide to Scripture, Theology and Canon Law*, New York: Pueblo, p. 42.

19 National Catholic Conference of Bishops' Committee on Priest Life and Ministry, 1982, *Fulfilled in Your Hearing*, Washington, DC: USCCB Publishing, no. 82.

20 Martin Marty, 1981, *The Public Church*, New York: Crossroad Press, p. 16.

21 Pope Francis, 24 November 2013, *The Joy of the Gospel*: Evangelii Gaudium, http://w2.vatican.va/content/francesco/en/apost_exhortations/documents/papa-francesco_esortazione-ap_20131124_evangelii-gaudium.html [accessed 15 August 2017], no. 10, also no. 111.

22 *The Joy of the Gospel*, no. 102.

23 Seminal here is the work of David J. Bosch, e.g., 1991, *Transforming Mission: Paradigm Shifts in Theology of Mission*, Maryknoll, NY: Orbis Books.

24 vanThanh Nguyen, 2015, 'Preaching in the New Testament', in Edward Foley (ed.), *A Handbook for Catholic Preaching*, Collegeville, MN: Liturgical Press, pp. 41–50, at p. 47.

25 Nguyen, 'Preaching in the New Testament', p. 48.

26 *The Joy of the Gospel*, no. 257.

27 *The Joy of the Gospel*, no. 257.

28 Cf. note 18 above.

29 Leonardo Boff, 1987, *Sacraments of Life: Life of the Sacraments*, Washington, DC: Pastoral Press, p. 68.

30 Cf. Pope Francis, 1 June 2013, 'The Scandal of the Incarnation', https://w2.vatican.va/content/francesco/en/cotidie/2013/documents/papa-francesco-cotidie_20130601_scandal-incarnation.html [accessed 8 August 2017].

31 Dalai Lama, 2011, *Beyond Religion: Ethics for a Whole World*, Boston/New York: Houghton Mifflin Harcourt, especially chapter 2, 'Our Common Humanity', pp. 21–9.

32 *The Joy of the Gospel*, no. 55.

33 *The Joy of the Gospel*, no. 154.

34 Benedict XVI, 29 June 2009, *In Charity and Truth:* Caritas in Veritate, http://w2.vatican.va/content/benedict-xvi/en/encyclicals/documents/hf_ben-xvi_enc_20090629_caritas-in-veritate.html [accessed 15 August 2017], no. 78.

35 Paul VI, 26 March 1967, *On the Development of Peoples:* Populorum Progressio, http://w2.vatican.va/content/paul-vi/en/encyclicals/documents/hf_p-vi_enc_26031967_populorum.html [accessed 15 August 2017], nos. 16 and 20.

36 Paul VI, *On the Development of Peoples*, no. 42.

37 Francis, 11 October 2015, 'A New Humanism in Christ Jesus', http://en.radiovaticana.va/news/2015/11/10/pope_francis_a_new_humanism_in_christ_jesus/1185723 [accessed 15 August 2017]; also 6 May 2016, 'Conferral of the Charlemagne Prize', http://w2.vatican.va/content/francesco/en/speeches/2016/may/documents/papa-francesco_20160506_premio-carlo-magno.html [accessed 15 August 2017].

38 On the value of a narrative approach in preaching, see Herbert Anderson, 2015, 'Narrative Preaching and Narrative Reciprocity', in Foley, *Handbook for Catholic Preaching*, pp. 169–79.

39 Cf. Dan McAdams, 1993, *The Stories We Live By: Personal Myths and the Making of the Self*, New York: William Morrow.

40 Paul J. Zak, 28 October 2014, 'Why Your Brain Loves Good Storytelling', *Harvard Business Review*, https://hbr.org/2014/10/why-your-brain-loves-good-storytelling [accessed 15 August 2017].

41 Richard Kearney, 2002, *On Stories*, London/New York: Routledge, p. 140.

12

Worship Through Sanctuary

MIGUEL A. DE LA TORRE

This coming Sunday, Christians will gather in their churches – self-segregated by race and class – and, for about an hour, worship the Lord of all creation. They will probably follow a specific liturgy based on their particular denomination. More than likely, a few hymns will be sung (probably 300-year-old tunes). Prayers will be offered, a sermon preached and a collection plate will be passed. If the church has evangelical leanings, a come-to-Jesus moment will bring worship to a close as an altar call is given. This pattern, with minor variations, will be followed in most Christian churches, a model that has been followed for decades, if not centuries. For the vast majority of congregants, this is how worship has always been done, so it must not only be right, it must be God-ordained. This is how my grandparents worshipped; this is how my parents worshipped; thus, this is how I worship. And long after my bones are interred in their final resting place, my children and their children will continue to worship in this matter.

How we do worship has become so ingrained, so second-nature, that seldom do we bother to ask if we are doing worship correctly. How we worship has been so normalized in our lives that we cannot even imagine another way of defining worship, and if we did, it would feel illegitimate. And yet, I wonder if our houses of worship slumber in the light of the good news, being no better than exclusive country clubs with a thin veneer of spirituality, where like-minded people meet weekly to gaze upon themselves. Should we then be surprised at the endless national decline in church attendance as more and more people, specifically millennials and Generation Z, see no reason to continue the façade? Our focus on orthodoxy, seeking and abiding with the 'correct doctrine', has made the church experience, for many, irrelevant.

I have no doubt God vomits at the sight of how we have come to do worship. According to the prophet Isaiah, God is nauseated at the stench of our liturgy when the pursuit of justice is absent. The prophet writes:

'The multitude of your sacrifices – what are they to me?' says the Lord. 'I have more than enough of burnt offerings, of rams and the fat of fattened animals; I have no pleasure in the blood of bulls and lambs and goats. When you come to appear before me, who has asked this of you, this trampling of my courts? Stop bringing meaningless offerings! Your incense is detestable to me. New Moons, Sabbaths and convocations – I cannot bear your worthless assemblies. Your New Moon feasts and your appointed festivals I hate with all my being. They have become a burden to me; I am weary of bearing them. When you spread out your hands in prayer, I hide my eyes from you; even when you offer many prayers, I am not listening. Your hands are full of blood! Wash and make yourselves clean. Take your evil deeds out of my sight; stop doing wrong. Learn to do right; seek justice. Defend the oppressed. Take up the cause of the fatherless; plead the case of the widow.' (1.11–17, NIV)

We appear less interested about the fullness of life for the marginalized than we are about the fullness of the collection plate; while God, on the other hand, appears less interested in our order of worship than about how we order our interaction with the oppressed. And while caring for the orphan and widow are noble causes, the term serves as a euphemism for those who are among the most vulnerable within the patriarchal society of Isaiah's era – those without a father, those without a husband, in short, those without a man. The question for us today is who are among the most vulnerable in our society?

Jesus tells us that whatsoever we do for the very least among us, we do unto Jesus. Jesus is more than simply in solidarity with the most vulnerable of society; Jesus is reincarnated among them. And while a multitude of social issues exists which provide access to the world's wretched, for the purposes of this chapter, we will only focus on one disinherited and dispossessed group: the undocumented immigrant residing within the boundaries of the United States. In Matthew 25.31–46, Jesus links his very being with the US immigrant experience of today. Hungry in their homelands, thirsty in the deserts, naked after having been robbed, sometimes at gunpoint, of their possessions, sick in the hospitals due to the death-causing conditions of crossing deserts, imprisoned in detention centres and, if they make it, estranged and marginalized, today's undocumented leave us with questions about the ways Christ is present in those we are so ready to ignore or reject, those from whom we wish to separate by building walls. I argue that the way the undocumented should be seen is through contemplation on how they embody the presence of Christ.

To be an undocumented immigrant is to live in fear, to live in the shadows, to live as if a criminal. And while we gather on any given Sunday to praise and celebrate the love and graces of a merciful God, the alien among us is persecuted by our government and by our church. And to do nothing, to ignore their suffering, is to be complicit with their maltreatment. What does it mean to participate in worship and liturgy that is pleasing unto the Lord? I argue that unless the church is committed to justice, it is no better than a social club, for God is absent in houses of worship that ignore the plight of the oppressed, during Isaiah's time and now. Becoming a sanctuary church – that is, a church that opens its hearts and doors to the alien among us – is a pleasing fragrance unto God. Liturgy is understood here as love-based praxis that seeks justice for the hungry, the thirsty, the naked and the alien among us. If there is no love-based praxis, then our liturgy is nothing more than a sounding brass or a clanging cymbal. This chapter explores the liturgy of sanctuary – not what liturgy might be used by a sanctuary church, but how the praxis of sanctuary itself is liturgy!

Constructing Relevant Worship

Communities of faith discover their reason for being and their own salvation when they focus more on orthopraxis, correct action, rather than orthodoxy, correct doctrine. Worship is meaningless when the focus is upon preaching personal piety instead of how we live out our faith in fear and trembling. If the goal of worship is to rejoice in the presence of God, then one enters this presence when the faith community interacts with the world's marginalized who are the incarnation of Deity – Emmanuel, God with us. We live in a world where the world's marginalized are lifted up, as living sacrifices, crucified so the elite few can have life, and life abundantly. All too often, churches full to the brim with power and privilege must reconcile the difference between justifying their unearned advantages at the expense of the disenfranchised and a gospel that calls for radical solidarity with the least of these. A form of worship must be created that ignores the gospel call to be Jesus in a hurting world.

We develop a liturgy that neuters the essential call of the gospel, so we can continue to profit from injustices. A national civil religion, and a corresponding form of worship, must be constructed to maintain and sustain US racism, classism, sexism and heterosexism. Faith leaders arise to dismiss utopian visions of justice, claiming as futile any attempts to establish just social order until the Second Coming (Billy Graham). Or championing social justice is constructed as contradictory to faith, thus calling believers to bolt from churches advocating social or economic justice (Glen Beck). Or arguing that any attempt to engage in social justice is a mistake for the church, which should instead concentrate on simply being the church as if the message of Christ was true (Stanley Hauerwas).

The fundamental problem with how churches conduct themselves is relegating moral reasoning to the sectarian realm of abstractions. North

American Christianity, and by extension how Christians conduct worship, has a problem with 'what you do' because of its focus on 'how you believe'. Accepting Jesus Christ trumps using his life as the paragon for how church members are to live. Through this sleight of hand, churchgoers can profess belief in Christ while refusing to create a more just social order, or worse, engage in activities diametrically opposed to Jesus' life and teachings. For the church to be church, congregants must learn how to live their faith, rather than simply talk about their faith. Or as St Francis of Assisi supposedly said, 'Preach the gospel at all times; whenever necessary, use words.' Churches become a light unto the world, rather than simply sleeping in the light, not by what they claim to believe, or how they construct their worship service, but by becoming training grounds that prepare congregants on how to stand in solidarity with the marginalized.

The Concept of Sanctuary

If worship is manifested as acts that demonstrate solidarity with the oppressed, then becoming a sanctuary church is one possible manifestation of worship. The concept of sanctuary pre-dates the biblical text. Within ancient culture, those who feared death due to blood-feud retaliation or sanctioned execution could temporarily seek sanctuary at the altar of their local deity. This concept found expression within the biblical text (Num. 35.6–34). Six villages were set aside within the new Promised Land to serve as sanctuary cities. They became refuges from those demanding 'a life for a life, an eye for an eye, a tooth for a tooth'. Those fearing death or amputation could flee to these sanctuary towns in hopes of breaking the revenge-based *quid pro quo* cycle.

This biblical concept was revised during the 1980s, when US foreign policy aided and abetted Central American dictatorships that were massacring their people. During this time, Southside Presbyterian Church in Tucson, Arizona, responded, providing sanctuary to over 13,000 refugees, according to then-Pastor John Fife. The church recognized that their faith was rooted in the biblical stories of immigrants: the refugees Adam and Eve; the foreigners Abram, Isaac, Jacob and Joseph; the migrants in Egypt for 400 years; the exiled in Babylon for 70 years; and a Messiah who himself found refuge south of the border when his life was threatened by the reigning political power structures. An immigrant thread runs throughout the fabric of the biblical text. No wonder the prophets consistently remind their people to welcome the alien within their midst, for they were once aliens in the land of Egypt. Cognizant of their calling, the congregation of Southside Presbyterian Church set out to become a sanctuary church.

During the 1980s, almost a million migrants escaped US-sponsored death zones seeking haven in the very country supporting the terror from which they were fleeing. And while the legal concept of refugee is understood as one who fears persecution due to their race, religion, nationality and/or their political views or involvement, the Reagan administration of the time refused to categorize these immigrants as political refugees because of the US government's support of Central American dictatorships and their death squads. These immigrants were being rounded up and sent back to face certain death. When the government failed to live up to its 'freedom and justice' rhetoric, churches sprang into action. Aware of the US tradition of the Underground Railroad and the overall failure of European churches to safeguard Jews during the Holocaust, church leaders during the 1980s committed themselves to provide sanctuary to Central Americans fleeing US-sponsored death squads.

Sanctuary during the 1980s, according to the movement leaders, spread to over 567 houses of worship representing different faith traditions. In all, over 1,000 congregations, denominations and religious associations throughout the United States were part of a modern underground railroad, which provided safe havens for those escaping the violence of their homeland, the same violence we as a nation were exporting. Seventeen municipalities, colleges and universities, and the State of New Mexico declared themselves as places of sanctuary. From its pre-biblical roots, sanctuary has come to mean the action taken by a community (of faith or secular) that stands in radical solidarity with the oppressed, committed to protect the basic human rights of those whose lives are threatened by the government while being a prophetic witness in holding said government accountable for its complicity in violating human rights.

Worship is best manifested when the church makes 'a preferential option for the oppressed', a liberation theology concept first expressed during the 1968 Medellín Conference. The preferential option recognizes God's special concern for the oppressed and their epistemological privilege of understanding reality and divinity. And here is why congregations who make this same preferential option are manifesting worship. If worship is the means by which churchgoers better grasp reality and divinity, then only through a preferential option can such understanding be obtained.

Doing Sanctuary as a Way of Worship

Churches were clear they were not engaged in civil disobedience. The purpose of civil disobedience is to change bad laws (e.g. Jim and Jane Crow). Instead, they were arguing that the Reagan administration was guilty of violating the 1980 Refugee Act, passed to align US immigration laws with the international standards set by the 1951 UN Convention. It was the US government that was engaged in civil disobedience, refusing to follow – in this case – good laws. What do you do when the state refuses to live up to its legal and moral international commitments? The Sanctuary Movement was not interested in changing laws it perceived as being good. What they sought was for the government to follow good laws.

Jim Corbett, one of the founders of the Sanctuary Movement, coined the term 'civil initiative' to 'correct the maladministration of an existing body of laws'. The strategy for the church was (1) neither evade nor seize police powers, but stand ready to be arrested, and, if this happens, demand a trial by jury; (2) be truthful, open and subject to public examination; (3) strive towards being catholic, protecting the rights of the abused regardless of their ideology or their political usefulness; (4) seek to be dialogical, treating government officials as persons, not simply adversaries, in the hope of reaching a reconciliation that does not compromise human rights; (5) remain germane to the needs of the oppressed to be protected and not simply focus on media attention; (6) be a volunteer-based operation; and (7) be community-centred.[1]

Worshipping Today

By the 1990s, while the need for Central American sanctuary came to an end, a new need was developing due to the ratification and implementation of the North American Free Trade Agreement (NAFTA). Executing NAFTA created a significant increase in border crossings. One year before NAFTA was ratified, the General Accounting Office (GAO) released a report stating that if NAFTA was implemented, the consequences would be an immediate migration flow increase from Mexico. According to the GAO report: 'the flow of illegal [sic] aliens across the southwest border is expected to increase during the next decade because Mexico's economy is unlikely to absorb all of the new job seekers that are expected to enter the labor force'.[2] The US government knew that the impact of NAFTA would be devastating on the Mexican economy and labour market, triggering an increase in immigration to the United States. The United States responded to this perceived threat by implementing Operation Gatekeeper. NAFTA went into effect on 1 January 1994. Nine months later in September, Operation Gatekeeper was initiated.

Operation Gatekeeper, devised during the Clinton Administration, was a response to the unprecedented disruption NAFTA had on Mexico's small business and rural sectors caused by the economic liberalization. Immigrants were pushed to hostile terrain where they faced the threat of death. Operation Gatekeeper is a government policy based on 'prevention through deterrence'. In a 1 August 2001 letter to the US Senate Committee on the Judiciary, Richard M. Stana of the GAO wrote that the ultimate goal of Operation Gatekeeper was 'to make it so difficult and costly for aliens to attempt illegal entry that fewer individuals would try'.[3] 'Costly' is understood to mean more than simply a financial expense; deterrence is also measured by loss of life. Every four days it is estimated that five brown bodies perish attempting to cross these hostile lands,[4] preventable deaths which remain invisible to the Euro-American public consciousness. Some die traversing these dangerous mountains and deserts – but that is fine, because their deaths will deter others from attempting the hazardous crossing. The death of these migrants is not some unforeseen consequence of Operation Gatekeeper, but acceptable 'collateral damage'. Crimes against humanity are institutionalized through the benign governmental policy of 'prevention through deterrence'. Even after decades of data that fails to show any empirical evidence that any migration was actually deterred, we continue with a policy where desperate people of colour are placed into life-threatening situations so as to protect the safe vanilla white spaces of Euro-Americans.

While churches sing their hymns about the mercies of God, few churches show mercy towards those dying at the borders of their churches, making their praises an abomination. Such churches are like whitewashed tombs full of the decaying rot of a Eurocentric theology that advocates belief over action, abstraction rather than praxis. A New Sanctuary Movement is arising within some churches where the work of a new generation of sanctuary leaders continues. They still define worship as encompassing the mission of saving lives; only this time, the lives being lost are on the border as a direct result of our immigration policies. John Fife, who was the pastor of the sanctuary church Southside during the 1980s, explained, 'It's not enough to write a letter to your congressional representative, it's not enough to picket in front of a federal building, especially when the lives of people are hanging in the balance. We HAVE done all that, but it is not enough.' When government policies lead to death, churches that preach life have a moral obligation to step up the challenge. As more bodies perished in the desert, several churches, starting again with Southside Presbyterian Church, called for a New Sanctuary Movement. I spoke with the current pastor of the church, Alison Harrington. 'The place of hopelessness,' she tells me, 'is where solidarity begins, where we commit to do the hard work.' This hard work to which the church commits itself is the saving of lives from injustices.

Worship in Action

On 7 August 2014, a 41-year-old house cleaner and mother of two, Rosa Imelda Robles Loreto, entered Southside Presbyterian Church and requested sanctuary. Robles Loreto is a hardworking woman who owns her own house, pays taxes on her earnings and has no criminal record. 'I have been living here for 16 years,' she tells me, 'and my work has always been housecleaning. I've only been stopped once. On my way to work in September 2010, I was stopped by a sheriff for a minor traffic violation. Instead of giving me a ticket, he called for immigration authorities and I was sent to detention.' Fearing separation from her US-born children, Robles Loreto sought sanctuary. 'When I entered in sanctuary,' she says, 'we thought it would be days, a month, before my case would be closed. But then came 40 days. Then 100. Then we celebrated Christmas in the church, and my children's birthdays. I missed the first all-star tournament of my son, José Emiliano, nine years old. My older son, Gerardo, 12 years old, went to Washington to intercede on my behalf. We celebrated my birthday here in July, and now my children have returned to school.'

How does the church decide when and to whom sanctuary is offered? According to the Harrington, the pastor, 'Sanctuary is not about going out into the community to find the person to be the poster child of the movement. It's about who shows up, knocking at your door, looking for help. While Rosa is a leader in this movement, she didn't need to fit into the mythical "good migrant" archetype – she's a mom who loves her kids, and that's enough for us.' The church, along with the movement, does not decide whom to assist based on who is worthy or not worthy, who is exceptional. All humans have worth and dignity because they contain the *imago Dei*. Instead, the church recognizes its calling to be in the struggle against injustice. Robles Loreto asked for sanctuary because she did not want to make her husband a widower, nor her children orphans. What does the church do in the face of a government that ignores the literal pronouncement of the prophets: 'Take up the cause of the [mother]less; plead the case of the widow' (Isaiah 1.17, NIV)?

Southside Presbyterian Church became Robles Loreto's new home. No one asked what was her religion, if she belonged to any church or even if she had faith. None of that matters. She was an alien in their midst, and the church, as an act of worship, embraced her and took her into their care. I asked her why she sought sanctuary. 'I know people are looking at me,' she responded. 'I'm not only fighting just for my family, but I am fighting for the thousands of other mothers that are in my same situation.' She lived in a 12-by-12-foot room (the pastor's former office) where she spent the majority of her days. The room is cramped, containing bunk beds, a television set for her to watch her novellas[5] and an assortment of chairs for visiting friends and family. A portrait of her family hangs on the wall, a constant reminder of how close and yet far they are from her. She spent her evenings surfing the internet. About a dozen individuals nationwide find themselves in a similar predicament, seeking sanctuary in a house of worship. This self-imposed prison is their last resort. Who knows? It might provide hope for others living in the shadows. 'We want to move from the shadows,' Robles Loreto says. 'We are tired of hiding, we want to live in the open. But don't separate us from our families, don't separate a mother from her child.'

The use of the church to house the alien, Jesus in the here and now, is not only the best usage of the church's resources, but is the best example of what true worship looks like. Obviously, Robles Loreto is physically saved by the actions of the church; and in return, the church finds its own salvation by the presence of Robles Loreto. In response to Europe's 2015 Syrian refugee migration, Pope Francis challenged a crowd in St Peter's Square after reciting the traditional noon Angelus prayer. He called the church to make migration a major social cause of the church. 'May every parish, every religious community, every monastery, every sanctuary in Europe host a family,' said the pontiff.[6] Muslims are to be housed in Christian churches, thus placing the focus on the trials and tribulations of the immigrant, not their religious faith (or lack thereof), nor their nationality, nor their political views. The focus is on the injustices faced by the immigrant. Houses of worship engage in true worship when they take in one family, which therefore personalizes the crisis, moving the immigration dilemma from some abstract number of people seeking refuge to the injustices being faced by one person whom church members house and with whom they worship and share a meal. Imagine if houses of worship were to take up the pope's challenge here in the United States when dealing with our own migrants.

Immigration reform would come about more quickly if the churches were to open their doors to the one gently knocking, asking to be let in. 'In the face of the tragedy of tens of thousands of refugees fleeing death in war or hunger, and who are on the road to hope of life,' the pope continues, 'the Gospel calls us, asks us to be near, the littlest and the abandoned.' Leading by example, the Vatican has offered sanctuary to several families.[7] For Pope Francis, the church – and not just Catholics – should globally open its doors to everyone, without exception. At times, he says, the church keeps Jesus 'prisoner' in its own institutions and does not let him out into the world. 'The house of God is a refuge, not a prison! And if the door is closed, we say: "Lord, open the door!" Jesus is the door that lets us enter and exit.'[8]

'I always ask myself,' says Robles Loreto, 'what it would be like if the American people and I had the opportunity to come to know each other.

People would realize that my family is equal to theirs. We are mothers and fathers who would give their lives for their children to fulfil their dreams. We are equals, and just because an immigrant made a mistake does not mean we all should be judged the same. And those who carry hatred against us would see that we are all brothers and sisters, children under the same God.' Robles Loreto was at Southside for 461 nights, cooking her meals in the church's kitchen and sleeping in the pastor's former study. On 10 November 2015, about 200 people gathered at the church to bid Robles Loreto farewell and watch her take her first steps towards freedom after an agreement was reached ensuring that she could safely leave sanctuary.

Not only was Robles Loreto's life radically changed, so was the life of the church. John Fife, former pastor of Southside, provides four enduring lessons that houses of worship can learn from the Sanctuary Movement:

> First, that the church can be an effective community base for active, nonviolent resistance to government violations of human rights. Second, the church has a responsibility, both legally and morally, to protect the victims of human rights violations. We called it civil initiative: the legal right and ethical responsibility to protect the victim of human rights violations when government is the violator. ... Third, the church is a global institution capable of forming effective relationships to protect the poor and persecuted across national borders. Fourth, by entering into protective community with the poor, the church becomes spiritually transformed.[9]

Pastor Harrington informs me that 'Every church should determine for itself how to be a disciple of Christ in the midst of scary injustices. What is our call, not just how do we prop up the institutionalized church so it can survive?' In a small courtyard at Southside there is a pile of stones with names written on them and dates. Every year, the church conducts a migrant Sunday worship service. The names of those who perished crossing the border over the past year are written upon these rocks. The word 'desconocido', Spanish for 'unknown', appears on many of these stones. I have been visiting this church for over a decade now. I am deeply grieved at how high the pile of stones has become.

Notes

1 Jim Corbett, 1986, *The Sanctuary Church*, Wallingford, PA: Pendle Hill Publications, pp. 19, 23–4.

2 US General Accounting Office, 1993, 'North American Free Trade Agreement: Assessment of Major Issues', GAO/GGD–93–137.

3 Richard M. Stana, 2001, *INS Southwest Border Strategy: Resource and Impact Issues Remain after Seven Years*, Washington, DC: US General Accounting Office, p. 1.

4 Fernanda Santos and Rebekah Zemansky, 20 May 2013, 'Arizona Desert Swallows Migrants on Riskier Trails', *The New York Times*.

5 Novellas or telenovelas are a type of limited-run serial drama or soap opera popular in Latin America.

6 Francis X. Rocca, 6 September 2015, 'Pope Calls on Europe's Catholics to Shelter Refugees', *The Wall Street Journal*.

7 Rocca, 'Pope Calls on Europe's Catholics'.

8 Joshua J. McElwee, 18 November 2015, 'Francis Cries Out for Welcoming Church', *National Catholic Reporter*.

9 John Fife, 6 July 2012, 'New Sanctuary Movement at the Border Can Spiritually Transform Us', *National Catholic Reporter*.

Appendix 1

Same-Gender Union

W. SCOTT HALDEMAN (19 JUNE 2004)

Gathering

Word

Response

Naming the Occasion

Presider: Sisters and brothers, the love of God surpasses all understanding. Yet being human beings, we need to see love embodied to know of its power to heal, to sustain hope, to forgive, to accompany through trials and tribulations. It is so easy to forget, to doubt, to lose our way. In a world of loneliness and conflict and pain, what else can be said when persons come together to make love, to make family, to make a commitment to accompany another through all that life may bring but: Praise God!

Praise the profligate lover who is as close to us as our very breath and so sustains our life!
Praise the One whose love is stronger than death!
Praise God!

And so, today, we gather to see love embodied, to witness as our friends declare divinely outlandish promises of love, faithfulness and care for one another. Despite realism about all of their frailties, doubts and past betrayals, today, these two *(or whatever number)* honour us by standing before us to embody love, to make vows, to show us a bit about what God's love looks and feels like.

Praise God!

Declaration of Consent

Presider: *Name*, do you come today, with a free spirit, a free conscience and your whole self, to publicly proclaim your love
for *name(s)*, to join in the reinvention of what it means to be
family in this nation and world, to enter a new phase of life
where this loving relationship that has sustained you is now
placed at the service of church and neighbour as evidence of
God's love for all?

Partner 1: I do.

Presider: *Name*, do you come today, with a free spirit, a free conscience and your whole self, to publicly proclaim your love
for *name(s)*, to join in the reinvention of what it means to be
family in this nation and world, to enter a new phase of life
where this loving relationship that has sustained you is now
placed at the service of church and neighbour as evidence of
God's love for all?

Partner 2: I do.

[repeat as needed]

Gathering Support

Presider: As ministers to us in the work of being love in flesh, you will
need help. I invite you now to solicit the support you need
as you enter this life of loving for the sake of the world.

Partners: We ask our chosen family to stand.
You who have been for us sisters and brothers in a land
hostile to our love, we ask you now, here among these witnesses, to continue as confidants and counsellors, to lend
us still your helping hands and loving hearts as we begin
a new phase of our lives together. Call us to account when
we cause you or one another pain, betraying the covenant
we make today. Celebrate with us our joy and do not leave
us isolated in times of sorrow and loss. Will you go with us
into the future as companions and friends?

Members of the chosen family:
We will, with God's help.

Partners: We ask members of our biological families to stand.

Many are not so fortunate to have mothers, fathers, sisters, brothers *(etc.)*, with them on days when they proclaim love that has been so often disdained. You have grown with us into new people with wider visions of what it means to be human, broader understandings of faithful ways to live. We thank you and praise God for the transformative work of grace and the sustaining of ties of blood through stress and strain and change. Will you go with us into the future as family not chosen but loving and happily tied to a future yet unseen and full of promise?

Members of the biological families:
We will, with God's help.

Partners: We ask all present to stand.

We have gathered you this day to witness our promises, to celebrate our love and the gift of love itself. We give thanks for you and ask for your support in the hard work of loving. Will you share the wisdom of your lives with us, marking for us ways to walk that sustain life and listening to us in times of insight, doubt and pain?

All those gathered:
We will, with God's help.

Making Vows

Presider: As ministers to us in the work of being love in flesh, I invite you now to make your vows to one another, divinely outlandish promises that will found anew your covenant, that are made in faith and are dependent upon the Spirit to sustain and bless as you embody love for us in your hospitality, mutual care and companionship through all life's trials and triumphs.

Partners (each in turn):
I love you. I am honoured by your love for me.
I have built a life with you. I commit myself to remain with you, to stand by you, to celebrate who you are and who you may yet become.
I will, with you, show hospitality to the many whom we love and welcome the stranger into our lives.
I will, with you, spread a bountiful table for those who grace

our home, delight in times of plenty and sustain you in times
of want.
I will, with God's help, fight fair, tell truth and seek reconciliation when we find ourselves at odds.
I am yours and will worship you with my body, even as we
worship the One who is source of all love and hope of all
who long for the age when justice reigns and every tear is
wiped away.

*[The partners may also revise this model vow or craft their own words to
declare their love for one another.]*

Blessing Prayer

*[The Presider lays hands upon the couple or lifts hands above them in a
sign of blessing; others in the gathered community may join in a similar
gesture.]*

Presider: Having made your promises before God and this gathered
community, we in turn ask God's blessing upon your relationship:

Fiery Passion, whose desire for all you have created con-
sumes distrust, betrayal and brokenness, burn fiercely this
day and evermore in the love of these your *daughters/sons*,
so that all who encounter them may know that you live and
that your promises of hope, love and justice for all endure.

Abundant Mercy, whose grace overwhelms all barriers of
difference, inequality and prejudice, pour down this day and
evermore on the lives of these your *daughters/sons*, so that
all might know that reconciliation, forgiveness and transformation are possible.

Everlasting Strength, whose comforting embrace endures
beyond all rejection, oppression and attack, hold this day
and evermore these *daughters/sons*, so that all might know,
even while the day of true equality seems far off, it is surely
coming and the struggle for justice will issue in peace.

Undaunted Courage, whose tenacity outlasts all resistance,
empower this day and evermore the witness of these your
daughters/sons, so that all might know the many forms of
human love, human family, human community are faithful
and right.

We bless you, Giver of all good gifts, and ask this day for your blessing upon these *sisters/brothers* so that they may fulfil their promises, live in harmony and be a blessing to others.

In the name of Love, let all God's people say: *Amen.*

Declaration

Presider: Having made your promises before God and this gathered community and through the power vested in me, not by the state nor by the church, but only by the force of divine love that is the source and the sustenance of your own, I now declare you joined and blessed by God as signs of love in the midst of the world.

[It is appropriate for the partners to kiss and for the gathered community to respond with applause, or other gestures of celebration, and with acclamations, and, perhaps, in song.]

Exchange of Symbols

Presider: Having made your promises before God and this gathered community, you are now invited to exchange a ring *(or other sign)* as a sign of your relationship.

Partner 1: Wear this ring as a sign of my presence in your life, of my love for you, of my promises to you.

[repeat as needed]

Commissioning

Presider *(to the gathered community)*: I commission all of you in the name of God to go forth in joy, to celebrate and enjoy the gift of love that has brought us together this day and to which we have been witnesses. Tell the despairing that love is alive and even now reaches out towards them.

(to the partners): I commission you in the name of God to live as witnesses to the power of life and love. Be light to those who dwell in darkness. Be a source of warmth to those

who remain in the cold. Fulfil your promises. Live in hope. Be of good courage.

Benediction

Presider: God is love and nothing can separate you from this love. So there is no longer any reason to be afraid. God goes before you to guide you on your way. God goes beside you to accompany you. God follows behind you to catch you if you stumble. Go in peace to love.

Appendix 2

The Marriage Service of
Benjamin Bauer and Nicholas Senn

The Order of Service for
Witnessing a Lifelong Covenant[1]

Gathering

The couple joins the assembly. The assembly stands as the couple takes their place. The Presider says the following, the people standing

> Blessed be God: Father, Son and Holy Spirit;
> And blessed be God's Kingdom now and forever.

The assembly is seated. Presider addresses the assembly in these words

> Dear friends, we have gathered together today to witness Benjamin Bauer and Nicholas Senn publicly committing themselves to each other in marriage according to the laws of the State of New York and to celebrate their union: a relationship of mutual fidelity and steadfast love, in which they forsake all others and hold each other in tenderness and respect, in strength and bravery, come what may, as long as they both shall live. Ahead of them is a life of joy and sorrow, of blessing and struggle, of gain and loss, demanding of them the kind of self-giving love made manifest to us in the life of Jesus the Christ.

The Presider then addresses the couple, saying

> *Nick* and *Ben*, you have come before this company of people in the presence of God to make public your commitment to one another and to ask God's grace in your married life.

The Presider addresses one member of the couple

Presider:	*Benjamin,* do you freely and unreservedly offer yourself to *Nicholas?*
Answer:	I do.
Presider:	Will you live together in faithfulness and love as long as you both shall live?
Answer:	I will.

The Presider addresses the other member of the couple

Presider:	*Nicholas,* do you freely and unreservedly offer yourself to *Benjamin?*
Answer:	I do.
Presider:	Will you live together in faithfulness and love as long as you both shall live?
Answer:	I will.

The assembly stands, the couple faces the people and the Presider addresses the families and guests, saying

Presider:	Will all of you here gathered uphold and honour this couple and respect the covenant they make today?
People:	**We will.**
Presider:	Will you pray for them in times of trouble and celebrate with them in times of joy?
People:	**We will.**
Presider:	Let us pray, then, that they may be strengthened for the promises they make this day, and that we will have the generosity to support them in what they undertake and the wisdom to see God at work in their life together.

The Collect of the Day

Presider:	The Lord be with you.
People:	**And also with you.**
Presider:	Let us pray.

The Presider says the following Collect

Gracious and ever-living God: assist by your grace *Benjamin* and *Nicholas,* whose pledge of a lifelong commitment of love and fidelity we witness this day. Grant them your aid, that with firm resolve they may honour and keep the covenant they make with each other; through Jesus Christ our Saviour, who lives and reigns with you in the unity of the Holy Spirit, one God, for ever and ever.

People: **Amen.**

The people sit. One or more passages of Scripture is read

Reading: 1 Corinthians 12.31b—13.13

A song may be sung

Song: 'Someone Like You' by Adele Laurie Blue Adkins and Daniel D. Wilson

The Homily

Witnessing of the Vows and the Blessing of the Covenant Commitment

The couple stands, facing the Presider

Presider: *Ben* and *Nick*, I invite you now to make your covenant before God, your families and your community of friends.

Each member of the couple, in turn, takes the hand of the other and says

I, *N.*, give myself to you, *N.* I will support and care for you by the grace of God: enduring all things, bearing all things. I will hold and cherish you in times of plenty, in times of want, in sickness and in health. I will honour and keep you with God's help: forsaking all others, as long as we both shall live. This is my solemn vow.

If rings are to be exchanged, they are brought before the Presider, who prays using the following words

Let us pray.
Bless, O God, these rings as enduring signs of the covenant *Nicholas* and *Benjamin* have made with each other, through Jesus Christ our Lord. *Amen.*

The two grooms place the rings on the fingers of one another, first the one, then the other, saying

> N., receive this ring as a sign of my love and faithfulness.

Pronouncement

Presider: Inasmuch as *Nicholas* and *Benjamin* have exchanged vows of love and fidelity in the presence of God and this company, I now pronounce that they are bound to one another in a holy covenant, as long as they both shall live, and united in marriage according to the laws of the State of New York.

Prayer for the Couple

As the couple stands or kneels, the Presider prays for God's grace in the married life of Nicholas and Benjamin

> Let us pray.
> Most gracious God, we praise you for your tender mercy and unfailing care for your creation and for the great joy and comfort bestowed upon us in the gift of human love. We give you thanks for *Benjamin* and *Nicholas*, and the covenant of faithfulness they have made. By your Holy Spirit keep them in your steadfast love; protect them from all danger; fill them with your wisdom and peace; lead them in holy service to each other and the world; in Jesus' Name. *Amen.*

The Prayers

Presider: Let us pray for N. and N. in their life together and for all people everywhere, responding 'Hear our prayer'.

A Deacon or another leader bids prayers for the couple

Leader: For *Benjamin* and *Nicholas*, seeking your goodness and mercy in their lives; Lord, in your mercy (*or* Lord, in your goodness)

People: **Hear our prayer.**

Leader:	For a spirit of loving-kindness to embrace them all their days; Lord, in your mercy (*or* Lord, in your goodness)
People:	**Hear our prayer.**
Leader:	For friends to support them and communities to enfold them; Lord, in your mercy (*or* Lord, in your goodness)
People:	**Hear our prayer.**
Leader:	For peace in their home and love in their family; Lord, in your mercy (*or* Lord, in your goodness)
People:	**Hear our prayer.**
Leader:	For the outpouring of your love through their work and witness; Lord, in your mercy (*or* Lord, in your goodness)
People:	**Hear our prayer.**
Leader:	For strength for all married couples to keep their vows and commitments; Lord, in your mercy (*or* Lord, in your goodness)
People:	**Hear our prayer.**
Leader:	For those who seek justice in our society, peace in the world and concord among nations; Lord, in your mercy (*or* Lord, in your goodness)
People:	**Hear our prayer.**
Leader:	For those who are sick and suffering, homeless and poor; Lord, in your mercy (*or* Lord, in your goodness)
People:	**Hear our prayer.**
Leader:	For victims of violence and those who inflict it; Lord, in your mercy (*or* Lord, in your goodness)
People:	**Hear our prayer.**
Leader:	For fellowship with all who have died and gone before us in the hope of rising again [especially _____]; Lord, in your mercy (*or* Lord, in your goodness)
People:	**Hear our prayer.**

The Presider concludes the Prayers with the following or another appropriate Collect

God the Giver of every gift, source of all goodness, hear the prayers we bring before you for *Nicholas* and *Benjamin*, and all for whom we pray; through your Son, Jesus Christ our Lord. Amen.

The Peace

Presider: The peace of the Lord be always with you.
People: **And also with you.**
Presider: I invite everyone here present to offer a gesture and words of
              peace to others.

Ben and Nick may kiss each other and then greet their families and friends

Note

1 The following is adapted from the Episcopal Church resource *I Will Bless
You, and You Will Be a Blessing*, a collection of liturgical resources and theological
reflection regarding the celebration of same-gender marriages and lifelong partnerships. The current version was revised and updated by the General Convention
of the Episcopal Church in 2015 from the 2012 original and includes adaptations
to the service included here for use in the celebration of a marriage. The revised
version also includes a gender-neutral adaptation of the 1979 *Book of Common
Prayer*'s 'Celebration and Blessing of a Marriage' for use with same-gender couples. The portions included here are printed with the permission of the Church
Pension Group of the Episcopal Church. See http://www.episcopalchurchsc.org/
uploads/1/2/9/8/12989303/lifelong_covenant_liturgy.pdf [accessed 27 July 2018].

Index of Names and Subjects